The Financialization of Housing

Due to the financialization of housing in today's market, housing risks are increasingly becoming financial risks. Financialization refers to the increasing dominance of financial actors, markets, practices, measurements and narratives. It also refers to the resulting structural transformation of economies, firms, states and households. This book asserts the centrality of housing to the contemporary capitalist political economy and places housing at the centre of the financialization debate.

A global wall of money is looking for High-Quality Collateral (HQC) investments, and housing is one of the few asset classes considered HQC. This explains why housing is increasingly becoming financialized, but it does not explain its timing, politics and geography. Presenting a diverse range of case studies from the US, the UK, the Netherlands, Germany, Italy and Spain, the chapters in this book include coverage of the role of the state as the driver of financialization processes, and the part played by local and national histories and institutions. This cutting edge volume will pave the way for future research in the area.

Where housing used to be something "local" or "national", the two-way coupling of housing to finance has been one crucial element in the recent crisis. It is time to reconsider the financialization of both homeownership and social housing. This book will be of interest to those who study international economics, housing systems, economic geography and financialization.

Manuel B. Aalbers is Associate Professor of Human Geography at KU Leuven/ University of Leuven, Belgium, where he leads an ERC project and research group on the intersection of real estate, finance and states.

Routledge Studies in the Modern World Economy

For a full list of titles in this series, please visit www.routledge.com/series/SE0432

The Financialization of Housing

A political economy approach

Manuel B. Aalbers

 Routledge
Taylor & Francis Group

LONDON AND NEW YORK

First published 2016
by Routledge
2 Park Square, Milton Park, Abingdon, Oxfordshire OX14 4RN

and by Routledge
711 Third Avenue, New York, NY 10017

First issued in paperback 2017

Routledge is an imprint of the Taylor & Francis Group, an informa business

British Library Cataloguing in Publication Data
A catalogue record for this book is available from the British Library

Library of Congress Cataloging in Publication Data
Names: Aalbers, Manuel, author.
Title: The financialization of housing : a political economy approach /
Manuel B. Aalbers.
Description: Abingdon, Oxon ; New York, NY : Routledge, 2016.
Identifiers: LCCN 2015047923| ISBN 9781138950580 (hardback) |
ISBN 9781315668666 (ebook)
Subjects: LCSH: Housing--Finance.
Classification: LCC HD7287.55 .A25 2016 | DDC 333.33/82--dc23
LC record available at http://lccn.loc.gov/2015047923

ISBN 13: 978-1-138-09290-7 (pbk)
ISBN 13: 978-1-138-95058-0 (hbk)

Typeset in Times New Roman
by Fish Books Ltd.

Photo: Martin Sokol

Contents

Figures

Tables

Credits and Acknowledgements

Chapter 2 has been previously published as: Aalbers, M.B. and Christophers, B. (2014) Centring housing in political economy. *Housing, Theory and Society* 31(4): 373-394. Chapter 3 has been published as: Aalbers, M.B. (2008) The financialization of home and the mortgage market crisis. *Competition & Change* 12(2): 148-166. I've added a new afterword. Chapter 4 has been published as: Aalbers, M.B. (2015) The Great Moderation, the Great Excess and the global housing crisis. *Journal of Housing Policy* 15(1): 43–60. And finally Chapter 5 has been published as: Fernandez, R. and Aalbers, M.B. (2016) Financialization and housing: Between globalization and Varieties of Capitalism. *Competition & Change* 20(2) doi:10.1177/1024529415623916. I'd like to thank the respective publishers and co-authors for allowing me to reprint these papers here as book chapters. I would also like to thank Laura Johnson and Emily Kindleysides at Routledge for navigating this book through its different stages, the reviewers for providing critical feedback, Nikola Stalevski for editing the four new chapters of the book, and Martin Sokol for providing not only Central European pilsners in Dublin but also the opening photo of this book. Finally, I'd like to acknowledge financial support from the European Research Council [grant number 313376: "The Real Estate/Financial Complex"] which has allowed me to spend time writing this book rather than being swamped in many of the other things academics are supposed to do.

1 Introduction

Financialization and Housing Studies

In contemporary Western societies, financial activities are a defining charac-teristic not only of the corporate economy, but also of politics, the welfare and social security system, and general culture.

(Knorr Cetina and Preda, 2005: 1)

What is Financialization?

The term finance is often used without any explicit conceptualization of what it means. This is not necessarily problematic; terms are often used without concep-tualizing or defining them, and many daily terms are not so easy to define. Yet, it may help to take a step back and ask the question: What is finance? Google this question and one of the first answers is Daniel Kurt's definition on investo-pedia.com:[1]

> 'Finance' is a broad term that describes two related activities: the study of how money is managed and the actual process of acquiring needed funds. Because individuals, businesses and government entities all need funding to operate, the field is often separated into three sub-categories: personal finance, corporate finance and public finance.

Other websites highlight that finance was originally a French term adopted into English to mean "management of money". Finance is sometimes also considered as the equivalent of the exchange of available resources:

> Finance is not restricted only to the exchange and/or management of money. A barter trading system is also a type of finance. Thus, we can say, Finance is an art of managing various available resources like money, assets, invest-ments, securities, etc.[2]

Combining these different definitions, finance can be considered as the management of funds one owns outright, raised funds (e.g. through shares) and borrowed funds (e.g. loans) for personal, corporate or public goals.

Financialization, in its most basic terms, is then the process by which something or someone is managed as a fund; thus a more elaborate definition would read:

> the increasing dominance of financial actors, markets, practices, measurements and narratives, at various scales, resulting in a structural transformation of economies, firms (including financial institutions), states and households.
>
> (Aalbers, in press)

There are many other definitions of financialization[3] and I am not arguing that my definition is necessarily the best one. Other definitions can be used. Some are more precise, but often definitions tend to be too specific and narrow to capture the essence of the process. Krippner's definition of financialization—'a pattern of accumulation in which profit making occurs increasingly through financial channels rather than through trade and commodity production' (Krippner, 2005: 14)—is very popular in the financialization literature, but is only useful if one studies patterns of accumulation and many of the studies that use Krippner's definition do not. Moreover, the idea of a "pattern of accumulation" has certain theoretical connotations that will be mobilized by such a definition. Many of the studies that cite Krippner seem to uncritically copy her definition, without reflecting on the meaning and use of the concept.

Financialization also has been criticized, either because the concept is considered imprecise, vague and chaotic or because the presented evidence supporting the financialization claim is disputed (e.g. Christophers, 2015). To some extent, the critics are right: financialization can be a very loosely defined concept that covers many processes, structures, practices and outcomes at different scales and in different time frames. Furthermore, sometimes financialization is the *explanandum* (the phenomenon to be explained), sometimes the *explanans* (the thing that explains) and sometimes as a mechanism intervening between causes and consequences (Aalbers, in press). In that sense, financialization is not that different from other concepts whose academic and media popularity rose quickly and which are simultaneously criticized for being imprecise and vague—globalization and neoliberalism are cases in point. Part of the intellectual journey of the use of concepts is that they problematize existing conceptualizations and understandings of what caused what. The literature on financialization thus is part of a larger attempt to understand the non-linear, multi-dimensional, multi-scalar complexity of contemporary societies and economies (Aalbers, in press).

In this book, I will demonstrate the specificities of housing as a central aspect of financialization. Currently, housing is a relatively minor theme in the financialization debate, and likewise, financialization receives little attention in the interdisciplinary field of housing studies—but this is beginning to change. A small but growing literature on the financialization of housing is emerging, covering financialization through overpriced and overextended loans (Newman, 2009; Waldron, 2014; Walks, 2013), through mortgage securitization (Aalbers,

2008; Gotham, 2009; Wainwright, 2009), through credit scoring of aspiring homeowners (Aalbers, 2008, 2011; Hall, 2012), through land use planning (Coq-Huelva, 2013; Kaika and Ruggiero, 2014; Savini and Aalbers, 2015), of private serviced residences (Trouillard, 2013), and of subsidized housing (Fields, 2014; Heeg, 2013; Uffer, 2014).

The financialization literature is commonly divided into three strands: financialization as a regime of accumulation (Régulation Approach political economy), financialization as the rise of shareholder value (critical social accountancy), and financialization of daily life (cultural economy) (see also Chapter 3). In these different strands housing either plays a minor role or is simply seen as one of the bearers of financialization. Despite the varied analyses of the financialization of housing and the importance of housing to financialization, the relations between housing and financialization remain under-researched and under-theorized. The financialization of housing is not a specific from of financialization, as it transcends several forms.

One key argument of this book is that housing and finance are increasingly interdependent and that the financialization of housing is the general mechanism through which we can analyse this growing interdependence. This mechanism has different drivers, including the "wall of money" (Chapter 5) and wider tendencies towards globalization, neoliberalism, privatization and "regulated deregulation" (in particular Chapters 4 and 7) but also include financial-technological changes such as credit rating, credit scoring and the construction of new financial markets (Chapter 3). The mechanism of the financialization of housing comes in different empirical forms: the securitization of mortgage loans (in particular Chapter 3), the rise of subprime and predatory lending (Chapter 3), rising mortgage debt for households (in particular Chapter 6), the entry of private equity firms, hedge funds and publicly listed real estate firms in subsidized rental markets (Chapter 7), and finally the reliance of non-profit housing associations on social housing bonds and complicated financial derivatives (Chapter 7).

The relationship between privatization and financialization is a complicated one. In some cases privatization directly created the conditions for financialization (e.g. the privatization of social housing, followed by rising mortgage debt and securitization). In other cases privatization itself was financialized (e.g. the sale of entire public housing companies to private equity firms—"financialized privatization"). Finally, financialization can be an indirect consequence of earlier rounds of privatization (e.g. the use of social housing bonds or derivatives by privatized housing associations). More generally speaking, markets first need to be created before privatization and financialization can be fully developed. Through a process of "regulated deregulation" (Chapter 7) markets are not so much deregulated or liberalized, as is often argued, but created and re-created—markets need regulation to make them work.

This book contributes to the debate in at least three ways. First, there are still very few studies that focus on the financialization of housing per se, with financialization often lingering in the backstory. Housing is a key field to witness, research and understand the financialization of non-financial firms and industries, that is traditionally non-financial firms and industries are increasingly partaking in practices that have been the domain of the financial sector and are being dominated by financial narratives and practices. This book places housing in the centre of the financialization debate, but also places financialization in the middle of housing and urban debates.

Second, this book contributes to the small but growing literature on the financialization of the semi-public and public sectors, by focusing on the role of states in financialization processes in general and by presenting evidence of the financialization of subsidized housing in particular. While some authors conceptualize financialization in terms of "less state and more market", I argue that states and semi-public institutions are increasingly dependent on financial markets and are also evaluated using similar tools applied to firms. The state is often the driver of financialization processes, for example by pushing families into housing debt, by enabling financial institutions to buy up subsidized housing, or by simply withdrawing from providing or regulating the housing sector and opening up the field to rent-seeking financial institutions. All these forms of financialization are investigated in this book. The financialization *of* and *through* the state is one of the research frontiers to be explored in the coming years.

Third, the financialization literature is dominated by studies from the UK and particularly the US. This book discusses how the financialization of housing takes place in sometimes similar and sometimes quite different ways. Examples from the US, UK, the Netherlands, Germany, Italy, and Spain illustrate not only the emergence and commonalities of housing financialization but also the key and persistent influence of national—and to some extent also local—histories and institutions. Some cases show how financialization takes place in the context where states that were traditionally deeply involved in regulating the housing market, to safeguard affordable housing for all (rather than only the very poor), are increasingly transferring social responsibilities, either actively or passively, to financial actors and financial markets.

This book aims to reach not only academics and libraries, but also students, housing sector practitioners and politicians. Some academics may find the tone of the book too journalistic or essayistic and not theoretical or methodical enough. They may consider the examples too simple, perhaps even simplistic, for an academic book, but I hope these examples and descriptions will help the other readers to understand what the financialization of housing really implies. Theoretical, conceptual sections (in particular Chapter 2 and parts of Chapters 3 and 5) are mixed with more descriptive and essayistic chapters. The real-world descriptions in Chapters 6 and 7, for example, serve to make the more abstract reasoning in earlier chapters clearer and more accessible. Chapter 4 is written in a more essayistic style and aims to bring together the conceptual with the more descriptive chapters. The concluding chapter is largely non-theoretical and may disappoint those readers expecting a big, sweeping conceptual conclusion—I hereby refer those readers to Chapters 2–5 of the book. Instead, the concluding chapter questions the idea of housing wealth and discusses a possible politics of de-financialization *of* as well as *beyond* housing.

The following questions will pique the interest of academic readers: Why has the financialization literature paid so little attention to housing, and why has the field of housing studies demonstrated relatively little interest in financialization? The next section will look at one type of studies within the interdisciplinary field of housing studies: comparative housing studies. I will present a sympathetic critique that suggests that, despite the label "comparative", a great deal of these comparative studies focus on *explaining* differences between national housing systems, rather than coming to an *understanding* of the remarkably common trajectories (but not necessarily convergence) shared between countries. These pathways are partly driven by globalization processes, not only in the economic sense but also including different ideologies (Doling and Ford, 2003; Ronald, 2008). In recent decades, these were in particular incarnations of neoliberal ideology that naturalize not only housing commodification and privatization but also financialization.

The financialization literature is primarily embedded in the wider interdisciplinary field of political economy, where social scientists of all stripes come together to discuss economic issues. The term is used widely by a range of different traditions, including political scientists, sociologists, geographers and other social scientists. It is not always easy to define political economy in its entirety, but it is possible to define political economy as opposed to mainstream economics.[4] Table 1,1 shows some of the features of political economy and its opposition to mainstream economics. In Chapters 2 and 5, I will show what a political economy approach implies for analysing the financialization of housing, using political economy's own terminology instead of relying on simple opposition to mainstream economics.

Students sometimes question my characterization of mainstream economics: *they cannot really believe that, can they? Perhaps a few economists think in this way but this cannot be a realistic summary of a large part of such a big discipline.* Or: *some of these assumptions are so absurd, why would anyone work with them?* I am as puzzled as they are, but the partial answer is: Many mainstream economists appear so dedicated to these key assumptions that they cannot give them up. Even if most are open to discuss these assumptions and argue their merits, their studies and the theories they rely on all too often demonstrate how strong these assumptions are embedded in their discipline.

A Critique of Comparative Housing Studies

Why study housing in the first place? Shelter is one of our most basic needs, but a house—not just a single-family house but all types of housing—is not just a roof over one's head; it is also a place to call "home". Furthermore, housing is necessary for social and physical reproduction: a house is a place to raise children and from a capitalist perspective a house in a necessary condition for the reproduction of labour. From this perspective, it could be argued that housing is

Table 1.1 Key Differences Between Mainstream and Political Economics

	Mainstream Economics	Political Economy
1	Actors have complete information.	Actors do not have full and complete information (uneven access).
2	Information is free.	Information is usually not free to most actors (power/knowledge).
3	All actors act in the same rational way according to exogenously given preferences.	Rationality is complicated and not singular (multiple rationalties).
4	Actors are oriented toward profit or utility maximization.	Actors may be oriented to other things, e.g. the long-term survival of their firm or a happy, fulfilled life.
5	State intervention negatively alters the workings of the market.	State intervention is a pre-condition for markets to exist; can do many things, not necessarily negatively impacting markets; corporations also use states.
6	Market equilibrium appears by itself as a result of market forces.	Market equilibrium is a rare occurrence; change is constant; markets differ from each other according to product and place.

a public good. In fact, housing is treated in most countries as a so-called merit good: a commodity that an individual or society should have and is not primarily delivered by the state but rather by the market.

There are only a few areas that link people's livelihoods so directly to the global economy as housing (the other being food and pension schemes). It is connected to other important life domains: health, environmental conditions (air, soil, water, etc.) and general well-being; access to food, services, education, employment, transportation, and so on (location); and poverty and inequality. Importantly, housing is not merely a reflection of but also closely shapes one's life opportunities. Indeed, it is hard to imagine domains of life not connected to housing in some way. Therefore, it should come as no surprise that the field of housing is where many disciplines come together, including a range of social sciences (like anthropology, sociology, human geography, economics and political science) as well as design and engineering sciences (like urban planning and design, architecture and civil engineering).

Housing has micro- and macroeconomic drivers and consequences; it has micro- and macro-political drivers and consequences; it has micro- and macro-sociological drivers and consequences; and it has micro- and macro-geographical drivers and consequences. The book focuses primarily on the macro level of these sectors, namely the national and international political economy of housing systems. This implies that it largely ignores a cultural economy and poststructuralist approach to the financialization of housing that focuses more on microstructures, rationalities, biopolitics and disciplining (e.g. Allon, 2010; Di Feliciantonio, in press; Langley,

2008; Rossi, 2013; Smith and Munro, 2008). A housing system is understood as "the full range of interrelationships between all of the actors (individual and corporate), housing units and institutions involved in the production, consumption and regulation of housing. It is thus a much broader term than housing market or sector" (Bourne, 1981: 12).

The housing market is an economic field structured by the power relations between different actors. The housing market, like any other market, cannot be characterized as a "natural" entity, but should be seen as the social product of the institutions that shape it. Comparative housing studies is a lively sub-field in the interdisciplinary study of housing, focusing on the institutions that shape different national housing systems. Comparative housing studies have devoted thousands of pages to describing differences and similarities between different national, and occasionally regional, housing systems. Some of these studies focus on a range of countries and compare entire housing systems; other studies focus on one aspect, such as housing finance or social housing, while other studies present in-depth comparisons between a few countries. Often, studies feature tables with detailed comparisons of specific policy instruments and housing practices.

Comparative housing studies have uncovered great insights about the remark-able diversity of housing systems around the world, especially in Europe,[5] as well as the "stickiness" or "path dependency" of earlier choices, for example, early twentieth-century developments "explaining" the specific housing diversity in the twenty-first century. I placed "explaining" between quotation marks here because demonstrating that differences exist and that they go back to decisions made decades ago is hardly an explanation for their continued relevance. Policy decisions are constantly being re-evaluated and revised. Calling something an explanation because it follows a seemingly stable trend is hardly an explanation, especially if one considers the massive social changes that happened in between. Stability is side-tracked as something that needs no explanation and the focus is diverted to change. But stability in the face of change all around begs for an explanation as much as the direction of change does.

I am not arguing that all comparative housing studies have neglected to explain stability, stickiness and persistent differences between systems. Some of the in-depth studies of institutional change in specific countries do a good job at not only explaining change but also stability and stickiness. Often such studies explain how change and stability work together to change the existing housing system step-by-step, sometimes leading to a radical overhaul, even though some of the institutions at the heart of the housing system appear stable. I could have placed "appear" between quotation marks as well because the fact that a rule, a practice or more generally speaking an institution remains in place says nothing about its relevance, its possibly changing nature and its relations to other institutions. Some institutions were originally associated with a set of policies, with a specific political approach and with a specific ideology, and over time became naturalized and de-politicized or associated with different policies, politics and ideologies.

The idea that stability is the norm is misleading: "Every era had gradual and constant change."[6] The fact that some of the formal institutions appear stable does not imply that the informal institutions and practices are stable. Mainstream economists are obsessed with stability and the only way their models can deal with change is to call the period of change exceptional and to see this period as part of a move towards equilibrium. Mainstream economists see equilibrium as a natural tendency, even though it is artificially constructed and not just rare but impossible to define because it suggests that there is some sort of "normal", namely a benchmark. Institutions and practices are relatively stable at most (rather than "at best").

Many of the table-ticking type of comparative housing studies implicitly assume a world of stability in which changes only take place at one given point in time rather gradually or constantly. The bigger problem is that such studies falsely suggest that the workings of housing systems can be explained through path dependency. Path dependency, as applied in many such studies, is not an explanation; it is an accepted way of saying "history matters". Of course history matters. This is a trivial truth. But why and how do some histories matter more or differently from others? Of course the present is a result of decisions and practices—of institutions—in the past (and the present). Often comparative housing studies conveniently mobilize path dependency to "explain" stability and shelve it again to explain change.

Another problem with comparative housing studies, in particular those funded through EU framework programmes, is that they often take an extended version of Esping-Andersen's (1990) *Three Worlds of Welfare Capitalism* (hereafter EA+) for granted. In his landmark study, Esping-Andersen distinguishes three types of welfare states: liberal (sometimes referred to as Anglo-Saxon), corporatist-statist (sometimes also referred to as conservative or continental) and social-democratic. The US, Germany and Sweden respectively are the ideal-typical examples of each. Canada and Australia are placed in the liberal model, France, Austria and Italy in the corporatist, and Denmark and Norway in the social-democratic model. Originally, Esping-Andersen did not classify the UK as a liberal welfare state, although it could be argued that, over the years, the UK has moved closer to this type, albeit perhaps less so in health care provision than in other sectors like housing.[7]

While many have criticized Esping-Andersen's typology, it has persisted, with a few additions, as the standard classification of the welfare state, even reaching paradigmatic status in several fields of study. It has been argued that many countries have components from different types or that changes in all three types make it hard to keep using certain countries as ideal types as such countries are subject to changes in their welfare systems as well. An important critique incorporated in EA+ is that Esping-Andersen's typology should be expanded with a fourth type, the Mediterranean or familial welfare state type that can be found in Italy, Spain and other Southern European countries. Esping-Andersen himself has been reluctant to expand his typology with a fourth type, arguing that the Mediterranean type is a sub-type of the corporatist type and that the theoretical support for a fourth type is not there. In later years, Esping-Andersen seems to have accepted the fourth type of welfare state. Over the last 25 years, however, a fifth type has almost silently been added to EA+, i.e. the post-socialist welfare state type, sometimes referred to as Central and East European (CEE) welfare state type.

These four or five types form the basis of the EA+ model, but several authors have argued that more types are needed to account for different types of welfare states. Scholars outside Europe have highlighted the Eurocentric tendencies of the model, arguing for the inclusion of other types of welfare states, such as Confucian (East-Asian). Although these expansions of EA+ may enjoy acceptance in certain regions of the world, they are not generally considered part of EA+, perhaps reflecting the continued Eurocentric nature of the typology. Indeed, Esping-Andersen explicitly developed his model for OECD countries and never argued that his typology could actually be applied worldwide.

The four or five types of EA+ are convenient labels for any researcher who seeks European funding sources. Indeed, EA+ is mobilized as a self-evident classification to justify case study selection. Take the following imaginary example:

> Our proposed case studies are Sweden, Germany, the United Kingdom, Italy and Hungary. Each of these countries represents one of the five types of welfare states. Sweden represents the social-democratic model, Germany the corporatist model, the United Kingdom the liberal model, Italy the Mediterranean model and finally Hungary the post-socialist model.

These terms suggest that Sweden's housing system is somehow representative of the social-democratic housing model and therefore representative of other Nordic countries, but this ignores a whole range of studies that problematize the translation (or actually, the lack thereof) from welfare state types to housing systems.

Esping-Andersen developed his typology by looking at the welfare and market sectors of education, health care and social services. He did not include housing in his models, perhaps because he wanted to limit himself to three fields of policy or perhaps because he knew little about housing. It could also be that Esping-Andersen considered housing policy too complicated to be integrated in his typology. As it turns out, housing behaves differently from the other three policy fields and its inclusion would make it harder to construct ideal types. In his well-cited article *Housing: the Wobbly Pillar under the Welfare State*, Ulf Torgesen spoke of an

> uneasy relationship between welfare state purposes and housing policy, and the way in which other purposes are introduced and mixed with welfare state designs. I believe that housing always will occupy a special and awkward position in welfare thinking due to the special nature of the commodity in question. [...] housing policy, unlike the other fields of welfare state endeavour, will contain much that is rather different from this perspective.
>
> (Torgesen, 1987: 116)

In other words, housing is different from other fields of welfare, and therefore, does not fit the EA+ typology (cf. Kemeny, 1992). If EA+ is applied to housing, the in-group differences are often as big as the between-group differences, rendering the use of these types to construct a housing systems typology irrelevant and useless. The Mediterranean type, which was not part of Esping-Andersen's typology, is perhaps the most coherent when housing systems are included (for a discussion, see Allen *et al.*, 2004); however, several non-Mediterranean countries (e.g. liberal Ireland, corporatist Belgium and post-socialist Hungary) could also fit the model. This apparent paradox raises the following questions: Why do these countries share so many similarities between their housing systems, despite the massive differences in welfare systems and housing histories? Why do social-democratic Denmark and the corporatist/social-democratic hybrid the Netherlands both rely so heavily on mortgage finance, a feature associated with liberal states like the US and the UK? And, why does Spain also appear to be converging towards the liberal model? In Chapters 4–6, I will attempt to answer these questions.

Most comparative housing studies prioritize the analysis of housing as a public policy of the welfare state rather than as public policy in its own right. Yet, in most—if not all—contemporary political economies, current housing policy reflects housing not only as a pillar of the welfare state but also as a pillar of the capitalist economy, especially important for growth in terms of GDP, employment, finance, and so on, as well as a pillar of the ideology of private property. To reduce the analysis of public policy to an analysis of housing policy as welfare policy is to reduce the study of housing systems to only one side of housing while ignoring the others. Much of housing policy does not come out of Housing Departments and Ministries but out of Commerce, Business and Labour Departments and Ministries or the Treasury. This book will shift the focus from housing as welfare policy to the connections between the ideology of private property, the growth impetus and the financial sector, on the one hand, and existing housing policy, on the other.[8] Housing policy, including its fiscal treatment, is one of the key arenas of financial regulation and policymaking, including many financial policies that impact lenders, landlords and investors.

Overview of the Book

The book makes the case for bringing the interdisciplinary fields of housing studies and political economy together: the field of housing studies would benefit from a political economy approach, while the field of political economy has ignored housing for far too long even though housing is central to the real political economy. As we argue in Chapter 2 (co-authored with Brett Christophers), the issue of "housing" has generally not been granted an important role in post-war political economy. Housing as policy was reserved for social policy analysis and a growing field of housing studies; housing as market was confined to mainstream economics. This book insists that political-economic analysis can no longer ignore the Housing Question; housing is implicated in the contemporary capitalist political economy in numerous critical, connected, and very often contradictory ways.

In Chapter 3, financialization is conceptualized as capital switching from the primary, secondary or tertiary circuit to the quaternary circuit of capital. The financialization of mortgage markets demands not just homes but also homeowners to be viewed as financially exploitable. It is exemplified by the securitization of mortgage loans but also by the use of credit scoring and risk-based pricing. In the past century, mortgage markets were transformed from being a "facilitating market" for homeowners in need of credit into a tool for facilitating global investment. Since mortgage markets are both *local* consumer markets and *global* investment markets, the dynamics of financialization and globalization directly connect homeowners to global investors, thereby increasing the volatility in mortgage markets, as the recent economic crisis showed all too well.

This book explores the relationships between local and national housing markets and recent historic transformations in global capitalism. In Chapter 4, a periodization of developments in housing markets, policies and practices is proposed. Here, I distinguish between, first, the pre-modern period; second, the modern or Fordist period; third, the flexible neoliberal or post-Fordist period; and fourth, the late neoliberal or emerging post-crisis period. This periodization is a heuristic device that helps to make sense of the interdependence of national housing markets and the global financial crisis. The argument is not that the crisis caused the breakdown of the post-Fordist housing model, but rather that the shift to this model introduced certain dynamics into housing markets that a few decades later culminated into a crisis. The start of the Great Moderation was also the start of the financialization of states and economies in various domains, including housing. In making this argument, I unpack the concept of the Great Moderation: what appeared to be a structural moderation of macroeconomic cycles was in fact the build-up of a bubble economy. The 1970s and early 1980s, as well as the years after the 2007 crisis, are critical junctures in the development of housing. The Great Moderation was also a Great Excess in terms of rising inequality and excessive growth of credit and debt, suggestive of a finance-led regime of accumulation (Boyer, 2000).

In Chapter 5 (co-authored with Rodrigo Fernandez), we demonstrate how housing ties into the real-world political economy, and propose a potential role and location within academic political economy. We argue that the political economy literature on the Varieties of Capitalism (VoC) is still coming to grips with both housing and finance. In order to enhance the analysis and under-standing of the varieties in real-world political economies, VoC needs to open up more to the literatures of financialization and housing, in particular the crucial role of the financialization of housing, not only as a bearer of financialization processes, but as a central concept for understanding contemporary real-world political economies.

In this chapter we investigate the rise of housing finance as an integral part of macro-economic policy and highlight the role of financial globalization in the rise of housing finance. Housing is seen as an absorber of "the wall of money", a profoundly uneven process. We construct four trajectories of national institutional structures and discuss how capital flows are absorbed in each of these ideal types. In Chapter 6, these trajectories are illustrated with country case studies: the US, Italy, Germany and the Netherlands each typify one of the four trajectories. In addition, Spain is discussed as a country that "jumped" groups and, therefore, has a unique trajectory not properly covered by any of the four.

The financialization of housing is not limited to homeownership and mortgage markets, but extends to rental housing, in particular subsidized rental housing. On the one hand, private equity firms have become important investors in subsidized housing. On the other hand, social housing providers have become active as investors in derivatives. The entry of private equity firms contributed to the restructuring of subsidized rental housing in Germany and the US, in turn increasing housing inequality in both countries. Furthermore, in the Netherlands and the UK many social housing associations started developing housing for profit and several of them also started adopting more complex financial techniques, such as lending money to other associations, borrowing on global capital markets and purchasing derivatives. I will argue that the changes in the housing sector that led to its financialization cannot be separated from the wider financialization of the state.

Until a few years ago the promotion of homeownership was ubiquitous, not just in Europe and the US but across the globe. Where housing used to be something local or national, the two-way coupling of housing and finance was one crucial element in the recent economic crisis. This financialization of housing should therefore be problematized, something I will do in the concluding chapter. It is time to reconsider not only the promotion of homeownership and the commodification of subsidized housing, but also the increasing interdependence between housing and finance.

Notes

1   See www.investopedia.com/ask/answers/12/finance.asp.
2   See http://kalyan-city.blogspot.be/2011/11/what-is-finance-meaning-definition.html.
3   Although Wikipedia is often frowned upon in academic circles, it provides a decent overview of a range of different definitions of financialization: https://en.wiki pedia.org/wiki/Financialization.
4   Mainstream economics includes, but is not limited to, neoclassical economics. Many schools of economic thought share many, but often not all, of the assumptions of neoclassical economics. Furthermore, many pluralist economists fail to challenge the basic assumptions of mainstream economics and integrate questionable theories—questionable in the eyes of political economists—into their pluralistic world.
5   This is not due to particularly large diversity in Europe, but rather because Europe has been the focus of most comparative housing studies.
6   The quote is from the introduction to Gill Scott-Heron's *The New Deal*, the lyrics of which (but not the introduction) can be found here: www.azlyrics.com/lyrics/gil scottheron/thenewdeal.html. If you don't know Scott-Heron, you should do yourself a favour and familiarize yourself with his work, perhaps starting with the iconic *The Revolution Will Not Be Televised*: www.youtube.com/watch?v=qGaoXAwl9kw.

7   I will not attempt to summarize the dimensions of Esping-Andersen's typology or the characteristics of the different types here; most readers will be overly familiar with them. Nor will I discuss individual countries and how they fit, or not fit, in Esping-Andersen's typology and the different alternative typologies developed over the years (e.g. Bambra, 2007). Interesting cases, such as the hybrid nature of the Netherlands, the special case of Switzerland or cases outside Europe—Japan, Singapore and Chile are three countries often discussed in the welfare state literature—are also not discussed here.

8   I do take the housing as welfare policy approach seriously, but as it is adequately covered in numerous studies, I do not present it extensively in this book.

References

Aalbers, M.B. (2008) The Financialization of Home and the Mortgage Market crisis. *Competition & Change* 12(2): 148–166.

Aalbers, M.B. (2011) *Place, Exclusion, and Mortgage Markets*. Oxford: Wiley-Blackwell.

Aalbers, M.B. (in press) Corporate Financialization. In: D. Richardson, N. Castree, M.F. Goodchild, A.L. Kobayashi and R. Marston (Eds), *The International Encyclopedia of Geography: People, the Earth, Environment, and Technology*. Oxford: Wiley-Blackwell.

Allen, J., Barlow, J., Leal, J., Maloutas, T. and Padovani, L. (2004) *Housing & Welfare in Southern Europe*. Oxford: Blackwell.

Allon, F. (2010) Speculating on Everyday Life: The Cultural Economy of the Quotidian. *Journal of Communication Inquiry* 34(4): 366–381.

Bambra C. (2007) Sifting the Wheat from the Chaff: A Two-dimensional Discriminant Analysis of Welfare State Regime Theory. *Social Policy & Administration* 41(1): 1–28.

Bourne, L.S. (1981) *The Geography of Housing*. London: Edward Arnold.

Boyer, R. (2000) Is a Finance-led Growth Regime a Viable Alternative to Fordism? A Preliminary Analysis. *Economy and Society* 29(1): 111–145.

Christophers, B. (2015) The Limits to Financialization. *Dialogues in Human Geography* 5(2): 183–200.

Coq-Huelva, D. (2013) Urbanisation and Financialisation in the Context of a Rescaling State: The Case of Spain. *Antipode* 45(5): 1213–1231.

Di Feliciantonio, C. (in press) Subjectification in Times of Indebtedness and Neoliberal/Austerity Urbanism. *Antipode*.

Doling, J. and Ford, J. (Eds) (2003) *Globalisation and Home Ownership: Experiences in Eight Member States of the European Union*. Delft: DUP Science.

Esping-Andersen, G. (1990). *The Three Worlds of Welfare Capitalism*. Cambridge: Polity Press.

Fields, D. (2014) Contesting the Financialization of Urban Space: Community Organizations and the Struggle to Preserve Affordable Rental Housing in New York City. *Journal of Urban Affairs* 37(2): 144–165.

Gotham, K.F. (2009) Creating Liquidity Out of Spatial Fixity: The Secondary Circuit of Capital and the Subprime Mortgage Crisis. *International Journal of Urban and Regional Research* 33(2): 355–371.

Hall, S. (2012) Geographies of Money and Finance II: Financialization and Financial Subjects. *Progress in Human Geography* 36(3): 403–411.

Heeg, S. (2013) Wohnungen als Finanzanlage. Auswirkungen von Responsibilisierung und Finanzialisierung im Bereich des Wohnens. *s u b \ u r b a n*. *Zeitschrift für Kritische Stadtforschung*. 1: 75–99.

Kaika, M. and Ruggiero, L. (2014) Land Financialization as a "Lived" Process: The transformation of Milan's Bicocca by Pirelli. *European Urban and Regional Studies* DOI: 10.1177/0969776413484166.

Kemeny, J. (1992) *Housing and Social Theory*. London: Routledge.

Knorr Cetina, K and Preda, A. (2005) Introduction. In: Knorr Cetina, K and Preda, A. (Eds) *The Sociology of Financial Markets*. Oxford: Oxford University Press.

Krippner, G. (2005) The Financialization of the American Economy, *Socio-Economic Review*, 3: 173–208.

Langley, P. (2008) Sub-prime Mortgage Lending: A Cultural Economy. *Economy and Society* 37(4): 469–494.

Newman, K. (2009) Post-Industrial Widgets: Capital Flows and the Production of the Urban. *International Journal of Urban and Regional Research* 33(2): 314–331.

Ronald, R. (2008) *The Ideology of Home Ownership Homeowner Societies and the Role of Housing*. Basingstoke: Palgrave Macmillan.

Rossi, U. (2013) On Life as a Fictitious Commodity: Cities and the Biopolitics of Late Neoliberalism. *International Journal of Urban and Regional Research* 37(3): 1067–1074.

Savini, F. and Aalbers, M.B. (OnlineFirst in 2015) The De-contextualization of Land Use Planning through Financialisation: Urban Redevelopment in Milan. *European Urban and Regional Studies*. doi:10.1177/0969776415585887.

Smith, S.J. and Munro, M. (Eds) (2008) The Microstructures of Housing Markets. *Housing Studies* 23(2): 159–367.

Torgersen, U. (1987) Housing: The Wobbly Pillar under the Welfare State. *Scandinavian Housing and Planning Research* 4(S1): 116–126.

Trouillard, E. (2013) Development of a Financialized Rental Investment Product: Private Serviced Residences in the Paris Region (Île-de-France). Working paper, *Transforming Cities: Urban Processes and Structure*. URL: researchrepository.ucd.ie.

Uffer, S. (2014) Wohnungsprivatisierung in Berlin. Eine Analyse verschiedener Investitionsstrategien und deren Konsequenzen für die Stadt und ihre Bewohner. In: A. Holm (Ed.) *Reclaim Berlin. Soziale Kämpfe in der neoliberalen Stadt*, pp. 64–82. Berlin: Assoziation A.

Waldron, R. (2014) *Mortgage Stress and the Impact of the Irish Property Crash*. PhD dissertation. Dublin: University College Dublin.

Walks, R.A. (2013) Mapping the Urban Debtscape: The Geography of Household Debt in Canadian Cities. *Urban Geography* 34(2): 153–187.

Wainwright, T. (2009) Laying the Foundations for a Crisis: Mapping the Historico-Geographical Construction of RMBS Securitization in the UK. *International Journal of Urban and Regional Research* 33(2): 372–388.

2 Centring Housing in Political Economy

With Brett Christophers

1. Political Economy and the Housing Question

Historically, property and land—their use, the desire to acquire them and the need to regulate their transfer—were among the fundamental reasons for the development of states. Property and land were, and still are, foundational to both power and wealth. The tensions present in acquiring and maintaining power and wealth are embedded in a property system that brings into play an entire social order, and in which housing relations today figure prominently. That, it seems to us, should be reason enough for political economy to take housing seriously; it is likewise reason for housing researchers to take political economy seriously.

But what do we mean by "political economy"? There are many schools of thought that call themselves political economy. Sometimes, the term is used to refer to a specific group of heterodox economists; or, to a cohort of political scientists especially interested in the economy, in what is often called "international political economy" or "comparative political economy". In addition, there is a different (but related) political economy within sociology and geography, heavily influenced by Marxist thinking (as we can clearly see in the work of David Harvey), though by no means exclusively so. What these different political economy traditions have in common, and what tends to distinguish them from mainstream economics, is that they analyse "the economy within its social and political context rather than seeing it as a separate entity driven by its own set of rules based on individual self-interest" (Mackinnon and Cumbers 2007, 14). In the present paper, we are mostly interested in reaching out to this interdisciplinary field of political economy outside the economics discipline.[1]

Yet despite our opening assertion that housing *should* be central to political economy thus conceived, it never really has been. Marx, like the classical "bourgeois" political economists who preceded him, gave it short shrift. And while Engels was the author of *The Housing Question* (1979[1887]) and had discussed housing at length in *The Condition of the Working Class in England* (1987[1845]), his perspective on housing was deeply ambivalent: he recognized its social and political importance but, for reasons we shall discuss below, resisted making it a core concern of radical political-economic theory.

Similarly, and partly because of that historical sidelining, the issue of housing has not been granted an important role in post-war political economy. Housing-as-policy became the preserve of social policy analysis and of a growing field of housing studies that have both shown relatively little interest in the issues that typically concern political economists. Housing-as-market was similarly largely siloed, within mainstream economics. The latter's pre-occupation with "free markets" and its lack of analysis of power relations or of state involvement— beyond the statement that the latter hampers the functioning of markets—has militated against an integrated analysis of housing as a crucial part of political economy. Equally, interest in housing within what was by now a very isolated Marxian political economy tradition (see especially Berry 1979) tended to restrict such interest not only to a limited set of analytical concerns but also to a productionist perspective. The important work of, in particular, Ball (1988) on "structures of housing provision" sought to break away from Marxian productionism, but only with modest success.

In recent years, however, there has been a growing and broadly based recognition of the increasing centrality of housing to the political economy of advanced capitalist societies in much more than a production-related sense. This recognition is most explicit in the work of Schwartz and Seabrooke (2009), who have introduced the concept of "varieties of residential capitalism", building on both the varieties of capitalism literature within political economy and debates within housing studies on the role of homeownership in welfare states. Based on the simple variables of owner-occupation rate and mortgages-as-a-share-of-GDP they have developed four sophisticated residential capitalist "ideal types" that each have a distinct set of housing politics. By doing this, Schwartz and Seabrooke offer an important and illuminating perspective on the role of housing in different varieties of capitalism; nevertheless, we continue to lack a coherent and relatively comprehensive conceptualization of the place of housing in the contemporary capitalist political economy, more generally.

This paper sets out to try to offer such a conceptualization—partly to help bring together existing but typically self-standing arguments about different elements of the political economy of housing; partly to help frame and connect up on-going research in this area; and partly to insist that political-economic analysis more generally *must* take housing seriously. We argue that housing is implicated in the contemporary political economy in numerous critical, connected, and very often contradictory ways. In doing so we lean on the housing studies literature to the extent that it addresses the questions that political economists are interested in and we connect these often fragmented and isolated insights to those of the relatively few political economists who have studied housing. And we present our argument specifically by going back to what it is arguably the central category of political economy, "capital", and identify the multiple (and ever more material) roles of housing when capital is considered from the perspective of each of its three primary, mutually constitutive guises: capital as process of circulation; capital as social relation; and capital as ideology.

The three main sections of the paper, therefore, consider housing's centrality to each such "modality" of capital. There then follows a short conclusion in which we reflect primarily on implied priorities and possibilities for future research. Before proceeding, however, two brief observations are necessary by way of framing. First, in view of space constraints, our discussion of rent is limited to the rent of housing and does not therefore encompass land rent. The latter is obviously a crucial vector of coordination of spatial economies of the built environment, and it shapes—and is shaped by—the political economy of housing, not least in relation to capital circulation, in significant ways (e.g. Harvey 1982; Ball 1985; Haila, 2015). Equally, we recognize that when we speak of house prices, we are in fact, in most instances, speaking of a combination of prices for the physical house and the underlying land. After all, differences between and particular developments in house prices are first and foremost a result of differences between and changes in the price of the land that a house sits on. But a proper consideration of the role of land as separate from housing is simply not possible here. Second, and related to this, it is important to distinguish between housing *per se* and the more ill-defined category of "property" with which housing is often used interchangeably, but which (equally often) also can include land not used for housing. Our paper is about housing. That said, some of its arguments, such as that pertaining to capital switching, apply equally to other forms of (e.g. commercial) property (though even here we would argue that housing is, today, especially material); but many of its arguments do not, but rather are specific to the housing phenomenon.

2. Housing and the Circulation of Capital

In political economy in general, and Marx in particular, capital is conceptualized as a process of circulation. Stripped down to its essentials, this process is typically seen to comprise the following main stages. First, money is advanced to secure the means necessary to produce goods and services; those means often include raw materials, and *always* include wage labour. Second, those collective means are mobilized in the production process to produce the goods or services in question. Third, these goods or services are offered for sale (realization) on the market in exchange for money: money now, in theory, comprising the quantum originally invested in production *plus* the "surplus" value created in production. This money—minus, *inter alia*, consumption expenditures and deductions for things like interest and rent—is then reinvested in production once more. And so, the circle having been squared, the process is renewed.

Our argument in this section is that housing is pivotal to this process of circulation in numerous key respects, and is increasingly so; or, to put it another way, it is that we cannot hope to understand the circulation of capital, least of all today, without recognizing the multifaceted materiality of housing to this process.

Perhaps, the most obvious and logical place to begin building this recognition is with housing's important figuration as itself an output of the production process: as, that is to say, the "thing" produced by labour and sold for profit (e.g.

Ball 1988). Housing may of course be produced by the labour that intends to consume the end product (i.e. it may be self-built), but increasingly in both advanced and less-advanced capitalist societies housing is not produced and consumed by the same people. Its creation is the locus of wage-labour-based production. Thus, housing construction and development is an important sector in narrow economic terms, whether measured in terms of added labour value and number of jobs created or in terms of contribution to GDP. Additional jobs are also created in other housing industries, e.g. housing renovation and refurbishment, furniture and housing accessories, kitchen and bathroom outfitters, and home improvement stores (Bourdieu 2005). This partly explains why the housing industry is often seen as an economic sector that needs to be stimulated in order to foster economic growth more widely. This was most visible in the first post-Second World War decades when Keynesian policies often singled out the housing sector as a prime beneficiary of government-induced economic growth (e.g. Florida and Feldman 1988).

Yet housing's physical materialization as a product of labour is only one small dimension of its significance to capital circulation. If we return to our basic picture of this process, we saw that some of the value that is realized through the sale of products and services is thrown back into production. But not all of it is. And even that which is, does not necessarily get used immediately. Value, under capitalism, also has to be stored. And while money—cash—is one vehicle of such storage, it is not the only one. Housing is another. Contrary to most other commodified consumer goods, it can pay to invest not only in the production of housing, but also in the ownership of it, for while the market price of a car or a laptop goes down merely by owning it (even without using it), the market price of a house often remains stable or appreciates whether one uses the house or not, largely because the price of the underlying land typically will not decrease in the long term. This simple fact—housing-cum-land's role as a store of value—turns out to be of enormous significance for understanding capital circulation in the contemporary world.

Consider first of all, in this regard, the fact that housing *itself circulates*. We buy and sell it among one other. We do so sometimes because we desire one house's "use value" over that of another. But we might also do so partly or exclusively to exploit housing's "exchange value", which derives from the fact that value is stored in housing-cum-land. In other words, one way to profit from owning a house is to sell it for a higher price than it was bought for, as one can also do with stocks or pieces of art, for example. Ownership for the exclusive reason of selling a product for a higher price is referred to by economists as "speculation" and housing speculation assumes many guises. First, there is the homeowner who lives in a house but hopes to resell it for a higher price and trade-up in the market. Second, there is the pure speculator who buys and sells houses without even considering occupying them or renting them out. Third, there is the speculator who tries to buy in one market segment and sell in another, i.e. speculators who benefit from—and often contribute to—the socio-spatial division of housing markets. "Blockbusters", for example in the US context, were real estate brokers who preyed on white homeowners' fear of the prospect of black neighbours and of the impact of their presence on housing prices by encouraging such homeowners to sell their houses for low prices "while they still could", then reselling the houses for higher prices to aspiring black homeowners who were often excluded from buying properties in other neighbourhoods and were willing to pay a premium (Gotham 2002). One can also think here of downmarket private landlords who buy up dilapidated housing in declining neighbourhoods and make money first by "milking" the property—minimizing maintenance and maximizing rents, often by renting to people lacking choice in the wider housing market (e.g. undocumented migrants)—and then by selling it for a higher price, either to landlords or developers preying on gentrification or zoning changes who plan to vacate and renovate (or vacate, demolish and new build) the housing, or to government agencies involved in urban renewal and revitalization schemes (Aalbers 2006).

Whether housing is exchanged for its use or exchange values or both, its circulation is highly material to the circulation of *capital* in the wider sense introduced above. For one thing, the exchange of housing has important "knock-on" effects within the production process at the heart of capital circulation—in relation both to the production of housing per se, and the production of other goods and services. In the case of the former, the significant fact is that in most markets the circulation of existing housing also sets the prices for newly constructed housing, thereby calibrating the value and surplus value that can be generated through housing production.[2] In the case of the latter, the pertinent issue is that housing's spin-off sibling industries include not only the aforementioned production-related sectors but also sectors implicated primarily in housing *exchange*: most notably, of course, the field of real estate agents, brokers and other intermediaries, who are all dependent on the circulation of housing (Bourdieu 2005).

For another thing, the exchange of housing often assumes a vital function in actually *enabling* capital to continue to circulate. One of Marx's great insights—and one of the things that distinguished his work most clearly from his "bourgeois" predecessors—was that circulation periodically, and for all manner of reasons, can break down. Capital's flow is rarely smooth and often interrupted. Indeed "crisis", for Marx, was—and for David Harvey and many Keynesian economists, even more so, is—a question in large measure of blockages to circulation. One such blockage concerns the question of what is called "effective demand", and it is in this context that the exchange of housing is especially relevant. An obvious problem that capitalism can face is that there simply is not enough demand in the market for the products and services that are being or can potentially be produced. If people cannot afford to buy things, or choose to hoard their savings instead of consuming them, circulation grinds to a halt: value cannot be realized, and thus re-invested; and if value cannot be realized, capitalists will soon stop producing it. This is called a crisis of "effective demand". But where does housing fit in? The answer is that housing, as an exchangeable store of value, furnishes means of funding effective demand when other sources dry up. If a buoyant housing market sees prices rising, demand for capitalist products and services tends to rise. Some people, after all, *are* wealthier—those who sell up, at a profit. But even those who do not actually crystallize their gains through sale may *feel* wealthier and spend accordingly—sometimes nominally crystallizing gains through equity release (where one "releases" cash by taking on more mortgage debt) (Wood *et al.* 2013).

Crouch (2011) and Watson (2010) discuss this dynamic in terms of an explicit government policy that they have respectively dubbed "privatized Keynesianism" and "house price Keynesianism", where households, rather than the government itself, are encouraged to take on debt—under the banner of "wealth effects"—to stimulate the economy. Privatized or house price Keynesianism is hereby seen as a way both to fuel the economy by propping up consumption and to "compensate" labour for decades of negligible or even negative real income growth. The result is that in many countries mortgage debt has increased much faster than homeownership rates or even than house prices (Stephens 2003; Aalbers 2008). This has vital implications for how we understand the propulsion of capital circulation. In the UK, for instance, approximately two-thirds of all bank lending in 2009 was for residential mortgages (Turner 2013): to the extent that they lubricate on-going circulation through credit creation, in other words, UK banks have increasingly replaced supply-side (i.e. corporate lending) with demand-side stimuli, with housing debt being overwhelmingly privileged.[3] Moreover, increasing homeownership latterly drew in more vulnerable households with an insecure labour market position as a result of economic and labour market restructuring (Ford, Burrows, and Nettleton 2001; Doling and Ford 2003; Smith, Searle, and Cook 2009). Such households enjoyed less price inflation and thus fewer "wealth effects", with commensurately less upside impact on effective demand—especially given that these households usually lacked the buffers to ride out succeeding price declines.[4]

Indeed, many Western economies have become so addicted to high and increasing house prices that it seems difficult for governments and households alike to deal with a situation of declining prices, which are seen as lowering people's economic perceptions and therefore as having a negative influence on the economy at large. Thus, although declining house prices could imply increased housing affordability, the mantra that "rising house prices are good" remains entrenched, buttressed as it is by pressure on states from the home-owning electorate and the housing market lobby to do everything in their power to protect price levels. Even in times of austerity, the housing sector is still seen as a key vehicle to foster economic growth beyond housing markets per se (Forrest and Yip 2011). Sometimes the dominant thinking appears to be: if only people would believe that their houses prices would go up again, they would start spending more, thereby kick-starting the economy. Whether this is really the case is not even that relevant; the fact that state institutions act based on this belief by promoting the circulation of housing, e.g. by (temporarily) lowering stamp tax, means that its effects on the housing sector and the wider economy are real.

If exchange practices in the housing sector can help relieve problems of effective demand and get capital flowing again, housing also constitutes part of the "fix" to other notable problems of capital circulation. The most important is that of "overaccumulation". Where a lack of effective demand entails too much output of products and services relative to the demand for such output, overaccumulation—which may be connected to problems of effective demand, but does not have to be—entails too much value being produced in the aggregate relative to profitable opportunities for reinvestment thereof. It represents, therefore, another way in which circulation can grind to a halt: if capitalists feel they cannot make money by reinvesting their wealth in the production of new products and services, they hoard their wealth instead, and economic growth—not to mention employment—is threatened accordingly

Housing helps avert crisis tendencies here, too, though it is housing *production* rather than exchange that comes to the rescue in this case. How? Harvey's (1985) work is particularly insightful here. Not only, Harvey argues, is surplus value generated through the production of housing, but surplus value generated in other sectors of the economy is pumped into the housing sector through a process that he calls "capital switching". The idea of capital switching, building on Keynesian foundations, needs to be situated against the backdrop of Harvey's wider (1982) argument that financial institutions see the built environment—which includes but is not limited to housing—as an asset in which money can be dis/invested by directing and withdrawing capital to the highest and best use. If the generic "circuit of capital" which we sketched above (revolving around the production of goods and services) represents the "primary" circuit of capital, then Harvey suggests that we can think of production and reproduction specifically of the built environment, including housing, as a "secondary" circuit of capital. To be sure, such production generates surplus *sui generis* insofar as labour is put to work. But, for Harvey, it does so much more: it serves as an overflow tank into which "surplus" (i.e. overaccumulated) capital can be switched—and then, effectively, parked, until such time as conditions of overaccumulation have eased—when capitalists are unable profitably to reinvest it in the primary circuit. In short, capitalists respond to signs of overaccumulation and try to avert a crisis in the primary circuit by investing in the secondary circuit—albeit eventually overinvesting in the built environment, too (Harvey 1985).

Harvey's capital switching may sound uncomfortably structural and abstract, but once we start looking at actual housing crises, it is easy to see how many of them have been caused by overinvestment in the previous years of housing boom. The boom periods, just like the bust periods in housing cycles, are produced in the wider political-economic sphere, not only because surplus capital is extracted from other sectors of the economy but also because this is politically facilitated. The deflation of the IT bubble and the inflation of the housing bubble are empirically and analytically related—it is a clear example of capital switching to the secondary circuit of capital (Ashton 2009; Gotham 2009; Christophers 2011). But switching of capital has also been facilitated by the state: the spread of mortgage securitization, for instance, was enabled by adapting existing legal frameworks for housing finance to the needs of lenders and investment banks who wanted to expand the existing secondary mortgage market to free up capital for other uses—i.e. to facilitate the switching of capital in and out of housing (Aalbers 2008; Gotham 2009; see Chapter 3). Similar stories can be told for subprime and predatory lending in the USA (Wyly *et al.* 2009), the demutualization of building societies in the UK (Martin and Turner 2000) and Ireland (Murphy 1995), and the entry of consumer banks into the domain of mortgage lending in a whole range of countries (Dymski 1999).

3.   Housing and the Social Relations of Capital

For Marx, capital was a social relation just as much as a process of circulation. This social relation, as he conceptualized it, was first and foremost a dualistic and antagonistic one: capitalists (the owners of the means of production) on the one side and labourers on the other. In today's world, where housing is so often discussed in the abstract, depersonalized terms of "exchange", Marx's inherently socialized framing of political economy remains as vital as ever, even if his particular dualistic depiction requires revisiting. Capital is constituted by social relations, and housing, we argue here, is multiply-implicated in the forms and dynamics thereof. To envision housing merely as a "commodity" is therefore to lapse into precisely the fetishism that Marx attacked, whereby relations between people—the people who build, own, rent and *live in* houses—are reduced to the politically and analytically impoverished status of relations between things.

How might we begin systematically to conceptualize housing and capital-as-social-relation beyond Marx? A logical place to start is with the manifestation of the very fact of uneven social relations in the shape of the inequalities of wealth generated *by* capital. When capital circulates, value, as we have seen, is accumulated, distributed and stored as what we term "wealth". Such wealth takes numerous forms, among them cash money and company securities (often held in pensions), but it is of immense significance that in many capitalist societies residential property is the largest individual wealth/asset class although at the same time many—in some countries most—households own no residential property whatsoever. As such, it is in housing that the vast wealth inequalities of capitalist societies, which we hear so much about today, are often most visible and most material.

Social relations and their dissonance are, in other words, writ large in the physical landscape of housing. Housing, not least due to characteristic spatial expressions of inequality in segregated towns and cities, is vividly representative of capital's production of haves and—strictly in terms of holdings of wealth—have-nots (Wilson 1987; Massey and Denton 1993; Van Kempen and Özüekren 1998). The latter come in many guises, of course, among them slum-dwellers, most (if not all) renters, and those whose home "ownership" means much less in practice than in name—either because their houses are of limited use or exchange value, or because the mortgage lender is the effective owner. But two other categories of have-nots testify to housing's mediation of unequal social relations more clearly still. One is the homeless (e.g. Somerville 1992; Fitzpatrick 2005); the other the growing army of live-in domestic servants not only in cities of the Global South but also increasingly in cities such as London and New York (Jelin 1977; Sassen 1996; Lutz 2002), a class whose re-materialization harks back to the Victorian age as well as to colonialism and their own sharp social inequalities (Hecht 1981; Higgs 1983). Not only can such servants typically not afford their own housing, they are compelled to service the homes and lives of those who can, with the divide between them inscribed in the social and physical space of the house itself.

While housing clearly crystallizes the dislocation of social relations, it also reproduces and reinforces such dislocation in an explicitly spatial—dis*location*— sense. The poor location of housing may, for instance, increase commuting times and hamper access to good schools, clean air, transportation and a wide range of other services, recreational and commercial spaces, and so forth. It may also increase residents' exposure to crime, environmental pollution, flooding and a whole range of other problems. The so-called "neighbourhood effects" literature has amply demonstrated this (e.g. Briggs 1997; Friedrichs, Galster, and Musterd 2003; Van Ham *et al.* 2012), albeit without sufficiently recognizing that the spatial relations of housing are not constitutive in a socially abstract sense but are themselves always and everywhere the outcome of social, power-laden processes (Aalbers 2011; Slater 2013). And of course, the location of housing influences not only its use value but also its exchange value—i.e. the geo-physical landscape of housing works through and impacts both on capital's social relations *and* on the capital circulation processes discussed in the previous section.

Meanwhile, the social inequalities manifested in the ownership of housing stock are potentially very problematic for capital. This is partly for reasons alluded to earlier, relating to the problems of realization and effective demand (the more unequal ownership is, the more "house price Keynesianism" becomes dependent on the demand provided by a privileged minority). But it is also problematic because, *ceteris paribus*, ownership correlates with access and the cost thereof, and affordable access to housing is a sine qua non of the very reproduction of capitalism and its social relations. Without the healthy social reproduction of labour, after all, circulation grinds to a halt.

Housing, in short, is central to the matter of social reproduction, and not only insofar as the domestic sphere is where much of the work of social reproduction occurs. The—literally—vital imperative of housing to social reproduction helps explain, in large part, the persistence and power of the discourse of a "right" to housing, as opposed, pointedly, to the "right" to buy and sell it (Lefebvre 1996; Bengtsson 2001; Rolnik 2013; Aalbers and Gibb, 2014). And the question of social reproduction and its viability also relates to housing in a way that brings to the fore a social-relational issue that is never far away when capitalist housing is in the spotlight: that of social conflict. For ultimately, there is surely only so much inequality, embedded *inter alia* in differential housing wealth, that society's have-nots will tolerate whilst still contributing to the circulation and reproduction of capital.

All of this helps to explain a further crucial aspect of housing's role in the negotiation of the social relations of capital. Given the importance of housing to social and (therefore) economic reproduction, interventionist states have often made housing provision, whether in the form of subsidized physical property itself or of housing "benefits" of some kind, part of their redistributive programs. Such programs aim, explicitly, to rebalance and redistribute—even if only modestly— the skewed social relations endemic to capital and intensified by it (and crystallized, of course, in unequal housing ownership and access); and in so doing, they aim, also more-or-less explicitly, to make social reproduction smoother. There are certain similarities here with the methods and objectives of the private "welfare capitalists" of the late nineteenth and early-twentieth centuries who supplied workers with housing. They, too, recognized that capital was endangered by *not* redistributing wealth in this way. Engels was scornful of such assistance—it tied to one-place workers whose mobility was seen to enhance their bargaining power—but recognized the (for capital) productive purposes it served.

To think about housing only as a store of wealth, as a prerequisite of reproduction and as a tool of redistribution however, is to overlook the fact that social exploitation occurs *in and through* housing, too. Such housing-centred exploitation has been shown to take place in a myriad different ways: in the infamous redlining practices of mortgage lenders (Harvey and Chatterjee 1974; Jackson 1985; Squires 1992; Aalbers 2011); in the discriminatory allocations of public housing companies and other urban gatekeepers (Pahl 1975; Pearce 1979; Henderson and Karn 1984); in the predatory lending and foreclosures of the subprime crisis (Squires 2004; Immergluck 2009; Saegert, Fields, and Libman 2009; Wyly *et al.* 2009); in the lack of rights or local knowledge of migrants, both documented and undocumented, in poor overpriced housing in both the owner-occupied (emergency buyers) and rental sectors (Teijmant and Schepens 1981; Karn, Kemeny, and Williams 1985; Aalbers 2006); in the creation of the domestic-servant class discussed above (Hecht 1981; Lutz 2002); in the dispossessions engineered by the architects of neighbourhood gentrification (Smith 1979; Marcuse 1985; Lees, Slater, and Wyly 2008); and in the evictions effected (Desmond 2012) and monopoly rents charged (Berry 1981; Harvey 1985; López-Morales 2011; Fields, 2015) by private landlords.

That private property rental *can* be exploitative, by virtue of its frequently monopolistic qualities, partly explains why the state has often endeavoured to control residential rental prices to one degree or another. Rent is a contractual social relation; rent regulation and control, which can take innumerable different forms, thus constitute another, indirect tool of redistribution, in contexts where housing is seen to enable the dislocation of such relations. At certain points in time, some states—often in conjunction with expanding direct control over the local housing stock—have regulated the private-rented sector, and in particular rent pricing, to the point where private landlords feel that is it difficult to extract profits and have thus opted out of housing, resulting in a declining private rental market (Harloe 1985). Although the private-rented sector, especially with a lack of tenant protection, can be vulnerable to exploitation, it can also be seen as a crucial part of the housing stock that potentially offers greater flexibility for tenants when both social-rented housing and homeownership are inaccessible/unattractive—whether the reason is waiting lists, income limits, mortgage lenders' requirements, citizenship restrictions or a desire to avoid long-term investment. It is a sector that defies sweeping generalization (Allen and McDowell 1989). Private rental markets are, for instance, usually the only segment that is accessible to the lion's share of newcomers to a housing market, including intra- and inter-national migrants, young people, ex-prisoners and others. A country like Germany, moreover, has shown that a private rental market—with rents and other variables suitably regulated—can be profitable to landlords as well as relatively free of tenant exploitation (Kleinman 1996). But as neoliberal, market-oriented reforms have swept the capitalist world in recent decades, rent regulation has been phased out in many countries, giving increasingly free rein to the "free" markets within which, seemingly paradoxically, monopoly pricing can thrive.

There is, to be sure, a legitimate question mark over whether "exploitation" is the right word in this regard. Engels, for his part, actually believed not. The landlord-rentier merely "cheated" the labourer (and tenant); only the factory capitalist truly *exploited* her, by stealing her unpaid labour time. This was a large part of the reason why Engels saw the housing question as only a secondary "evil". It was pointless, as he saw it, to strive to abolish such evils—as the likes of Proudhon urged—while maintaining the capitalist mode of production that was the basis for the generation of those evils. To eliminate interest on mortgages, for instance, was, in Engels' view, merely to advantage the industrial capitalist vis-à-vis the rentier, not the worker vis-à-vis the industrial capitalist. Nor, we should say, is this mere semantics: exploitation, for both Engels and Marx, could occur only in production because it was only in production, and not in exchange or the secondary circuit of capital, that value was created.

These issues help to foreground what became, in the 1970s and 1980s, a lively and influential debate over the relationship between housing and the particular dimension of social difference emphasized by Marx and Engels: that of class. On the one side were Marxists, who insisted that one's position in the housing market is a result of one's position in the labour market, i.e. social class determines housing position (Ball 1986; Barlow and Duncan 1988). On the other side were Weberians, who maintained that this was a reductive reading that underplayed housing's role in actively *shaping*, as opposed to merely crystallizing, social relations. They suggested that perhaps, social position is derived from housing position, instead, i.e. position in the housing market determines social class (Rex and Moore 1967; Pahl 1975; Saunders 1984). Pahl (1975), for example, argued that capital gains from housing would blur inequalities arising in the labour market and create a division between owners and renters. Saunders (1984) took the Weberian view the furthest, arguing that the housing market gives rise to a new class division. Over time, a more balanced view of so-called "housing classes" has emerged: Murie and Forrest (2001), for example, point to an essential reciprocity: housing position is class (labour market) dependent, but housing itself also transforms this class division.

What is also clear, crucially, is that such divided social relations, and housing's role in their realization/reproduction, are not reducible to class dimensions alone. Race/ethnicity and gender palpably intersect with class, in all manner of different and complex ways, in producing the variegated landscape of social difference and inequality we associate with capitalist societies. Of course, social scientists have researched and demonstrated these intersections much more widely than in relation to housing alone. But housing's intimate implication in what we *do* choose to refer to here as processes of exploitation does appear to be especially emblematic of the intersections in question. This has nowhere been more evident than in regard to the recent financial crisis and its subprime epicentre, where race/ethnicity and gender were centrally bound up with class in the systematically uneven predations of mortgage finance and foreclosure (Squires 2004; Wyly *et al.* 2009; Aalbers 2012; Ashton 2012; Roberts 2013).

In short, we know, and political economy must therefore recognize, that housing serves as a principal crucible for the exacerbation of multiply-constituted social inequality. And in closing this section, we can usefully consider one axis on which such inequalities play out that we have not yet addressed: the generational axis. This axis is complicated because it needs to be examined from more than one perspective. Inequality *between* generations is certainly one: with widespread deregulation of housing and financial markets having spurred owner-occupancy and driven huge real house-price inflation in large parts of the capitalist world in recent decades, older generations, where ownership of housing wealth is inevitably concentrated, have benefited disproportionately. But inequalities *within* those older generations are important, too, as they do not just die away with the latter—through various pre- and post-mortality inheritance mechanisms, rather they are passed on to descendants (Allen *et al.* 2004; Helderman and Mulder 2007), and magnified, as the gap between those who benefit from housing wealth and those unable to access it grows ever larger, in particular, now that in the post-boom landscape, access to mortgages has decreased and reliance on intergenerational wealth transfers increased (Forrest and Yip 2011). Equally importantly, meanwhile, these fractured social relations are being handed down not just to any generation—but to a generation seemingly more obsessed than any that came before with the ideology of homeownership.

4.   Housing and the Ideology of Capital

As well as a process and a constellation of social relations, capital is quite clearly also an ideological institution. As depicted by both critics and champions over the course of more than two centuries, this ideological institution has three critical components. One is the absolute centrality of private property, the monopoly power over which is, says Harvey (2002, 97), "both the beginning point and the end point of all capitalist activity". A second is the primacy of markets, characterized by "free" competition, as the superior mechanism for the allocation of resources. And the third is the imperative of the accumulation of wealth.

"Accumulate, accumulate! That is Moses and the prophets!", as Marx famously wrote of capitalist ideology in Volume 1 of *Capital*.

Our argument in this section is that housing, for at least two reasons, is fundamental to this ideology. First, because the ideology in question is arguably nowhere more explicit and pronounced than in relation to housing; which is to say that the ideology of housing today *epitomizes* capitalist ideology more generally, inasmuch as private property ownership, market allocation mechanisms and accumulation strategies are decisively privileged. And second, because housing not only epitomizes but *buttresses* that wider capitalist ideology: it is in and through housing that much of the political work of reproducing and reinforcing the ideology of capital is performed.

Private property ownership is an ideological institution that is most dominant and absolute in capitalism but also present in many other state/market forms. Private property is not truly "private" because it is protected by the state and because it confers a very public power over resources and others (Gray 1991, 304). Indeed, private property rights presuppose states and are presented as natural and normal even though they are quite meaningless without being validated by the state's apparatus, whether that is the law or the state's monopoly on violence. In "pre-modern" states, the state and powerful landowners relied mostly on the monopoly on violence, but in advanced capitalist societies the law is the institution par excellence to embed the ideology of private property rights in wider societal relationships. But if the institution of law turns out to be insufficient to enforce private property rights, property owners will often try to mobilize the state's monopoly on violence, e.g. in the case of evicting squatters. Private property is not only about power over an object, it is fundamentally about the ability to exclude others from the use of it (Davies 2007).

Furthermore, while it may now seem like a long time ago that land and property ownership was a *condicio sine qua non* for formal political participation, in various places around the world communities are still, or again, effectively governed by homeowner associations and other private forms of government based on the ownership of housing (McKenzie 1994; Atkinson and Blandy 2005). Thus, private property is not only about the power over an object and the ability to exclude others from it; it is also related directly to political participation. Even in the present day and age, the acquisition of housing sometimes entitles people to citizenship rights. Spain has recently been in the spotlight for trying to rejuvenate its housing market by offering second citizenship to those purchasing property for more than €160,000. But outside the spotlight, a few dozen countries as diverse as Latvia, the Czech Republic, Austria, Panama, the Bahamas, St. Kitts and Nevis (e.g. Grabar 2012), and in some way also the US (O'Toole 2012) have a type of "citizenship-by-investment" programme or policy. The idea—and for some philosophers and policy-makers the ideal—of a capitalist property-owning democracy (Rawls 1971; Daunton 1987; O'Neill and Williamson 2012) is not only an historical artefact but also standing practice in some countries.

As both material artefact and ideology, private property is also contested and at the forefront of ideological battles within capitalism, as illustrated by social movements related to, for example, squatting and the right to housing. Furthermore, debates on the privatization, neoliberalization and financialization of housing go to the core of debates about capitalist ideology and practice, more generally (Aalbers 2008; Ronald 2008; Saegert, Fields, and Libman 2009; Rolnik 2013). There are many reasons for this, but one is that housing is tied directly to *each* individual, household and community as well as to the very heart of what states and markets do, and the debate over what they should do. Since the dichotomies of state and market, of public and private, are by their very nature problematic in the field of housing, the latter is a febrile place to study the political economy of actually existing capitalisms.

The fetishization of the ideology not only of private property but also of wealth-accumulation and markets is, of course, writ large in the political project of expanding homeownership (Kemeny 1981; Ronald and Elsinga 2012), which has characterized the vast majority of capitalist states—new and old—in the post-war era, particularly since the 1980s and (in post-communist states) 1990s, important exceptions such as Germany and Switzerland notwithstanding (Kleinman 1996; Lawson 2009). The often-mentioned advantages of homeownership—including but not limited to so-called "wealth effects" (Case, Quigley, and Shiller 2005); saving-in-brick for (and lower expenses during) retirement and therefore lower state expenditure on senior citizens (asset-based welfare) (Regan and Paxton 2001); "better", more involved and empowered citizens (Rohe, Van Zandt, and McCarthy 2002)—are generally not so much intrinsic features of homeownership as they are consequences of the political project of pushing homeownership at the expense of other tenures. This is not only a political project in the most general meaning of political, but also in the narrow meaning of what politicians and political parties do. It was Engels who warned against the embourgeoisement of the working class as it would minimize their autonomy by making them dependent on income from labour and therefore diminish the chance of them starting a revolution. It is exactly for this reason that politicians of various stripes have promoted working-class homeownership (often alongside suburbanization): as a bulwark against communism and revolts by giving working class residents a stake in the system, by making them dependent on wage labour, and by locating them further from the urban centres of oppositional movements.

Widened homeownership, crucially, may also erode support for various kinds of welfare state intervention. Kemeny (1995) and Castles (1998) have shown that the expansion of homeownership in countries that traditionally had bigger housing rental markets and bigger and often publicly funded pension systems has been accompanied by declining support for welfare state intervention in general and public pension systems in particular. They have termed this "the really big trade-off", suggesting that people's housing situation is fundamental to welfare state support, and (thus) that the politics of housing are fundamental to the political economy of advanced capitalist states more widely. The policy ideal of "asset-based welfare"—in fact, housing asset-based *wealth*—certainly suggests—explicitly or implicitly—that state redistribution can be diminished if more low-income households are homeowners who can reap the ostensible benefits of homeownership (Regan and Paxton 2001; Doling and Ronald 2010).

The political promotion of homeownership takes many forms, but none perhaps more transparent than housing privatization initiatives—from the Right-to-Buy in the UK and housing-privatization-as-shock-absorber in many post-communist countries to many demolish-subsidized-housing-and-replace-by-private-housing schemes throughout advanced capitalist countries (Clapham *et al.* 1996; Forrest and Murie 1988; Murie *et al.* 2005). Such policies are often clad in the language of "giving property back to the market" even though, with the exception of the restitution of private properties that made up a minor part of the privatizations in post-communist countries, most of these properties were never produced as commodities, as goods for market exchange. All such privatization schemes are the outcome of political processes and gave social and economic consequences, not only for those displaced by privatization, but also for new homeowners—who are predominantly low- and moderate-income and are often not as well situated to reap the full benefits of homeownership or bear the costs of maintaining a house—and for real estate agents, mortgage lenders and others who benefit from an increase in housing circulation. That privatization boosts circulation is, indeed, a vital point, for it is in privatization that we arguably witness most clearly the indissolubility of capital's three modalities and of housing's mediation thereof: housing privatization reflects and reproduces ideologies of capital; it augments the circulation of capital by making "dead" public capital private and liquid; and, in the process, it represents an explicit reworking of social relations, a socio-economic "enclosure" process whereby individualized private accumulation is facilitated by the dispossession of public resources (Hodkinson 2012a).

To appreciate this is to appreciate why housing is often discussed in terms of its three major segments or tenures: owner-occupied, public or social-rented, and private-rented housing. As owner-occupation in capitalist societies has increasingly been privileged both ideologically and economically—for instance through preferential tax treatment—so the other tenure types have been ideologically and materially squeezed, even in nominally social-democratic states where tenure equality has long been brandished as a central political philosophy (Kemeny 1981; Christophers 2013). Under capitalism and its different currents such as neoliberalism, ordoliberalism and welfare state capitalism, "things" in general become increasingly regarded as commodities, and this is certainly the case for housing. The different commodified forms of housing—and owner-occupation in particular—become naturalized and normalized while non- and partially commodified forms are othered and denormalized, even though all forms of housing are the product of a specific context and a specific ideology (Kemeny 1981). Social rental is the most "abnormal" of all, but even private rental has been ideologically devalued. And, in keeping with the growing centrality of market allocation mechanisms to (neoliberal) capitalist ideology, states' appetite for using rent regulation to override market forces in the private rental sector has over time (and as noted in the previous section) ineluctably diminished in many countries.

While the aforementioned tenure categories are often useful in describing and analysing housing, however, this threefold distinction is not as straightforward as it seems (Barlow and Duncan 1988; Lee and Murie 1999) and is itself ideologically charged. The segment of public- and social-rented housing includes a wide range of housing that is managed on a not-for-profit basis, whether this is owned by state institutions or by private non-profit and hybrid organizations that often receive government subsidies. Yet, not all so-called social housing is built with state support and a great deal of housing that is not classified as either public or social is built with government support or is managed on a non-profit basis, such as the housing owned by community development corporations and mutual housing associations in the USA. Moreover, not only tenants of public and social housing receive government subsidies; so do numerous tenants of private-rented housing and many homeowners. For the USA, Wyly and DeFilippis (2010) have even argued that all housing, and in particular owner-occupied housing, is public housing as it is supported by public funding, most importantly in the form of mortgage interest tax deductions from which wealthy homeowners benefit most. But we could also think of the government support of tax and other breaks given to housing developers that further problematize the dichotomy between public and private housing. This is exactly how Singapore has classified most of its housing: as *both* social *and* owner-occupied housing (Chua 1997).

Besides the evidently blurred boundaries it relies upon, the conventional three-way segmentation of housing also needs to be problematized in view of the great diversity within each segment and the different meanings each segment has in different places (Ruonavaara 1993). In places where public or social housing makes up only a few per cent of the housing stock, for example, it tends to be more marginalized, impoverished and stigmatized than in countries where 30 or more per cent of the housing stock is classified as such. It makes a big difference if public/social housing is considered to be a residual sector for the poorest of the poor or a sector for "the masses", i.e. including people from all walks of life. In a provocative thesis that would be hard to extrapolate beyond the USA, Wacquant (2009) has famously compared public housing to prisons, arguing that both are part of a penal state in which the poor are housed in the worst possible conditions and residents of the former have become increasingly likely to end up in the latter at some time in their life, especially if they are male and of a different ethnicity or colour than the dominant groups in society.

The diversity within the owner-occupied segment is also substantial (e.g. Hamnett 1999). The most common distinction made here is between housing that is owned outright and housing that is mortgaged. If we observe how easy it often is for lenders to "repossess" housing (as if taking back what was already rightfully theirs) where mortgage payments are in arrears, it makes absolute sense that so many homeowners say they "rent from the bank". Of course, the differences within owning-outright and renting-from-the-bank are often equally striking. Many homeowners in post-communist countries were either given their formerly rental units or were able to acquire them for a symbolic price; yet, they often acquired poorly maintained properties; frequently do not earn enough to put money aside for maintenance; and sometimes cannot make necessary structural repairs since their properties are found in mid- and high-rise complexes with structural defects affecting the entire building (Murie *et al.* 2005). Likewise, some mortgaged homeowners have manageable mortgage payments and maintenance costs while others have been sold mortgages (e.g. "predatory loans") that they are unable to service (Squires 2004; Wyly *et al.* 2009).

Last but not least, there are other housing segments than the three main ones, including but not limited to (and often overlapping): free housing (often provided by relatives); housing as part of a labour contract (including the aforementioned live-in domestic servants as well as nannies and people living in factory housing or service housing, but also some expatriates); second homes (which are not really owner-*occupied* and are in reality sometimes third or fourth homes and so forth); squats (i.e. non-owner occupied housing); sub-lets ("room tenants" often include many students and other young people as well as poor people and migrants);[5] trailer-park housing (accommodating more than 10% of the population in a country like the USA); a wide range of institutionalized housing forms (accommodating not only prisoners but also many students, senior citizens, mentally and physically challenged people, and others); and of course the "un-housed", i.e. the homeless, many not necessarily rough sleeping (or at least not all the time), and many also part of the institutionalized group. In short, the commonly accepted labels for different housing segments and different residents reflect deeper socially constructed distinctions between haves and have-nots, deserving and undeserving residents (and labourers), property owners and property subjects, public and private, and state and market. All these terms are ideologically loaded and politically-economically reproduced—reflecting, and re-embedding, the ideology and political economy of capital.

5. Conclusion: The Housing Question Revisited

For all our attempts in this paper to formulate a generalizable conceptualization of housing in political economy, we are only too aware that it emphasizes certain dynamics while relatively underplaying others. This strikes us as unavoidable, however. And instead of seeing such imbalances as a negative, we would much rather cast them in a positive, *enabling* light: as issues to be further explored, theoretically *and* empirically, in relation to the provisional heuristic framework we have offered here. It is important also to stress that we do not present political economy as a method but more as a *perspective* necessary to frame, contextualize and ultimately understand the role of housing in society. A political-economic perspective can be mobilized in combination with a wide range of methods and modes of analysis, both of the quantitative and qualitative variety and both of the empirical and more hermeneutic and discursive kind. An open political-economic approach does not privilege certain methods; but it does force the researcher to always embed the empirics, theories, policies and markets of housing in their political-economic context—to *not* study housing in isolation from its societal context.

Comparative political economists, for example, will likely judge that we have paid far too little attention to the state, and its role in shaping different housing outcomes in different historical and geographical political-economic conjunctures. We have certainly tried to demonstrate that in regard to each of the three "modalities" of capital, the role of housing in the wider political economy is heavily tied to the role of the state. But of course, there is wide variation in how housing enters each national (and to some extent, each local) political economy. Housing is a central part of the national and local political-economic configuration, which implies housing is different everywhere and has different meanings and implications. Common terms such as "homeownership" and "social housing" may even have very different meanings in different contexts. Furthermore, states may make new, and sometimes unexpected, connections *between* the different modalities (e.g. asset-based welfare). In our view, however, this does not gainsay the generic pertinence of the modalities identified but instead calls for adding more flesh to the framework thus provided, for instance, through comparative studies of the role that housing plays in different political economies, building on existing comparative studies that have taken seriously both housing and one or more of the modalities of capital in question (e.g. Kemeny 1981; Harloe 1985; Allen *et al.* 2004; Lawson 2006; Ronald 2008; Schwartz and Seabrooke 2009; Aalbers 2011).

Meanwhile, political economists interested more in *changing* the world than in interpreting it will doubtless be frustrated by our lack of discussion of housing in relation to progressive or *different* (even non-capitalist) political economies. What are the alternatives to commodified housing provision under capitalism? How might they be advanced? And what macro-scale political-economic reconfigurations might they require? While we are not naïve enough to imagine that "fixing" the housing question will fix capitalism's problems more generally—the very Proudhonian fancy that Engels ridiculed—we would insist, equally, that there can be no meaningful and sustainable progressive socio-economic change *without* the housing question being directly addressed (cf. Turner 1976; Ward 2002; Harvey 2012; Hodkinson 2012b).

One particularly intriguing prospect in relation to the figuration of political-economic change, we believe, is to focus critically on the *contradictions* of housing under capitalism, and on the spaces for change that such contradictions potentially open up (Dymski 2001; Harvey 2014). It is, in our view, no coincidence that Harvey identifies housing as a principal locus of capitalism's manifold contradictions. Not the least of these, of course, is the contradiction between housing's use value and exchange value, and the tensions that result from expecting and encouraging the former to be delivered by a system which relentlessly prioritizes the latter (cf. Christophers 2010).

But housing manifests, and indeed generates, various other contradictions, too; and we want to suggest that the framework developed here can help to expose these for critical analysis. For, the different modalities of capital we have analysed in relation to housing are intimately interconnected with one another (as we have noted at several points, despite discussing them mostly in isolation). More than that, however, they *depend upon* one another for mutual reinforcement: capital could not and would not circulate in the way it does, for example, if it were not for the distinctive ideologies that characterize it. It is precisely in the conjoining of these modalities—and in housing's implication therein—that contradictions tend to emerge. We have explicitly encountered one of these: namely, the fact that the unequal social relations arising from the circulation of capital, and expressed in housing wealth, tend to endanger the very social reproduction required for circulation safely to continue. But there are many more such contradictions to housing's role in our contemporary political economy, and exploring and understanding these represents a vital step in figuring different (housing) futures.

Taking housing seriously also implies bringing housing into the future of political economy *not* just in terms of the study of political-economic institutions but also in terms of policies and politics. In this sense, our conceptualization of housing as a crucial part of political economy is also a call to re-integrate housing-as-policy with housing-as-market. Housing plays such a vital role in actually existing political economies that it is no longer justifiable—if it ever was—for political economists to cede housing analysis either to economists who ignore or reduce the importance of power, politics and the state, or to a separate field of housing/social policy where the wider political economy is equally invisible. Researchers in the field of housing studies, similarly, could make a greater effort to connect their analyses and arguments to the questions of political economy—not because political economy is necessarily the privileged approach to tackle housing questions, but because housing cannot be discussed sensibly without relating it to its political economy.

Acknowledgements

We are grateful to Phil Ashton, Mirjam Büdenbender, Rodrigo Fernandez, Andrea Lagna and Tom Slater for reading and commenting on an earlier draft. The arguments developed here, and especially any shortcomings, remain however ours alone. The work of Manuel Aalbers was supported by the European Research Council [grant number 313376].

Notes

1   That does not imply, however, that we are not interested in seeking a dialogue with political-economy-within-economics (see Aalbers 2012; Dymski 2012). But we think this requires a different kind of argument since the relationship between political-economy-within-economics and housing-as-a-field-of-research is quite a different one; more political-economists-within-economics have taken housing seriously, albeit very selectively.

2   House prices rarely (if ever) merely reflect the cost of labour added to the costs of materials. They also reflect, *inter alia*, the cost of land, depreciation, rent potential, and, of course, what people are willing and able to pay. Thus, housing production through labour not only reflects the social relations embedded in the labour process, but also its key role in the circulation of surplus values.

3   Although we should not forget that banks do provide a stimulus on the supply side of the housing market, too—much of the one-third of UK bank lending *not* destined for residential mortgages financed housing construction instead, meaning that credit (often provided by the same financial institutions) underpinned both sides of the market.

4   It could be argued that "privatized Keynesianism" is fundamentally about debt rather than housing: that, in other words, the latter is merely a contingent vehicle for the crystallization of the former. In our view, however, this is not the case: household debt could not have grown to contemporary levels, and hence have driven effective demand to the extent that it has, without the debt "security" or "collateral" that housing, uniquely, nominally provides the non-commercial borrower. In this respect, it bears remembering that the famous phrase "safe as houses" originally referred to the relative risklessness of mortgage lending, not of home ownership: i.e. to the "safety" enjoyed by the financial institution, rather than by the homeowner with whom the phrase is typically now (mis-)associated.

5   Although it would seem convenient to include sub-letting in the category of private-rented housing, many sub-letters are also found in housing classified as owner-occupied or social/public housing, contributing to a further blurring of the categories.

References

Aalbers, M.B. 2006. "'When the Banks Withdraw, Slum Landlords Take Over': The Structuration of Neighbourhood Decline through Redlining, Drug Dealing, Speculation and Immigrant Exploitation." *Urban Studies* 43(7): 1061–1086.

Aalbers, M.B. 2008. "The Financialization of Home and the Mortgage Market Crisis." *Competition & Change* 12(2): 148–166.

Aalbers, M.B. 2011. *Place, Exclusion, and Mortgage Markets*. Oxford: Wiley-Blackwell.

Aalbers, M.B., ed. 2012. *Subprime Cities: The Political Economy of Mortgage Markets*. Oxford: Wiley-Blackwell.

Aalbers, M.B., and K. Gibb. 2014. "Housing and the Right to the City." *International Journal of Housing Policy* 14(3): 207–213.

Allen, J., J. Barlow, J. Leal, T. Maloutas, and L. Padovani. 2004. *Housing & Welfare in Southern Europe*. Oxford: Blackwell.

Allen, J., and L. McDowell. 1989. *Landlords and Property*. Cambridge: Cambridge University Press.

Ashton, P. 2009. "An Appetite for Yield: The Anatomy of the Subprime Mortgage Crisis." *Environment & Planning A* 41(6): 1420–1441.

Ashton, P. 2012. "'Troubled Assets': The Financial Emergency and Racialized Risk." *International Journal of Urban & Regional Research* 36(4): 773–790.

Atkinson, R., and S. Blandy. 2005. "Introduction: International Perspectives on the New Enclavism and the Rise of Gated Communities." *Housing Studies* 20(2): 177–186.

Ball, M. 1985. *Land Rent, Housing, and Urban Planning: A European Perspective*. London: Croom Helm.

Ball, M. 1986. "Housing Analysis: Time for a Theoretical Refocus?" *Housing Studies* 1(3): 147–166.

Ball, M. 1988. *Rebuilding Construction: Economic Change and the British Construction Industry*. London: Routledge.

Barlow, J., and S. Duncan. 1988. "The Use and Abuse of Housing Tenure." *Housing Studies* 3(4): 219–231.

Bengtsson, B. 2001. "Housing as a Social Right: Implications for Welfare State Theory." *Scandinavian Political Studies* 24(4): 255–275.

Berry, M. 1979. *Marxist Approaches to the Housing Question.* Birmingham, AL: University of Birmingham.

Berry, M. 1981. "Posing the Housing Question in Australia: Elements of a Theoretical Framework for a Marxist Analysis of Housing." *Antipode* 13(1): 3–14.

Bourdieu, P. 2005. *The Social Structures of the Economy.* Cambridge: Polity.

Briggs, X. de Souza. 1997. "Moving Up versus Moving Out: Neighborhood Effects in Housing Mobility Programs." *Housing Policy Debate* 8(1): 195–234.

Case, K.E., J.M. Quigley, and R.J. Shiller. 2005. "Comparing Wealth Effects: The Stock Market versus the Housing Market." *Advances in Macroeconomics* 5(1): 1534–1601.

Castles, F.J. 1998. "The Really-big Trade-off: Home Ownership and the Welfare State in the New World and the Old." *Acta Politica* 33(1): 5–19.

Christophers, B. 2010. "On Voodoo Economics: Theorizing Relations of Property, Value, and Contemporary Capitalism." *Transactions of the Institute of British Geographers* 35(1): 94–108.

Christophers, B. 2011. "Revisiting the Urbanization of Capital." *Annals of the Association of American Geographers* 101(6): 1347–1364.

Christophers, B. 2013. "A Monstrous Hybrid: The Political Economy of Housing in Early-twenty-first Century Sweden." *New Political Economy* 18(6): 885–911.

Chua, B.H. 1997. *Political Legitimacy and Housing: Stakeholding in Singapore.* London: Routledge.

Clapham, D., J. Hegedüs, K. Kintrea, and I. Tosics, eds. 1996. *Housing Privatisation in Eastern Europe.* Westport, CT: Greenwood.

Crouch, C. 2011. *The Strange Non-death of Neoliberalism.* Cambridge: Polity.

Daunton, M.J. 1987. *A Property Owning Democracy? Housing in Britain.* London: Faber and Faber.

Davies, M. 2007. *Property: Meanings, Histories, Theories.* Abingdon: Routledge-Cavendish.

Desmond, M. 2012. "Eviction and the Reproduction of Urban Poverty." *American Journal of Sociology* 118(1): 88–133.

Doling, J., and J. Ford, eds. 2003. *Globalisation and Home Ownership: Experiences in Eight Member States of the European Union.* Delft: DUP Science.

Doling, J., and R. Ronald. 2010. "Home Ownership and Asset-based Welfare." *Journal of Housing and the Built Environment* 25(2): 165–173.

Dymski, G.A. 1999. *The Bank Merger Wave: The Economic Causes and Social Consequences of Financial Consolidation.* Armonk, NY: Sharpe.

Dymski, G.A. 2001. "U.S. Housing as Capital Accumulation and the Transformation of American Communities." In *Seeking Shelter on the Pacific Rim: Financial Globalization, Social Change, and the Housing Market*, edited by G. Dymski and D. Isenberg, 63–96. Armonk, NY: Sharpe.

Dymski, G.A. 2012. "Subprime Crisis and Urban Problematic." In *Subprime Cities: The Political Economy of Mortgage Markets*, edited by M.B. Aalbers, 293–314. Oxford: Wiley-Blackwell.

Engels, F. 1979[1887]. *The Housing Question.* Moscow: Progress.

Engels, F. 1987[1845]. *The Condition of the Working Class in England.* Harmondsworth: Penguin.

Fields, D. 2015. "Contesting the Financialization of Urban Space: Community Organizations and the Struggle to Preserve Affordable Rental Housing in New York City." *Journal of Urban Affairs* 37(2): 144–165.

Fitzpatrick, S. 2005. "Explaining Homelessness: A Critical Realist Perspective." *Housing, Theory and Society* 22(1): 1–17.

Florida, R.L., and M.M.A. Feldman. 1988. "Housing in US Fordism." *International Journal of Urban and Regional Research* 12(2): 187–210.

Ford, J., R. Burrows, and S. Nettleton. 2001. *Home-ownership in a Risk Society*. Bristol: Policy Press.

Forrest, R., and A. Murie. 1988. *Selling the Welfare State: The Privatisation of Public Housing*. London: Routledge.

Forrest, R., and N.-M. Yip, eds. 2011. *Housing Markets and the Global Financial Crisis*. Cheltenham: Edward Elgar.

Friedrichs, J., G. Galster, and S. Musterd. 2003. "Neighbourhood Effects on Social Opportunities: The European and American Research and Policy Context." *Housing Studies* 18(6): 797–806.

Gotham, K.F. 2002. "Beyond Invasion and Succession: School Segregation, Real Estate Blockbusting, and the Political Economy of Neighborhood Racial Transition." *City and Community* 1(1): 83–111.

Gotham, K.F. 2009. "Creating Liquidity out of Spatial Fixity: The Secondary Circuit of Capital and the Subprime Mortgage Crisis." *International Journal of Urban and Regional Research* 33(2): 355–371.

Grabar, H. 2012. "Buy a House, Get a Visa: Coming Soon Everywhere?" The Atlantic Cities. Accessed October 22. www.theatlanticcities.com/housing/2012/11/buy-house-get-visa-coming-sooneverywhere/3959/.

Gray, K. 1991. "Property in Thin Air." *The Cambridge Law Journal* 50(2): 252–307.

Haila, A. 2015. Urban Land Rent: Singapore as a Property State. Oxford: Wiley-Blackwell.

Hamnett, C. 1999. *Winners and Losers. Home Ownership in Modern Britain*. London: UCL.

Harloe, M. 1985. *Private Rented Housing in the United States and Europe*. New York, NY: St. Martin's.

Harvey, D. 1982. *The Limits to Capital*. Oxford: Blackwell.

Harvey, D. 1985. *The Urbanization of Capital. Studies in the History and Theory of Capitalist Urbanization*. Oxford: Blackwell.

Harvey, D. 2002. "The Art of Rent: Globalization, Monopoly and the Commodification of Culture." *Socialist Register* 38: 93–110.

Harvey, D. 2012. *Rebel Cities: From the Right to the City to the Urban Revolution*. London: Verso.

Harvey, D. 2014. *Seventeen Contradictions and the End of Capitalism*. London: Profile Books.

Harvey, D., and L. Chatterjee. 1974. "Absolute Rent and the Structuring of Space by Governmental and Financial Institutions." *Antipode* 6(1): 22–36.

Hecht, J.J. 1981. *The Domestic Servant Class in Eighteenth-century England*. Westport, CT: Hyperion.

Helderman, A., and C. Mulder. 2007. "Intergenerational Transmission of Homeownership: The Roles of Gifts and Continuities in Housing Market Characteristics." *Urban Studies* 44(2): 231–247.

Henderson, J., and V. Karn. 1984. "Race, Class and the Allocation of Public Housing in Britain." *Urban Studies* 21(2): 115–128.

Higgs, E. 1983. "Domestic Servants and Households in Victorian England." *Social History* 8(2): 201–210.

Hodkinson, S. 2012a. "The New Urban Enclosures." *City* 16(5): 500–518.

Hodkinson, S. 2012b. "The Return of the Housing Question." *Ephemera* 12(4): 423–444.

Immergluck, D. 2009. *Foreclosed: High-risk Lending, Deregulation, and the Undermining of America's Mortgage Market*. Ithaca, NY: Cornell University Press.

Jackson, K.T. 1985. *Crabgrass Frontier. The Suburbanization of the United States*. New York: Oxford University Press.

Jelin, E. 1977. "Migration and Labor Force Participation of Latin American Women: The Domestic Servants in the Cities." *Signs: Journal of Women in Culture and Society* 3(1): 129–141.

Karn, V., J. Kemeny, and P. Williams. 1985. *Home Ownership in the Inner City: Salvation or Despair?* Aldershot: Gower.

Kemeny, J. 1981. *The Myth of Home Ownership*. London: Routledge & Kegan Paul.

Kemeny, J. 1995. "'The Really Big Trade-off' between Home Ownership and Welfare: Castles' Evaluation of the 1980 Thesis, and Reformulation 25 Years On." *Housing, Theory and Society* 22(2): 59–75.

Kleinman, M. 1996. *Housing, Welfare and the State in Europe: A Comparative Analysis of Britain, France and Germany*. Cheltenham: Elgar.

Lawson, J. 2006. *Critical Realism and Housing Studies*. London: Routledge.

Lawson, J. 2009. "The Transformation of Social Housing Provision in Switzerland Mediated by Federalism, Direct Democracy and the Urban/Rural Divide." *European Journal of Housing Policy* 9(1): 45–67.

Lee, P., and A. Murie. 1999. "Spatial and Social Divisions within British Cities. beyond Residualisation." *Housing Studies* 14(5): 625–640.

Lees, L., T. Slater, and E. Wyly. 2008. *Gentrification*. London: Routledge.

Lefebvre, H. 1996. *Writings on Cities*. Oxford: Blackwell.

López-Morales, E. 2011. "Gentrification by Ground Rent Dispossession: The Shadows Cast by Large-scale Urban Renewal in Santiago de Chile." *International Journal of Urban and Regional Research* 35(2): 330–357.

Lutz, H. 2002. "At Your Service Madam! The Globalization of Domestic Service." *Feminist Review* 70(1): 89–104.

Mackinnon, D., and A. Cumbers. 2007. *An Introduction to Economic Geography. Globalization, Uneven Development and Place*. Harlow: Pearson.

Marcuse, P. 1985. "Gentrification, Abandonment, and Displacement: Connections, Causes, and Policy Responses in New York City." *Journal of Urban & Contemporary Law* 28(1): 195–240.

Martin, R., and D. Turner. 2000. "Demutualization and the Remapping of Financial Landscapes." *Transactions of the Institute of British Geographers* 25(2): 221–241.

Massey, D.S., and N.A. Denton. 1993. *American Apartheid: Segregation and the Making of the Underclass*. Cambridge, MA: Harvard University Press.

McKenzie, E. 1994. *Privatopia: Homeowner Associations and the Rise of Residential Private Government*. New Haven, CT: Yale University Press.

Murie, A., and Forrest, R. 2001. "Whose City Now?: Housing, Competition and Conflict in the Post-privatised City". Paper presented at the RC21 Conference: Social Inequality, Redistributive Justice and the City, Amsterdam.

Murie, A., I. Tosics, M.B. Aalbers, R. Sendi, and B. Černič Mali. 2005. "Privatisation and After." In *Restructuring Large Housing Estates in European Cities*, edited by R. Van Kempen, K. Dekker, S. Hall and I. Tosics, 85–103. Bristol: Policy Press.

Murphy, L. 1995. "Mortgage Finance and Housing Provision in Ireland, 1970–1990." *Urban Studies* 32(1): 135–154.

O'Neill, M., and T. Williamson. 2012. *Property-owning Democracy*. Boston, MA: Wiley-Blackwell.

O'Toole, J. 2012. "Citizenship for Sale: Foreign Investors Flock to the U.S." CNN Money. Accessed October 22. http://money.cnn.com/2012/06/11/news/economy/citizenship-foreign-investment

Pahl, R.E. 1975. *Whose City?* London: Longman.

Pearce, D.M. 1979. "Gatekeepers and Homeseekers: Institutional Patterns in Racial Steering." *Social Problems* 26(3): 325–342.

Rawls, J. 1971. *A Theory of Justice*. Cambridge: Harvard University Press.

Regan, S., and W. Paxton. 2001. *Asset-based Welfare: International Experiences*. London: IPPR.

Rex, J., and R. Moore. 1967. *Race, Community, and Conflict*. London: Oxford University Press.

Roberts, A. 2013. "Financing Social Reproduction: The Gendered Relations of Debt and Mortgage Finance in Twenty-first-century America." *New Political Economy* 18(1): 2142.

Rohe, W.M., S. Van Zandt, and G. McCarthy. 2002. "Home Ownership and Access to Opportunity." *Housing Studies* 17(1): 51–61.

Rolnik, R. 2013. "Late Neoliberalism: The Financialization of Homeownership and Housing Rights." *International Journal of Urban and Regional Research* 37(3): 1058–1066.

Ronald, R. 2008. *The Ideology of Home Ownership*. Basingstoke: Palgrave Macmillan.

Ronald, R., and M. Elsinga, eds. 2012. *Beyond Home Ownership: Housing, Welfare and Society*. London: Routledge.

Ruonavaara, H. 1993. "Types and Forms of Housing Tenure: Towards Solving the Comparison/Translation Problem." *Scandinavian Housing and Planning Research* 10(1): 3–20.

Saegert, S., D. Fields, and K. Libman. 2009. "Deflating the Dream: Radical Risk and the Neoliberalization of Homeownership." *Journal of Urban Affairs* 31(3): 297–317.

Sassen, S. 1996. "Service Employment Regimes and the New Inequality." In *Urban Poverty and the Underclass*, edited by E. Mingione, 64–82. Oxford: Blackwell.

Saunders, P. 1984. "Beyond Housing Classes: The Sociological Significance of Private Property Rights in the Means of Consumption." *International Journal of Urban and Regional Research* 8(2): 202–227.

Schwartz, H.M., and L. Seabrooke, eds. 2009. *The Politics of Housing Booms and Busts*. Basingstoke: Palgrave Macmillan.

Slater, T. 2013. "Your Life Chances Affect Where You Live: A Critique of the 'Cottage Industry' of Neighbourhood Effects Research." *International Journal of Urban and Regional Research* 37(2): 367–387.

Smith, N. 1979. "Toward a Theory of Gentrification a back to the City Movement by Capital, Not People." *Journal of the American Planning Association* 45(4): 538–548.

Smith, S.J., B.A. Searle, and N. Cook. 2009. "Rethinking the Risks of Home Ownership." *Journal of Social Policy* 38(1): 83–102.

Somerville, P. 1992. "Homelessness and the Meaning of Home: Rooflessness or Rootlessness?" *International Journal of Urban and Regional Research* 16(4): 529–539.

Squires, G.D., ed. 1992. *From Redlining to Reinvestment: Community Responses to Urban Disinvestment*. Philadelphia, PA: Temple University Press.

Squires, G.D., ed. 2004. *Why the Poor Pay More: How to Stop Predatory Lending*. Westport, CT: Praeger.

Stephens, M. 2003. "Globalisation and Housing Finance Systems in Advanced and Transition Economies." *Urban Studies* 40(5–6): 1011–1026.

Teijmant, I., and W. Schepens. 1981. *Noodkopers: een onderzoek onder eigenaar-bewoners in twee Amsterdamse stadsvernieuwingswijken*. Amsterdam: Sociologisch Instituut.

Turner, A. 2013. *Credit, Money and Leverage: What Wicksell, Hayek and Fisher knew and Modern Macroeconomics Forgot*. http://ineteconomics.org/sites/inet.civicactions.net/files/Adair%20Turner%20Stockholm%20School%20of%20Economics%20September%2012.pdf.

Turner, J.F. 1976. *Housing by People: Towards Autonomy in Building Environments*. London: Marion Boyars.

Van Ham, M., D. Manley, N. Bailey, L. Simpson, and D. Maclennan, eds. 2012. *Neighbourhood Effects Research: New Perspectives*. Dordrecht: Springer.

Van Kempen, R., and A.Ş. Özüekren. 1998. "Ethnic Segregation in Cities: New Forms and Explanations in a Dynamic World." *Urban Studies* 35(10): 1631–1656.

Wacquant, L. 2009. *Prisons of Poverty*. Minneapolis, MN: University of Minnesota Press.

Ward, C. 2002. *Cotters and Squatters: The Hidden History of Housing*. Nottingham: Five Leaves.

Watson, M. 2010. "House Price Keynesianism and the Contradictions of the Modern Investor Subject." *Housing Studies* 25(3): 413–426.

Wilson, W.J. 1987. *The Truly Disadvantaged. The Inner City, the Underclass, and Public Policy*. Chicago, IL: The University of Chicago Press.

Wood, G., S. Parkinson, B. Searle, and S.J. Smith. 2013. "Motivations for Equity Borrowing: A Welfare-switching Effect." *Urban Studies* 50(12): 2588–2607.

Wyly, E., and J. DeFilippis. 2010. "Mapping Public Housing: The Case of New York City." *City & Community* 9(1): 61–86.

Wyly, E., M. Moos, D. Hammel, and E. Kabahizi. 2009. "Cartographies of Race and Class: Mapping the Class-monopoly Rents of American Subprime Mortgage Capital." *International Journal of Urban and Regional Research* 33(2): 332–354.

3 The Financialization of Home and the Mortgage Market Crisis

Introduction

Financialization as Capital Switching

Financialization is often defined a pattern of accumulation in which profit-making occurs increasingly through financial channels rather than through trade and commodity production (Arrighi 1994; Krippner 2005).[1] It refers to the increasing role of finance in the operations of capitalism (Magdoff & Sweezy 1972) and implies that 'the inverted relation between the financial and the real is the key to understanding new trends in the world' (Sweezy 1995: 8). Due to the slowing down of the overall growth rate and the stagnation of the real economy, capitalism has become increasingly dependent on the growth of finance to enlarge money capital (Foster 2007; Sweezy 1995). Therefore the capital accumulation process becomes financialized, focused on the growth of finance not to benefit the real economy but to benefit actors within financial markets such as investors. Boyer (2000) speaks of a finance-led regime of accumulation. Financialization is not merely a concept used to signify the rise of the idea of shareholder value in different economic sectors and associated changes in management priorities (Engelen 2002; Froud *et al.* 2000; Lazonick & O'Sullivan 2000); in addition, it signifies that the financial industry has been transformed 'from a facilitator of other firms' economic growth into a growth industry in its own right' (Engelen 2003: 1367). Furthermore, some commentators argue that under a finance-led regime, financial investment is replacing physical investment (e.g. Stockhammer 2004).

Much like globalization, financialization can be seen as 'a *process* that has introduced a new form of competition within the economy and that has the capacity to become ever more pervasive' (French *et al.* 2011: 8, emphasis in original). Financialization is by no means limited to financial markets and entails the financialization of non-financial sectors of the real economy that become heavily involved in capital and money markets. Of course, actors (e.g. firms) in the real economy have always been dependent on credit, but with financialization they are increasingly ruled by financial actors and their interests: 'finance more and more sets the pace and the rules for the management of the cash flow of non-financial firms' (Foster 2007: 7). The rules and logics of Wall Street are increasingly becoming the rules and logics outside Wall Street. Financialization not only refers to the growth of financial actors such as banks, lenders, private equity and hedge funds, but is reflected in the operations of non-financial firms in different parts of the economy, such as the car industry (Froud *et al.* 2002), the 'new economy' (Feng *et al.* 2001) and real estate (Smart & Lee 2003). Finally, financialization not only affects businesses, but increasingly also consumers: 'It asks people from all walks of life to accept risks into their homes that were hitherto the province of professionals. Without significant capital, people are being asked to think like capitalists' (Martin 2002: 12; cf. Mandel 1996).

Financialization is not just a finance-led regime of accumulation, but can also be reinterpreted as a new stage in the process of capital switching. David Harvey speaks of capital switching when capital flows from one sector of the economy to the other. He argues that for financial institutions, the built environment is seen as an asset in which money can be invested and disinvested by directing capital to the highest and best uses, and by withdrawing and subsequently redirecting capital from low pay-offs to potentially higher ones (Harvey 1982, 1985). Capital switching entails the flow of capital from the primary circuit (production, manufacturing, industrial sector) to the secondary circuit. The secondary circuit comprises the built environment for production (e.g. infrastructure) and for consumption (e.g. housing). Harvey also identifies a tertiary circuit, the circuit of social infrastructure, identified as investment in technology, science, conditions of employees, health and education. Switching from the primary to the secondary circuit takes place when there is a surplus of capital in the primary circuit and signs of over-accumulation emerge. Capital switching is a strategy to prevent a crisis, but because of the inherent contradictions of capitalism, investment in the secondary circuit will only delay, not take away, the crisis. Moreover, since investments in the built environment are generally long-term investments, there are tendencies to over-accumulate and to under-invest, resulting in a cyclical model of investment in the built environment. The resulting 'spatial fix', while trying to resolve the internal contradictions of capitalism, 'transfers its contradictions to a wider sphere and gives them greater latitude' (Harvey 1985: 60).

Financialization can be characterized as capital switching from the primary, secondary or tertiary circuit to what I call the quaternary circuit of capital. Financialization not only implies the financialization of existing economies—i.e. the restructuring of existing markets into producer and consumer markets that are heavily tied to financial markets—but also the rise of financial markets for their own good; that is, the rise of financial markets not for the facilitation of other markets but for the trade in money, credit, securities, etc. Or, in the words of Cox (1992: 29), finance is increasingly becoming 'decoupled from production to become an independent power, an autocrat over the real economy'. What further distinguishes the quaternary circuit from the other circuits of capital is that in the quaternary circuit control over the economy has shifted from corporate boardrooms to financial markets (Foster 2006: 5). The essence of a quaternary circuit is not that power shifts from the non-financial to the financial, but that financial and non-financial firms alike become increasingly involved in financial markets. And this is not a direct result of a lack of equity, but a direct result of financialization, which rewrites the rules of capital accumulation.

Like capital switching to the secondary circuit, capital switching to the quaternary circuit is liable to lead to over-accumulation and eventually to crises. But capital switching to the quaternary circuit is in at least one way fundamentally different from capital switching to the secondary circuit: where the secondary circuit generally *competes for* financing in the capital market, the quaternary circuit *represents* the capital market as an investment channel in its own right. In that sense financialization can be characterized as the capitalist economy taken to extremes: it is not a producer or consumer market, but a market designed only to make money. Although it can be argued that there exists a necessary link 'between *stable* income sources and financial speculation' (Leyshon & Thrift 2007, emphasis added), this is not necessarily so: many of the recent crises have their roots in *unstable* income sources and over-accumulation, as both the Enron debacle and the current mortgage crisis demonstrate. In a finance-led regime of accumulation, risks that were once limited to a specific actor in the production–consumption chain become risks for all of the actors involved in a specific industry. In that sense, the quaternary circuit, which is in the first place a heuristic tool, is strongly attached to the other circuits of capital. Financialization as capital switching does not deny the necessary link between the different circuits—quite the contrary, it stresses the increased interdependence between the circuits of capital. In addition, it highlights how one of these circuits, the quaternary, comes to dominate the other circuits, possibly to the disadvantage of all circuits.

Mortgage Markets and Financialization

Mortgage markets are a special kind of financial market. They were originally designed as credit markets facilitating capital switching to the secondary circuit of capital. Mortgage loans not only facilitated households who wanted to buy a home, but also fuelled house prices. Since more people gained access to mortgage credit, competition for homes increased, resulting in higher house prices. In other words, first the development of mortgage markets, and second the loosening of mortgage requirements—both increasing access to capital for homebuyers—made it possible for households to acquire more expensive properties, but also led to higher house prices. The banks pursued a policy of cheap money: to keep the market going mortgage requirements were loosened further (cf. Aalbers 2005, 2007; DNB 2000).

As I will argue in this paper, the expansion of mortgage markets has recently entered a new stage in which mortgage markets no longer only facilitate capital switching to the secondary circuit—i.e. are no longer purely designed to facilitate homeownership—but are increasingly, but not exclusively, designed to facilitate capital switching to the quaternary circuit of capital. This financialization of mortgage finance—i.e. the transformation from mortgage markets as facilitating markets to mortgage markets as markets in their own right—implies not only capital switching from the primary to the secondary circuit, but also capital switching from the secondary to the quaternary circuit of capital. The result is not that there is more or less capital switching to the secondary circuit; the point is that the fate of the secondary circuit is increasingly tied to what happens in the quaternary circuit. Real estate has always been dependent on finance, but today investment in real estate markets is more than ever before dependent on the development of financial markets. But of course the linkages go in two directions: if two markets become entangled, they effectively become interdependent. In the end, the development of financial markets is also dependent on the development of real estate and housing markets.

This development is not unique to the secondary circuit; financialization also takes place in the primary and tertiary circuits of capital. Stock markets are no longer designed to facilitate production-oriented companies; hedge funds for example are designed to extract capital from the primary circuit thereby switching capital to the quaternary circuit. Pensions funds are another interesting example, not only because they are important global players in financial markets, thereby increasing the flow between the tertiary and quaternary circuit in both directions, but also because pensions are increasingly not merely privatized, but financialized (Engelen 2003). The financialization of pension funds ties the fate of individual pension beneficiaries and workers to the fate of financial markets because capital meant for the tertiary circuit switches directly to the quaternary circuit.

In this paper I limit myself to mortgage markets and thus to capital switching to the quaternary circuit and to the financialization of the secondary circuit. Mortgage markets are not only important due to their sheer volume—€4.7 trillion outstanding mortgage loans in the European Union at the end of 2004; €11.3 trillion worldwide (EMF 2005)—but also because most homeowners depend on them and because they fuel the economy both directly and indirectly (through equity withdrawal). The push for homeownership, combined with the privatization of public/social housing in various types of (welfare) states (e.g. Murie *et al.* 2005) has increased the importance of homeownership at both the individual and the societal level (Aalbers 2005). For most of the twentieth century, homeownership was generally seen as relatively free of risks and as a good way to acquire wealth. Unsustainable homeownership, negative equity and arrears were seen as temporary problems linked to economic fluctuation. According to Ford and colleagues (2001; see also Forrest *et al.* 1999), however, this is no longer the case: homeownership is now also surrounded by increasing insecurity. This is mainly due to processes outside of the housing market, particularly in the labor market and social security provision. Part-time and flexible forms of work have now become the rule rather than the exception, and life courses have therefore become not only more flexible, but also more unpredictable and insecure. Consequently, people are at higher risk of being unable to meet their financial commitments. Existing institutions were not designed to deal with the fragmentation of the life course that occurred because of deregulation, liberalization and privatization tendencies and strategies.

The expansion of the mortgage market is not just meant to increase homeownership, but is also intended as a means to further the neo-liberal agenda of private property, firms and growing profits. In this process, homeowners also become more dependent on financial markets. Old arrangements of social rights have been replaced and continue to be replaced by new arrangements in which social rights and guarantees are transferred from the state to financial markets. Indeed, the restructuring of welfare states has resulted in a 'great risk shift' in which households are increasingly dependent on financial markets for their long-term security (Hacker 2006). Due to the financialization of home, housing risks are increasingly financial market risks these days—and vice versa. The restructuring—or in some countries, retreat—of the welfare state is coupled to the restructuring of the mortgage market. The financialization of home forces more and more households to see acquiring a house not just as a home, as a place to live, but as an investment, as something to put equity into and take equity from. This can be a financially gainful experience, but is not necessarily so. As homeownership has increased primarily among low-income groups, there are also more groups that have become vulnerable to the risks of homeownership. It is these groups that experience the most insecurity because of changes in the labor market, the welfare state and the mortgage market crisis.

The remainder of this paper consists of two substantial sections. In the next section I will lay out a short history of mortgage markets to show how the mortgage market first enabled capital switching to the secondary circuit, but is now increasingly financialized itself because mortgages have been drawn, or better, are being drawn, into the quaternary circuit. In addition, the financialization of the mortgage market demands that not just homes but also homeowners become viewed as financially exploitable. The second substantial section, which flows into the conclusion, argues that the current crisis in (subprime) mortgage markets exemplifies how the fate of homeowners is increasingly tied to the fate of financial markets. In its origins, this is not because of rising default rates and foreclosures trouble financial markets, but because the financialization of mortgages and homeowners has led to the extraction of capital from homeowners to financial investors. In other words, the mortgage crisis is a direct result of the financialization of both mortgage markets and homeowners. In this case the crisis in the quaternary circuit, very much in line with Harvey, is a result of overaccumulation, giving the contradictions of capitalism greater latitude. Although the current crisis has its origins in the US, it is by no means limited to the US. This is not just a result of the financialization of the US mortgage market, which has seen it becoming interdependent with global financial markets, but also because many mortgage markets outside the US are increasingly financialized. As an example of the latter argument, the paper not only draws on developments in the US but also on developments in the Netherlands, a country where default rates are low and where a mortgage market crisis seems, at least at present, far away, but also a country in which the mortgage market is not only the most expanded in the world (in relative terms), but also increasingly financialized.

In presenting home as a case of financialization, I connect the different strands in the financialization literature (see French *et al.* 2011; Krippner 2005) by arguing that the restructuring of mortgage markets (regulation school political economy), the securitization of mortgage portfolios (critical social accountancy) and the financialization of homeowners through credit scoring (financialization of daily life) are intrinsically linked. That is, securitization and risk-based pricing are not possible without credit scoring; and the restructuring of the mortgage market that made this possible is not just a result of mortgage lenders expanding their business, but is also a highly political project. The financialization of home is not just another example of financialization but a crucial one, as mortgage markets are crucial markets in the present economy, while homes are as crucial as ever for households, but have increased their importance as indicators of the economy. Indeed, home equity affects what homeowners can spend, how much credit they can get and how they think of the economy at large. In addition, this paper adds a capital switching perspective to the financialization literature, by arguing that financialization can be seen as capital switching to the quaternary circuit. Finally, it highlights connections between the local, the national and the global, and how these connections have been redrawn in the restructuring of the mortgage market. This paper pays attention to the geographical differences in the financialization of home, but a fuller account of how space intersects with the political economy of mortgage markets and the financialization of homeowners remains a task for the future. Another future task would concern the socio-economical and spatial implications of the current mortgage market crisis.

The Restructuring of the Mortgage Market

The History of Mortgage Markets: Enabling Capital Switching

Mortgage markets were first developed in the Mediterranean and then spread throughout Europe, but it was in the US that they first became the important routes to homeownership, equity and economic growth that they are today. Throughout the twentieth century, US state institutions were instrumental in designing, implementing and executing such innovations. Immergluck (2004) aptly speaks of the *visible hand of government* in the US mortgage market. Structural changes in mortgage markets originate from the US and then spread to other parts of the world.

The entrance of commercial banks into the mortgage market coupled with the economic optimism of the 1920s led to a rapid growth of US mortgage markets. The boom of the 1920s was followed by the Wall Street crash of 1929 and the crisis of the 1930s in which many homeowners lost not only their jobs, but also their homes. Many homeowners were unable to refinance their loan because of the withdrawal of financial institutions from the mortgage market. In the early 1930s the average number of foreclosed mortgage loans was 250,000 per year; half of all home mortgages in the US were in default (Dennis & Pinkowish 2004; Immergluck 2004).

What followed was a crucial episode in the history of mortgage markets. In the 1930s, the modern mortgage market emerges in the US, along with its standardized guideline and the introduction of long-term, amortized mortgages. Under presidents Hoover (1929–33, Republican) and Roosevelt (1933–45, Democrat), the state firmly enters the market: home construction became subsidized, the construction process less regulated, the state starts providing liquidity to commercial banks and a central credit facility to mortgage lenders, and a state-created institution, the *Home Owners Loan Corporation* (HOLC), starts providing emergency relief to homeowners in order to forestall foreclosures. The HOLC 'introduced, perfected, and proved in practice the feasibility of the long-term, self-amortizing mortgage with uniform payments spread over the life of the debt' (Jackson 1985: 196) thereby replacing the five-year, non-amortizing mortgage with a balloon payment at the end of the loan period. The HOLC set the standards for mortgage lending to this day and systematized appraisal methods across the US. The introduction of such standards facilitated not only homeownership, but also the switching of capital from the primary to the secondary circuit of capital.

A further standardization comes with the creation of the *Federal Housing Administration* (FHA) and the *Veterans Administration* (VA), both of which insure mortgage loans, thereby decreasing the risk for lenders, lowering the interest rate for borrowers, increasing loan-to-value ratios (which lowers the necessary down-payment) and increasing the loan maturity to 25 or 30 years. FHA's standardization made it easier, less risky and cheaper to buy a home, thereby fuelling the development of the mortgage market. FHA may only have been active in the US, but the changes it implemented in the US also had their effect in other (mostly developed) countries, where, throughout the second half of the twentieth century, interest rates for mortgage loans generally dropped and smaller down-payments became possible (e.g. Aalbers 2007: 181–186). Again, this facilitated capital switching to the secondary circuit, not only benefiting homeowners, but also all others involved in real estate and credit markets, including construction companies, real estate agents, banks and other lenders, and, arguably, states.

Following the institutionalization of mortgage standards by the HOLC and the FHA, the next steps were taken by two private, yet government-created and 'government-sponsored' institutions and one public institution: the *Federal National Mortgage Association*, known as *Fannie Mae*; the *Federal Home Loan Mortgage Corporation*, known as *Freddie Mac*; and, the *Government National Mortgage Association*, known as *Ginnie Mae*. They created a standardized mortgage instrument used in all US states. An elaborate discussion of these organizations is beyond the scope of this paper (see Dennis & Pinkowish 2004; Gotham 2006; Immergluck 2004; Ross & Yinger 2002; Stuart 2003), but let me briefly mention here why they require special attention. They played a pivotal role in integrating mortgage markets throughout the US into one single mortgage market, and were instrumental in implementing and institutionalizing some other important changes in mortgage markets, changes which either facilitate or embody the financialization of mortgage markets: the rise of securitization and secondary mortgage markets, and the rise of credit scoring and risk-based pricing.

Primary and Secondary Mortgage Markets: The Financialization of Finance

In a primary mortgage market, mortgages are closed between the borrower and the lender; in a secondary mortgage market, investors can buy mortgage portfolios from lenders. Fannie Mae, Freddie Mac and Ginnie Mae were created to buy such mortgage portfolios, but are not the only investors; pension funds, for example, also have an important stake in this market. Nonetheless, not only lenders planning to sell their portfolios to the three big institutions, but in fact a large majority of mortgage lenders follow the guidelines of Fannie Mae and Freddie Mac who 'continually set the industry standards' (Dennis & Pinkowish 2004: 93). The importance of the secondary mortgage market has increased over the last ten years. In the secondary market so-called mortgage-backed securities (MBS) are sold to investors. This process, called securitization, provides liquidity to lenders because loans are placed off-balance; it moderates the cyclical flow of mortgage capital; it assists the flow of capital from surplus areas to deficit areas; and it decreases the geographical spread in interest rates and allows for portfolio diversification because risks are spread geographically (Dennis & Pinkowish 2004: 208–209). Fannie Mae and Freddie Mac take the role of securitizers (known as 'special purpose vehicles'): they are the market makers who buy mortgage portfolios from lenders ('originators'), package them and resell them as MBS to investors.

Securitization requires not only a vastly expanding market, but also the deregulation and internationalization of domestic financial markets (Sassen 2001: 72) leading to a rapid growth in trade of securities, of which MBS are only one element.[2] Again, it is the state that re-regulated the mortgage market to enable growth: the US government was actively involved in making the trade in MBS possible, in de-linking investment from place,[3] and in facilitating liquidity/tradability, thereby creating opportunities for both risk-averse and high-risk investors (Gotham 2006; Wyly *et al.* 2006). Because securitization increasingly connects the mortgage market to the stock market, securitization embodies the financialization of the mortgage market. It increases the volatility of the mortgage market (and as the current crisis demonstrates, it also increases volatility in the wider credit market) because stock markets by their very nature are volatile markets.

Securitization of mortgage loans takes on different dimensions in different countries. In the US, 'the secondary market is government backed, enjoys implicit government guarantees and therefore provides cheaper sources of funding' (Coles & Hardt 2000: 778). As a result, secondary mortgage markets have grown tremendously and now represent two-thirds of the mortgage market; in the year 2005, MBS have been issued to a value of almost 2,000 billion US dollars. In Europe, government support is more limited than in the US and MBS face a 50 per cent capital weight requirement (20 per cent in the US). And although MBS have been introduced in Europe much later than in the US, the MBS market is rapidly growing: it tripled in less than four years to 326 billion euros (and estimates for 2007, despite the mortgage market crisis, stand at 531 billion euros). Recently, secondary market securitization has become more established in the UK, Spain, the Netherlands and Italy, and to a lesser extent also in Germany, France and Portugal (Forum Group on Mortgage Credit 2004; IFS 2006). In the Netherlands, for example, 15 per cent of the mortgage market was securitized in 2005 and this share is increasing each year; MBS issuance in that year was valued at 36 billion euros. In the UK, in absolute terms the largest European MBS market, MBS were issued for a value of 145 billion euros in 2005. MBS are sold to both national and foreign investors, and today there exists an international market for MBS. Securitization increasingly takes places in global cities; highly concentrated command points that function as a global marketplace for finance (Sassen 2001; see also Langley 2006; Pryke & Lee 1995), such as New York and London.[4]

This is possible because MBS are, in theory, much more transparent than mortgage products in the primary market. Local knowledge, which is so important in the primary market and a barrier for foreign mortgage companies, is much less important in the secondary market because products have been standardized and made more transparent, to make them more interesting for investors (cf. Clark & O'Connor 1997). Investors, in return, have the ability to compare the price, risk and expected profitability of MBS between countries, and also to compare them to other possible investments. As a result of securitization, mortgage markets indirectly become more globalized, not through mortgage lenders in the primary market, but through investors in the secondary market. While the primary mortgage markets remain firmly national, the secondary market becomes globalized and at the same time localized in a few global cities (Aalbers 2009a). Throughout the twentieth century, state interventions have resulted in national mortgage markets replacing local mortgage markets. Likewise, state interventions have supported the globalization of finance, witnessed by the securitization of mortgages and ultimately the growth of a patchwork of globalized secondary mortgage markets, traded in a few global cities (so in one sense highly localized), with sellers and buyers from all over the world.

Credit Scoring and Risk-Based Pricing: The Financialization of Homeowners

Mortgage portfolios sold in the secondary mortgage market are usually classified by risk profiles, because risk determines their selling price (risk-based pricing). Therefore, mortgage lenders classify loan applicants according to the risks that they pose to both lenders and investors. The calculation of housing costs and other financial obligations in proportion to income determines the likelihood that an applicant will be *able* to pay back a mortgage, but moneylenders also attempt to assess whether they are *willing* to pay it back (Aalbers 2005; Stuart 2003). Credit scoring uses available information to make predictions about future payment behavior; it is a form of customer profiling. Credit scores are based on such common variables as 'occupation, length of employment, marital status, bank account, gender and geographical address' (Leyshon & Thrift 1999: 444), which are also analyzed by computer systems and statistical methods in order to predict credit performance.

Moneylenders and information bureaus analyze the customers of mortgage providers. These analyses identify important indicators and allow the determination of mutual connections. In this way, a 'score card' is made, and a limit can be established to determine whether a client qualifies for acceptance. In order to determine a credit score, statistical methods are used to assess whether a potential client possesses certain qualities that increase the credit balance. This process involves the combination of a number of factors and their reduction to numerical values, which are called credit scores. A score that exceeds a fixed upper limit indicates that the risk is too high, and the applicant with such a score will be rejected. Applicants whose scores are lower than the fixed lower limit are accepted. Scores between the upper and lower limits do not lead to definite rejection or acceptance. In this case, the outcome depends on the policies of the specific institution and its employees. In some situations, a score between the upper and lower limits may qualify an applicant for a mortgage with less-favorable conditions, such as price differentiation and the application of additional criteria for acceptance. According to former US and Dutch banker, Hilhorst,[5] it is 'a sport among all banks to retrieve increasingly better information about the social profile of the client. The fact that this occurs is unknown, but not a secret. Credit scoring is everyday practice. The systems, the content and the criteria that banks put together to provide mortgage loans, however, are confidential.'[6] Minor moneylenders usually work with computer programs developed by the American companies Experian and Fair Isaac. Major moneylenders, such as well-known banks, use these companies as consultants, but also have their own computer divisions that constantly improve their systems.

Credit scoring is not only indispensable if lenders want to sell their mortgage portfolios in the secondary market, but also facilitates risk-based pricing by charging higher interest rates for borrowers with low scores ('bad risk') and charging lower interest rates for borrowers with high scores ('good risk'): 'As lenders become more confident about their ability to predict default, they also become more willing to issue credit, at a relatively high price, to higher-risk borrowers' (Ross & Yinger 2002: 23), as well as at a relatively low price, to lower-risk borrowers. Risk-based pricing presents a new chapter in the standardization of mortgage loans, not by making loans one-size-fits-all, but by breaking them up into classes with the use of credit scoring, and re-selling these loans in classes in the secondary market.

The application of credit-scoring models not only implies the reduction of individuals to membership of an assumed group; it paradoxically also disregards geographical differences. Although social-geographical data can be used as input for these models, credit-scoring models simultaneously ignore the local context by applying the same type of models in different contexts. This process of homogenization and standardization excludes the necessary role of local knowledge and expertise (Scott, 1998: 6). Standardized 'facts' are aggregate 'facts', and are either impersonal or simply a collection of facts about individuals (ibid.: 80) that are considered outside of local contexts and the particularities of place and time. Credit scoring and other forms of credit risk management rely on impersonal yet highly specialized and seemingly individual tests, in which trust takes a more calculative form. While such calculative trust systems do consider available information, in principle, they arise from a lack of full information at the individual level, reflecting 'reliability in the face of contingency' (Giddens 1990: 34). As Martin (2002: 195) demonstrates, 'the redefinition of the family home as an object of speculation and credit (...) displaces domestic life'.[7] Not only did finance become socialized; the social also became financialized.

Over-Accumulation, Predatory Lending and the Mortgage Market Crisis

Expanding Access to Credit: the Netherlands and the US

Financialization has resulted in an increase in the number of homeowners, but also, and more importantly, in a rapid and huge increase in the value of homes. It is not recent homeowners who benefit most, but those who have been property owners for decades. The financialization of home is of course the most beneficial for those who invested earlier and who were able to invest more: the 'upward pressure on house prices restricts access to homeownership and adds to the wealth of the "insiders" at the expense of the "outsiders"' (Stephens 2007: 218). In more developed societies, most households see their capital grow more through homeownership than through any other form of personal capital accumulation. When real wages were hardly keeping up with inflation, it was housing equity that spurred the real economy. In that sense, the financial and the real are reconnected. Of course, this is only possible as long as home prices keep on rising. The National Bank of the Netherlands estimated that during the half decade of exorbitant home price increases in the late 1990s, half of the economic growth was due to home equity rather than to real growth of the economy (DNB 2000). A less extreme version of this 'home equity fuels the real economy' phenomenon can be witnessed in almost all other developed countries, including the US and the UK. In the US, the wealth effect associated with housing may be twice as large as that associated with the stock market; the difference is even bigger in several European countries (Case *et al.* 2001).

Although the financialization of the mortgage market has reached the furthest in the US, it is not limited to the US.[8] The experience of the Dutch mortgage market illustrates the processes described above. The Dutch mortgage market is not unique, as similar developments have occurred in other countries with highly developed mortgage markets, although the timing and intensity of these developments have differed. Although the Netherlands has proportionately fewer homeowners than most other European countries, it experienced a period of strong development during the 1990s. In recent years, however, there has been a dramatic expansion of homeownership and of the mortgage market. The current rate of homeownership stands around 55 per cent. A number of factors have fuelled this trend. First, the government has actively supported homeownership by offering tax incentives to buyers and encouraging landlords to consider selling their rental stock. Second, structurally low interest rates and bank policies of accepting higher risks for home mortgages have made it easier to purchase a home. Since the early 1990s, the acceptance policies of banks have become increasingly lenient, and credit limits (i.e. the maximum amount that can be borrowed through a mortgage) have expanded. In the second half of the 1990s, all banks that provided mortgages widened their average credit limits by similar margins. For example, in the past, a second income within a household was not taken into consideration when calculating credit limits; today, however, all banks include such income in their calculations. Within five years, credit limits widened by 86 per cent for households with one income of €30,000 and one income of €11,000 (i.e. the average 1.5-income household) (DNB 2000). State policies together with the changing attitudes and policies of lenders have facilitated capital switching to the secondary and quaternary circuits of capital.

The percentage of the assessed value that is used to calculate the size of a mortgage has also increased. The assessed value is the value that a house would have if it had to be sold immediately, and is lower than the market value. When financing a house, moneylenders do not consider the purchase price of a house, but rather its assessed value. The number of new mortgages that exceed 75 per cent of the assessed value tripled between 1995 and 1999, which has increased the amount of risk faced by banks. Higher loan-to-value loans were necessary in order to enable people to buy homes, because the average household income was not increasing as quickly as average house prices. In return, these larger loans contributed to higher house prices. The boom in the housing market provided fuel for the boom in the mortgage market, and vice versa (Aalbers 2005).

Another factor that fuelled the mortgage market was that home mortgages were used for purposes of credit repair or the repayment of consumer credit. As in some other countries, such as the UK and the US, alternative mortgage products became popular in the Netherlands—so popular indeed that they can no longer be considered *alternative* mortgage products. While possibly financially beneficial, these loans also entail higher risk levels, in some cases for the applicant as well as the lender. The high-risk 'investment mortgage' overtook the traditional 'annuity mortgage' (in which the monthly payments are constant, with the installment portion increasing and the interest portion decreasing) as the most popular mortgage at the end of the 1990s. In addition, financial intermediaries and mortgage brokers had an incentive to sell these loans, as they often received higher sales fees on high-risk mortgage loans. In short, the Dutch mortgage market became financialized.

Bigger mortgage loans and easier access to credit enable homeownership. Since access has increased for almost everyone, it also implies increased competition and increasing house prices. Capital switching from the primary to the secondary circuit of capital may, at first sight, seem to benefit people who want to buy a house, but since it has resulted in dramatic increases in house prices, homeownership has paradoxically become more accessible *and* more expensive. The expansion of the mortgage market has not so much facilitated homeownership as it has facilitated capital switching to the quaternary circuit of capital.

In the US the housing bubble that was created as a result of similar processes, in combination with a rapid increase in consumer debt, equally stimulated consumer spending. Although home equity related growth was arguably nowhere as high as in the Netherlands, the US financial system made other types of credit more and more dependent on home equity. Simply put, owning a home made it easier and cheaper to get credit and, in addition, the growth of the US economy in recent decades has become increasingly dependent on credit rather than on income. Home equity was and is an important part of the accumulation regime that needs to keep the system going. Consequently, the current mortgage crisis in the US and the related fall in house prices affect not just households that need to refinance their homes or that want to sell their homes, but the whole economy. Home equity has become so entangled with the other parts of the economy, that problems in housing must affect other parts of the economy. A crisis in the mortgage market is therefore a crisis in the accumulation patterns of financial-ization and affects the economy at large. If a rise in home equity can keep the market going, a stagnation or decrease in home equity can result in a stagnation of other sectors of the economy and can depress economic growth.

Sub-Prime and Predatory Lending: A Crisis in the Making

Financialization demands that tradables become more liquid. Mortgages therefore need to be standardized so they can be priced in packages in the secondary mortgage markets. Credit scoring not only facilitates risk-based pricing, but also facilitates the securitization of mortgages. MBS are usually packaged by credit score and MBS representing high-risk credit scores are priced differently from those with low-risk credit scores: 'What was avoided before as "bad risk" becomes sought after as a high return, growth-fuelled dynamic market segment, as distinct from a "safe", sclerotic, "middle of the road" market' (Marron 2007: 126). Indeed, the fastest growing part of the secondary mortgage market is the trade in sub-prime MBS, i.e. MBS with high-risk credit scores.[9] The danger is that when the bubble bursts, as is currently the case in the mortgage market, MBS— which in theory are supposed to be very transparent, liquid products—become illiquid because traders start developing doubts about their value. In other words, one of the basics of the mortgage crisis is that MBS have become less liquid and are thus less easy to trade. Indeed, in a financialized world, illiquidity spreads rapidly and unpredictably (Boyer 2000). The origins of the current mortgage crisis are therefore *not* in the growing number of defaults and foreclosures—these are symptoms of the crisis. The crisis originates in selling risky loans to risky borrowers (sub-prime lending) and in selling exploitative loans to all exploitable borrowers (predatory lending). A sub-prime loan is 'a loan to a borrower with less than perfect credit. In order to compensate for the added risk associated with subprime loans, lending institutions charge higher interest rates. In contrast, a prime loan is a loan made to a creditworthy borrower at prevailing interest rates' (NCRC 2002: 4; cited in Squires 2004). A predatory loan is:

> an unsuitable loan designed to exploit vulnerable and unsophisticated borrowers. Predatory loans are a subset of subprime loans. A predatory loan has one or more of the following features: (1) higher interest and fees than is required to cover the added risk of lending to borrowers with credit imperfections, (2) abusive terms and conditions that trap borrowers and lead to increased indebtedness, (3) fails to take into account the borrower's ability to repay the loan, and (4) violates fair lending laws by targeting women, minorities and communities of color
>
> (ibid.).

Predatory lending is a form of price discrimination that roughly targets the same people and the same places that were excluded in the past as a result of redlining policies, i.e. older residents and minority populations, or neighborhoods with relatively large groups of the elderly or minorities (Hernandez 2009; Squires 2004; Wyly *et al.* 2006). In addition, as we saw with alternative mortgage products in the Netherlands, mortgage brokers had an incentive to sell these loans as they often received higher sales fees on sub-prime and predatory loans. Moreover, 'disparities in lending cannot be explained solely by differences in creditworthiness' (Taylor *et al.* 2004: 25). Indeed, most predatory, exploitative loans are sold to borrowers who could have applied for cheaper loans.[10] Therefore, the high risk and exploitative character of these loans is of more importance than the high risk of the borrowers. Residents are either offered loans that are more expensive than the risk profile of the borrower would suggest, or they are offered overpriced mortgage insurance that they often do not even need. This frequently leads to mortgage foreclosures at the individual level and housing abandonment at the neighborhood level. Most predatory lending is legal, although legislators are trying to catch up by adapting the rules of the game (McCoy & Wyly 2004; Squires 2004).

Predatory lenders are a specific type of sub-prime lender, and they make profit 'by stripping equity and wealth from home owners in underserved communities through high-cost refinance loans' (Taylor *et al.* 2004: 27). Predatory lending is so widespread that it can no longer be dismissed as anecdotal or isolated in a few places (Wyly *et al.* 2008; see also, Squires 2004), nor is predatory lending just something that is done by small banks; it is also, and increasingly, the practice of large banks or their subsidiaries. This is partly a result of banking deregulation (cf. Dymski 1999). Many of these loans are not designed to increase homeownership—despite the marketing and lobbying machine of these lenders intended to make one believe so—but are designed to take ownership ('repossession') and withdraw equity. Indeed, 'the magic of finance is its ability to take by giving' (Martin 2002: 16). It is both a classic and an extreme case of accumulation-by-dispossession (cf. Harvey 1982), as well as of rent-seeking behavior based on onerous terms (Ashton 2008; Immergluck & Smith 2004). Teaser rates and other tricks are used to sell these loans (2/28 mortgages, for example, have two years of low, 'teaser rate' interest and 28 years of high interest). Next, rapidly increasing interest rates ('adjustable rate mortgages') and balloon payments are used to increase returns, but more importantly, to increase the likeliness of default. Repeated default then allows lenders to repossess homes and acquire equity. In this way lenders do not enable homeownership but effectively strip home equity from borrowers. That some of these borrowers should have never received a mortgage loan in the first place is of little or no concern to most predatory lenders. As long as house prices rise and interest rates stay low, the problems are limited to individual borrowers, but once house prices stagnate or decline, default rates increase, and investors start doubting the value of MBS, the secondary market collapses.

But as Dymski (2007; see also, Lordon 2007) clearly demonstrates, this is only part of the story. It is not just borrowers taking out risky loans; it is also lenders allowing more risk in their organizations, as both default risk and liquidity risk have increased as a result of the restructuring of the mortgage market:

> Banks transformed their revenue-generation strategies due to macro- and micro-distress at the onset of the neoliberal age. These changes also transformed the structural relationships between loan-making and risk-taking, on one hand, and between banks' management and absorption of risks, on the other. That is, banks hit upon strategies that appeared to fundamentally reduce risks associated with banking and financial intermediation activities. However, in adopting these strategies, banks ceased to perform some of their key roles in the economy as a whole. When banks generate default risk and liquidity risk through loan-making, and absorb those risks on their balance sheets, these are built-in breaks in tendencies toward speculative and overly-risky lending
>
> (Dymski 2007: 1)

Thus, the restructuring of the mortgage market—which, by and large, can be viewed as a financialization of the mortgage market meant to facilitate capital switching to the secondary and later also to the quaternary circuit of capital—resulted not only in overly risky loans for too many borrowers, but also in too much risk-taking behavior on the part of many lenders, thereby threatening the continuation of the accumulation strategy.

The Downside of Financialization

Housing is a central aspect of financialization. Through the rise of securitization and the vast expansion of secondary mortgage markets, not only in the US but also in other countries, the mortgage market becomes financialized. Increasingly, lenders become intermediaries who sell mortgages, but don't manage, service or fund them (Aalbers 2009a; Dennis & Pinkowish 2004). But the financialization of homeownership is not limited to the development of secondary mortgage markets; it can also be witnessed in the financialization of (potential) home-owners. The financialization of home was never designed to enable homeownership; it was first and foremost designed to fuel the economy. The expansion of the mortgage market was a necessary component in the financial-ization of home, but wider access to mortgage loans resulted in higher house prices (e.g. Aalbers 2007; Stephens 2007). Access does not equal affordability. The result is not improved access to homeownership, but an increase in risk and insecurity. Higher mortgage loans enabled not only homeownership, but also higher house prices; subsequently, access needed to be widened further to enable continued capital switching. It is a vicious circle that is now reaching its absolute limits.

By simultaneously expanding the mortgage market, by means of granting bigger loans (as a percentage of income and as a percentage of home value), and by giving access to more households (so-called 'underserved populations'), the growth machine kept on working smoothly for a while. Yet, every growth machine or accumulation regime needs to keep on growing to function smoothly and it seems that the current mortgage crisis has announced the beginning of the end of ever-expanding mortgage markets. If access to the mortgage market will not be further increased, the growth of the mortgage market as well as the rise in house prices will mostly depend on growth rates in the real economy. If households cannot get bigger loans, they can only acquire more expensive homes if their real income rises. If interest rates go up and mortgage markets become less accessible, households will find it harder, or more expensive, to acquire a mortgage loan, which may result in stagnating or falling home prices. Since home equity fuels other sectors of the economy, a stagnation or decline in home equity will affect other economic sectors, in particular consumer markets. In addition, the reduced liquidity of mortgages in the secondary market will make it harder for lenders to securitize loans. And considering that two-thirds of the US mortgage market is securitized, the impact can only be massive. This is why major bank lenders are hit hard and have lost billions of dollars in the crisis, but the ones going bankrupt (e.g. New Century Financial Corporation) or closing down (e.g. American Home Mortgage) are the non-bank lenders that fully rely on the secondary mortgage to sell their portfolios.

The financialization of home in its current form is unsustainable. I do not intend to imply that all financialized mortgage and housing markets will burst; I simply conclude that they cannot continuously expand without the expansion of the real economy. It is likely that the mortgage crisis will not become a global crisis, simply because the situation in the US is in many respects unique. Securitization has reached much higher levels in the US than elsewhere. A crisis in the liquidity of MBS therefore affects the US much more than markets in countries where mortgages are hardly securitized. In addition, the exploitative predatory loans that are now causing many of the defaults and foreclosures are much more widespread in the US than in any other country. This does not mean mortgage markets in other countries will not be affected.

As we can already see in the UK, the market is affected and this hits actors that are active in, or dependent on, the secondary market particularly hard. It may be considered ironic that Northern Rock, the mortgage lender that in 2005 won the 'International Financing Review Securitisation Award', has been the biggest victim of the mortgage crisis on the UK side so far. Simply put, the more financialized the mortgage market in a country, the bigger the risk of a mortgage crisis. The more mortgage markets are dependent on securitization, the more volatile they will be, because they will be more dependent on the ebb and flow in other financial and financialized markets. But the crisis is not just reaching beyond the US, it is also reaching beyond the mortgage market. This is partly a result of the sheer size of the mortgage market, partly a result of the unique role of banks as both commercial firms and essential nodes in the economy, and partly a result of financialization, which has not only made the mortgage market dependent on other financial and financialized markets, but also vice versa. This further implies that the impact is not limited to American homeowners or even to American homeowners, lenders and investors, but to investors worldwide. And since pension funds are important global investors in MBS, it indirectly also affects workers worldwide. This is exactly why buzzwords like financialization and the globalization of finance are not just buzzwords, but are about processes affecting even those seemingly disconnected from high finance and international investment.

The financialization of the mortgage market means that it is not only the global and the local that have become interdependent, but also the financial and the built environment. The financialization of the real economy not only implies that Wall Street is governing more and more economic sectors, it also implies that money is increasingly being invested in finance itself and not in the real economy. This form of capital switching to the quaternary circuit is being used as a way to resolve a crisis in the primary circuit; but, according to Harvey, capital switching can only delay a crisis, not withhold it. Moreover, capital switching has a tendency to enlarge a crisis, both in size and in geographical scope. Although credit scoring can be thought of as a way to control over-expansion of the mortgage market, it has in effect contributed to over-accumulation, because it has widened access to capital for high-risk borrowers. Credit scoring has fuelled risk-based pricing, and, taken together, credit scoring, risk-based pricing and securitization have resulted in the development of a mortgage market for sub-prime and predatory loans. Predatory loans, whether securitized or not, by definition, do not present a *stable* income source and are therefore, in a very literal sense, prone to accumulation-by-dispossession. The collapse of mortgage markets in 2007 (and 2008?) is undeniably at least in part a result of the rapid growth of both sub-prime and predatory lending (facilitated by credit scoring) and the spread of secondary mortgage markets.

Crises have often been blamed on a lack of openness and transparency. Yet, the current crisis originates in a market made open, liquid and transparent, located in a country that prides itself on its free, open markets. In addition, an analysis of financial crisis since 1945 demonstrates that financial liberalization, whether *de jure* or *de facto*, precedes the majority of crises (Kaminsky & Reinhart 1999)— the current crisis is no exception (cf. Dymski 1999; Gotham 2006). Apparently, liberalization-enabled securitization and financialization, by embracing risk rather than avoiding it, act against the interests of long-term investments (cf. Minns 2001: 108). Although securitization was designed to limit risk by spreading it over a wider area and to increase efficiency as a result of economies of scale, it now turns out that the spread of risk gives the crisis wider latitude, not only affecting sub-prime loans, but also prime loans; not only affecting mortgage markets, but also other credit markets; and not only affecting the US, but also other places around the globe. Through financialization, the volatility of Wall Street has entered not only companies off Wall Street, but increasingly also individual homes. While the expansion of the mortgage market facilitates capital switching to the secondary circuit, MBS facilitate capital switching to the quaternary circuit through the commodification of mortgage portfolios. Since the secondary circuit of capital is itself becoming financialized, decisions about the home are now, more than ever before, decisions about finance.

Postscript to Chapter 3

This chapter was written in late 2007 and originally published in June 2008. At the time of writing, the housing crisis in the US was still novel. When I attended the RC21 urban studies conference in Vancouver in August 2007,[11] our session on "The Sociology and Geography of Homeownership and Mortgage Markets" was attended by the usual crowd seen at a typical housing session at an urban studies conference. The session included several papers that analysed the housing and mortgage crisis in the US, and although the conference featured many sessions on urban governance, social movements, inequality and ethnicity, most conference attendees at the time did not realize that these topics were directly tied to the fate of housing and mortgage markets. The word "crisis" appeared in none of the 32 session abstracts.[12]

At the time, subprime had already gone prime time, as Elvin Wyly remarked at our session. In hindsight, it appears that many Americans at the time still thought that the crisis could be contained and would not spread much beyond housing and mortgage markets. Many Europeans felt that the crisis would be limited to the US. At the time there was quite some *Schadenfreude* regarding the perceived punishment of the Americans for their Wild West Capitalism and the seeming confirmation of the European Model, praised for its mixed economy "balance" between market and public needs. Few Europeans could see that the European Model, or at least most of the different European models, was not as balanced as was believed and as prone to a systemic crisis as the American.

Guy Verhofstadt,[13] in the short spell between his Belgian and his European political career, worked on a book on the financial collapse, *The Financial Crisis: How Europe can Save the World*. He praised Europe's Social Economy, arguing that Europe will lead the way out of the crisis and provide an example for how to create a sustainable economy. To Verhofstadt, the US and the BRIC countries do not have a viable solution for the volatility of the global economy, and Europe is the only geopolitical block that can drag the world out of the crisis.

Not long after its publication in the spring of 2009, European economies started to fall like dominos. Not just individual countries, but the euro and the European Union as a political and monetary block fell into a deep crisis from which it is yet to recover. While growth returned to the US, most European countries continue on a path of zero growth. Clearly, Europe did not save the world. The "balanced" European model turned out to be a patchwork of balanced, not-so balanced and completely unbalanced European models, stitched together by a common currency and a set of post-democratic institutions, but no common and democratic politics.

If we compare the cover of Verhofstadt's book to Robert Shiller's best-selling *The Subprime Solution: How Today's Global Financial Crisis Happened, and What to Do about It* (2008), one can only conclude that Verhofstadt's is a poor copy of Shiller's.[14] Verhofstadt's European arrogance towards the American Model contrasts squarely with the fact that his publisher could not do any better than publish his book with poorly executed copy of its supposed American counterpart, perhaps indicative of the poorly executed copy of the American model pushed by European politicians. In the crisis it became clear that since Thatcher, *Die Wende,* the Third Way and the Eurozone, Europe, and in particular the EU, had slowly but surely squandered its Social Economy, exchanging it for a Financialized Economy. While different from American financialized capitalism, it is nevertheless clearly related and arguably influenced by it.

When I presented *The Financialization at Home* to a Dutch audience in 2008 and a research proposal along the same lines to the Netherlands Organisation for Scientific Research (NWO), the responses included sentences such as "This will not happen in Europe"; "House prices in the Netherlands can be explained by the fundamentals"; and "This is all very interesting, but what are you going to do when the crisis has passed next year and we go back to business as usual?" House prices in many European countries dropped, with the Netherlands ranking among those with biggest losses (see Chapter 6). The crisis did not pass in a year. The financial sector, real estate lobbyists and some politicians have been trying hard to return to business as usual, at the costs of what remained of the balanced Social Economy, namely at the costs of entire countries like Greece and at the expense of populations at large as austerity measures, heavily pushed by the EU and often against democratic decisions, will hurt all Europeans who at some point in their life need to rely on the welfare state. While Greece's territory is literally commodified and its welfare state dismantled, privatization and financialization in the rest of Europe have accelerated. Health care, education, social services—Esping Andersen's three pillars of the welfare state (see Chapter 1)—as well as the housing pillar have all suffered. Today, one can speak of the four wobbly pillars of the welfare state.

Acknowledgements

The author would like to thank Sheila Hones, Gary Dymski and Ewald Engelen, as well as the editors and referees of this journal for their comments on an earlier draft of this paper.

Notes

1   As Krippner (2005: 181) argues, this definition of financialization 'is capable of encompassing alternative usages of the term', such as (1) the ascendancy of 'shareholder value' as a mode of corporate governance; (2) the growing dominance of capital markets over systems of bank-based finance; (3) the increasing political and economic power of a 'rentier class'; and (4) the explosion of financial trading associated with the proliferation of new financial instruments.

2   As Langley (2006: 292) argues, 'an on-going securitization programme is impossible without a growing portfolio of underlying assets'.

3   Gotham (2006) speaks of 'deterritorialized investment'.

4   London not only handles most European securitizations, but also half of Australia's MBS market and a small but significant share of US and Asian MBS issuance.

5   Currently director of the financial advice bureau *Independer*.

6   Cited in Damen (2003); authors' translation.

7   Compare Habermas' (1987) 'colonization of the life-world'.

8   French *et al.* (2011: 13) argue that, 'financialization is at present surprisingly limited in geographical scope'. Although it is clear that the US economy is, in many respects, increasingly financialized (Krippner 2005), and there is little doubt that the US is the most, or at least one of the most, financialized countries in the world, the debate is open on the level of financialization in other countries. Some countries, like the Netherlands, may at first sight appear to be a 'coordinated market economy' or represent a 'Rhineland model of capitalism' like Germany; a closer look reveals relatively high and increasing levels of financialization (cf. Engelen *et al.* 2010), not only through the opening up of the market and the internationalization of the stock holders of its largest companies, but also through its very large and internationally important pension funds and the expansion of its mortgage market, the world's largest in relative size.

9   Burton *et al.* (2004) make a distinction between traditional sub-prime suppliers and new subprime suppliers. The first focuses on low-income borrowers and often collect the repayments door-to-door; the second on out-of-the-box solutions for customers who are categorized as 'non-standard' because of their financial history, e.g. entrepreneurs.

10 A survey on sub-prime loans issued in 2005 and 2006 found that 55 per cent, respectively 61 per cent, of these borrowers had credit scores high enough to obtain conventional, prime, mortgage loans (Brooks & Simon 2007; cited in Dymski 2007).

11 See: www.rc21.org/conferences/vancouver.php. A selection of the papers was eventually published as a special issue of the *International Journal of Urban and Regional Research* (Aalbers, 2009b).

12 Even two years later, at the RC21 conference in São Paulo (2009), only 3 of the 30 sessions mentioned the crisis.

13 Prime Minister of Belgium between 1999 and 2008, and Member of the European Parliament as well as leader of the Alliance of Liberals and Democrats for Europe since 2009.

14   Amazon is one of the few places where you can still find the cover image of Verhofstadt's book: http://ecx.images-amazon.com/images/I/415kkybSe1L._SX321_BO1,204,203,200_.jpg. Shiller's is much easier to find.

References

Aalbers, M.B. (2005) 'The quantified customer', or how financial institutions value risk, in P. Boelhouwer, J. Doling and M. Elsinga (eds), *Home Ownership: Getting In, Getting From, Getting Out* (Delft: Delft University Press), pp. 33–57.

Aalbers, M.B. (2009a) The globalization and Europeanization of mortgage markets, *International Journal of Urban and Regional Research*, 33(2): 389–410.

Aalbers, M.B. (ed.) (2009b) The sociology and geography of mortgage markets: Reflections on the financial crisis, *International Journal of Urban and Regional Research*, 33(2): 281–442.

Aalbers, M.B. (2007) Geographies of housing finance: the mortgage market in Milan, Italy, *Growth and Change*, 38(2): 174–199.

Arrighi, G. (1994) *The Long Twentieth Century: Money, Power, and the Origins of our Times* (London: Verso).

Ashton, P. (2008) Advantage or disadvantage? The changing landscape of underserved mortgage markets, *Urban Affairs Review*, 43(3): 352–402.

Boyer, R. (2000) Is a finance-led growth regime a viable alternative to Fordism? A preliminary analysis, *Economy and Society*, 29(1): 111–145.

Brooks, R. and Simon, R. (2007) As housing boomed, industry pushed loans to a broader market, *Wall Street Journal*, 3 December, p. A1.

Burton, D., Knights, D., Leyshon, A., Alferoff, C. and Signoretta, P. (2004) Making a market: the UK retail financial services industry and the rise of the complex sub-prime credit market, *Competition and Change*, 8(1): 3–25.

Case, K.E., Quigley, J.M. and Shiller, R. (2001) Comparing wealth effects: the stock market versus the housing market, working paper no. 8606 (Cambridge, MA: National Bureau of Economic Research).

Clark, G. and O'Connor, K. (1997) The informational content of financial products and the spatial structure of the global finance industry, in K. R. Cox (ed.), *Spaces of Globalization: Reasserting the Power of the Local* (New York: Guilford Press), pp. 89–114.

Coles, A. and Hardt, J. (2000) Mortgage markets: why US and EU markets are so different, *Housing Studies*, 15(5): 775–783.

Cox, R.W. (1992) Global Perestroika, in R. Miliband and L. Panitch (eds), *Socialist Register 1992: New World Order?* (London: Merlin Press), pp. 26–43.

Damen, T. (2003) Langs de financiële meetlat van de bank, *Het Parool*, 8 February.

Dennis, M.W. and Pinkowish, T.J. (2004) *Residential Mortgage Lending: Principles and Practices*, fifth edition (Mason, OH: Thomson South-Western).

DNB (2000) *Het bancaire hypotheekbedrijf onder de loep. Rapport over de ontwikkelingen op de hypotheekmarkt in de periode 1994–1999 gebaseerd op onderzoek naar de hypothecaire kredietverlening bij Nederlandse financiële instellingen* (Amsterdam: De Nederlandse Bank).

Dymski, G.A. (1999) *The Bank Merger Wave: The Economic Causes and Social Consequences of Financial Consolidation* (Armonk, NY: Sharpe).

Dymski, G.A. (2007) From financial exploitation to global banking instability: two overlooked roots of the subprime crisis, working paper (Sacramento, CA: University of California Center Sacramento).

EMF (2005) *Hypostat 2004* (Brussels: European Mortgage Federation).

Engelen, E. (2002) Corporate governance, property, and democracy: a conceptual critique of shareholder ideology, *Economy and Society*, 31: 391–413.

Engelen, E. (2003) The logic of funding European pension restructuring and the dangers of financialisation, *Environment and Planning A*, 35(8): 1357–1372.

Engelen, E., Konings, M. and Fernandez, R. (2010) Geographies of financialization in disarray: the Dutch case in comparative perspective. *Economic Geography*, 86(1): 53–73.

Feng, H., Froud, J., Haslam, C., Johal, S., Haslam, C. and Williams, K. (2001) A new business model? The capital market and the new economy, *Economy and Society*, 30(4): 467–503.

Ford, J., Burrows, R. and Nettleton, S. (2001) *Home-ownership in a Risk Society* (Bristol: Policy Press).

Forrest, R., Kennett, P. and Leather, P. (1999) *Home ownership in crisis? The British Experience of Negative Equity* (Aldershot: Ashgate).

Forum Group on Mortgage Credit (2004) *The Integration of the EU Mortgage Credit Markets* (Brussels: European Commission).

Foster, J.B. (2006) Monopoly-finance capital, *Monthly Review*, 58(7): 1–14.

Foster, J.B. (2007) The financialization of capitalism, *Monthly Review*, 58(11): 1–12.

French, S., Leyshon, A. and Wainwright, T. (2011) Financializing space, spacing financialization, *Progress in Human Geography*, 35(6): 798–819.

Froud, J., Haslam, C., Johal, S. and Williams, K. (2000) Shareholder value and financialization: consultancy promises, management moves, *Economy and Society*, 29(1): 80–110.

Froud, J., Haslam, C., Johal, S. and Williams, K. (2002) Cars after financialisation: a case study of financial under-performance, constraints and consequences, *Competition and Change*, 6(1): 13–41.

Giddens, A. (1990) *The Consequences of Modernity* (Cambridge: Polity).

Gotham, K.F. (2006) The secondary circuit of capital reconsidered: globalization and the U.S. real estate sector, *American Journal of Sociology*, 112(1): 231–275.

Habermas, J. (1987) *Theorie des kommunikativen Handelns* (Frankfurt am Main: Suhrkamp) [English edition published by Polity, Cambridge].

Hacker, J.S. (2006) *The Great Risk Shift: The Assault on American Jobs, Families, Health Care and Retirement—and how you can fight back* (New York: Oxford University Press).

Harvey, D. (1982) *The Limits to Capital* (Oxford: Blackwell).

Harvey, D. (1985) *The Urbanization of Capital: Studies in the History and Theory of Capitalist Urbanization* (Oxford: Blackwell).

Hernandez, J. (2009) Redlining revisited: mortgage lending patterns in Sacramento 1930–2004, *International Journal of Urban and Regional Research*, 33(2): 291–313.

IFS (2006) *Securitisation* (London: International Financial Services).

Immergluck, D. (2004) *Credit to the Community: Community Reinvestment and Fair Lending Policy in the United States* (Armonk, NY: Sharpe).

Immergluck, D. and Smith, G. (2004) *Risky Business: An Econometric Analysis of the Relationship Between Subprime Lending and Neighborhood Foreclosures* (Chicago, IL: Woodstock Institute).

Jackson, K.T. (1985) *Crabgrass Frontier: The Suburbanization of the United States* (New York: Oxford University Press).

Kaminsky, G.L. and Reinhart, C.M. (1999) The twin crises: the causes of banking and balance-of-payment problems, *American Economic Review*, 89(3): 473–500.

Krippner, G. (2005) The financialization of the American economy, *Socio-Economic Review*, 3: 173–208.

Langley, P. (2006) Securitising suburbia: the transformation of Anglo-American mortgage finance, *Competition and Change*, 10(3): 283–299.

Lazonick, W. and O'Sullivan, M. (2000) Maximising shareholder value: a new ideology for corporate governance, *Economy and Society*, 29(1): 13–35.

Leyshon, A. and Thrift, N. (1999) Lists come alive: electronic systems of knowledge and the rise of credit-scoring in retail banking, *Economy and Society*, 28(3): 434–466.

Leyshon, A. and Thrift, N. (2007) The capitalization of almost everything: the future of finance and capitalism, *Theory, Culture and Society*, 24(7–8): 97–115.

Lordon, F. (2007) Spéculation immobilière, ralentissement économique. Quand la finance prend le monde en otage, *Le Monde diplomatique*, Septembre.

Magdoff, H. and Sweezy, P.M. (1972) *The Dynamics of U.S. Capitalism* (New York: Monthly Review Press).

Mandel, M.J. (1996) *The High-risk society: Peril and Promise in the New Economy* (New York: Random House).

Marron, D. (2007) 'Lending by numbers': credit scoring and the constitution of risk within American consumer credit, *Economy and Society*, 36(1): 103–133.

Martin, R. (2002) *Financialization of Daily Life* (Philadelphia, PA: Temple University Press).

McCoy, P.A. and Wyly, E.K. (2004) Guest editors' introduction, *Housing Policy Debate,* 15: 453–466.

Minns, R. (2001) *The Cold War in Welfare: Stock Markets Versus Pensions* (London: Verso).

Murie, A., Tosics, I., Aalbers, M.B., Sendi, R. and Černič-Mali, B. (2005) Privatisation and after, in R. van Kempen, K. Dekker, S. Hall and I. Tosics (eds), *Restructuring Large-scale Housing Estates in European Cities* (Bristol: Policy Press), pp. 85–103.

NCRC (2002) *Anti-predatory Lending Toolkit* (Washington, DC: National Community Reinvestment Coalition).

Pryke, M. and Lee, R. (1995) Place your bets: towards an understanding of globalisation, sociofinancial engineering and competition within a financial centre, *Urban Studies*, 32(2): 329–344.

Ross, S.L. and Yinger, J. (2002) *The Color of Credit: Mortgage Discrimination, Research Methodology, and Fair-lending Enforcement* (Cambridge, MA: MIT Press).

Sassen, S. (2001) *The Global City: New York, London, Tokyo*, second edition (Princeton, NJ: Princeton University Press).

Scott, J.C. (1998) *Seeing Like a State: How Certain Schemes to Improve the Human Condition Have Failed* (New Haven, CT: Yale University Press).

Shiller, R.J. (2008) *The Subprime Solution: How Today's Global Financial Crisis Happened, and What to Do about It* (Princeton, NJ: Princeton University Press).

Smart, A. and Lee, J. (2003) Financialization and the role of real estate in Hong Kong's regime of accumulation, *Economic Geography*, 79(2): 153–171.

Squires, G.D. (ed.) (2004) *Why the Poor Pay More: How to Stop Predatory Lending* (Westport: Praeger).

Stephens, M. (2007) Mortgage market deregulation and its consequences, *Housing Studies*, 22(2): 201–220.

Stockhammer, E. (2004) Financialisation and the slowdown of accumulation, *Cambridge Journal of Economics*, 28(5): 719–741.

Stuart, G. (2003) *Discriminating Risk: The U.S. Mortgage Lending Industry in the Twentieth Century* (Ithaca, NY: Cornell University Press).

Sweezy, P.M. (1995) Economic reminiscences, *Monthly Review*, 47(1): 1–11.

Taylor, J., Silver, J. and Berembaum, D. (2004) The targets of predatory and discriminatory lending: who are they and where do they live?, in G.D. Squires (ed.), *Why the Poor Pay More: How to Stop Predatory Lending* (Westport: Praeger), pp. 25–38.

Verhofstadt, G. (2009) *The Financial Crisis: How Europe Can Save the World* (London: Shoehorn).

Wyly, E., Atia, M., Foxcroft, H., Hammel, D. and Philips-Watts, K. (2006) American home: predatory mortgage capital and neighbourhood spaces of race and class exploitation in the United States, *Geografiska Annaler B*, 88: 105–132.

Wyly, E., Moos, M., Foxcroft, H. and Kabahizi, E. (2008) Subprime mortgage segmentation in the American urban system, *TESG, Tijdschrift voor Economische en Sociale Geografie*, 99(1): 3–23.

4 The Great Moderation, the Great Excess and the Global Housing Crisis

Introduction: A Periodization of Housing Structures

It has been well documented how the national subprime mortgage market in the US was one of the roots of the global financial crisis (e.g. Aalbers, 2009a, 2012; Gotham, 2009; Sassen, 2009; Wyly, Moos, Hammel, & Kabahizi, 2009). Not only in the US, but in many countries across different continents, the rapid increase in national house prices in the years or even decades before the global crisis is considered the main reason why house prices started to decline between 2007 and 2009. Thus, the underlying cause of house price decline is essentially seen as national in origin: house prices went down nationally because they had been rising nationally. Yet, the timing of the international house price decline is more global in nature: the financial crisis happened around the globe and was—is—related to a recession, or at least to the slowing of economic growth, a sovereign debt crisis and rising unemployment.

More than anything, this paper is part of a sustained effort seeking to understand the relation between the global financial crisis (2007–20??) and national housing markets. Never before had so many housing markets entered a crisis at the same time. To make sense of how housing policy and crisis became internationally synchronized, I present a periodization of developments in housing markets, policies and practices to structure the changes that have happened over time. I distinguish between four periods: first, the pre-modern period; second, the modern or Fordist period; third, the flexible neoliberal or post-Fordist period; and, fourth, the emerging post-crisis or late neoliberal period. I will not discuss the first, pre-modern period, but focus primarily on the shift from the modern/Fordist to the flexible neoliberal/post-Fordist period and the breakdown of the latter model in the global financial crisis and national housing crises. My argument is not that the crisis caused the breakdown of the flexible neoliberal/post-Fordist model, but rather that the shift to this model introduced certain dynamics to housing markets that a few decades later culminated in a global crisis.

I use (some might say misuse) the concept of 'the Great Moderation' in analysing the shift from the second to the third period. Economists refer to the Great Moderation as the macroeconomic cycle that began in 1984 characterized by more economic stability and observed in terms of smaller GDP and interest rate fluctuations than in previous cycles. In this paper, I unpack this concept by arguing that the so-called Great Moderation was not so much a moderation of macro-economic cycles as it was the start of the financialization of states and economies in numerous domains, including housing. In this period, credit flowing into the real economy decreased, while credit to finance and real estate increased in relative terms. What appeared to be a structural moderation of fluctuations was, in fact, the build-up of the bubble economy that burst in 2007 and the following years. The shift from the Fordist to the post-Fordist period is often understood to have been achieved through the so called Great Moderation of 1984, but had in fact already started in the 1970s with the end of the gold standard, the associated breakdown of the Bretton Woods institutions and the international recessions that took place in that decade. The recent global financial crisis signalled the end of the Great Moderation and the beginning of a new late neoliberal period, the features of which are only just beginning to become apparent.

The aim of this paper is three-fold. First, it is argued that to understand the housing crisis that hit many countries in the years following 2007, we need a historical perspective to understand how the regime of accumulation in housing that previously dominated was established in the first place. To do this, a period-ization of developments in housing is presented. It is argued that this periodization helps us to understand the post-World War II development of housing in different countries—the second goal of this paper. The third aim of this paper is to problematize the concept of the Great Moderation. It is argued that the moderation in interest rates and macroeconomic cycles, defining characteristics of this period, was also a Great Excess in terms of rising inequality and excessive credit and debt, suggestive of a finance-led regime of accumulation. The second and third are necessary elements in reaching the first goal of this paper but, as I suggest in the concluding section, they also open up new avenues for future research into connections between developments in (inter)national macroeconomics, on the one hand, and housing markets, policies and practices on the other.

The structure of this paper is rather straightforward. The next section intro-duces global and international developments in housing markets and discusses how these have resulted, at least to some extent, to similarities between different housing systems. Subsequent sections discuss the different periods and critical junctures one at a time. Finally, it is concluded that the period that started in the 1980s should not be regarded as the Great Moderation but rather as the Great Excess or the Great Financialization in which households became increasingly indebted to enable homeownership. The concluding section will also put forward some hypotheses that could be analysed within the analytical framework intro-duced here.

The Partially Global Nature of Housing

The periodization presented in this paper is a heuristic device. It does not provide a fully accurate picture of real developments, but an approximation that should enable us to better understand what happened to housing and how we ended up where we are now. In other words, it is my goal to use a periodization of housing to understand actually existing housing markets and policy developments better, particularly regarding the international synchronization of housing booms before 2007 and their subsequent bust. It is not intended as a model of the world or a straitjacket that should fit all countries. Like all periodizations (Mayhew, 2005) it is problematic in that it may stress similarities within a selected time frame and overemphasise changes between periods whereas, in reality, every era has gradual and constant change.

Since part of my argument is that some trends (e.g. homeownership politics, commodification and housing finance) have become increasingly—but far from completely—similar in different countries, the consequence is that the periodization is less accurate in the earlier periods than it is in the later periods. Countries move from period one to two at very different times in history, but there is significant synchronization in countries moving to periods three and four. This suggests, among other things, that in the first phase, developing countries are not exactly following the previous trajectories of developed countries. That is, they do not go through the same stages of development, only decades later, but are actually 'catching up' and may even skip a phase. One effect of globalization is that contemporary countries go through the same developments at roughly the same time. This does, of course, not imply that globalization has the same effects around the globe. On the contrary, globalization is a process of uneven development at the global scale and on a global scale.

There is a specific reason why I speak of international house price decline but not of a global financial crisis. House prices did not go down globally as there are dozens of countries that escaped house price decline. Yet, it would be hard to point at any country whose financial system and financial agents escaped the financial crisis completely. This is, at least in part, a result of the global nature of financial flows and financial agents. Even countries that continued to see economic growth and rising house prices, such as China, were hit by the global financial crisis (Wu, 2015). It is tempting to conclude that the financial sector is very globalized in nature, but that the housing sector continues to be national in nature. Not all housing finance is globalized: in many countries, most mortgage lenders are national and there is continued divergence in different financial models (Aalbers, 2009b). More salient to the readers of this journal is that housing is not only national in nature, but also local and global. As is well understood, housing is local in nature because housing markets work locally but, in the majority of countries, most housing market institutions and the lion's share of housing policies are embedded at the national scale.

Housing is also global in nature because, first, some agents of housing markets work globally, and, second, the ideology of housing as well as of states and markets is shaped in a complex fashion at the intersection of national and international trajectories. First, there are some real estate agents, buyers, developers and financiers that work internationally. Members of the 1 per cent may buy a house in London as easily as they do in New York, Dubai or São Paulo, even though they may not be registered citizens in any of these places. However, this does not imply they buy houses everywhere: their primary interest is in politically stable global cities and global leisure places. (And even in those places the 1 per cent typically only buy in a small part of the market, both in terms of price range and location.)

Likewise, real estate agents, consultants and developers may be globally active, but most of them are also selectively located in a small number of globally connected places. There are exceptions to this rule: some international real estate agencies, in particular franchises, are active outside global and capital cities. The popularity of Real Estate Investment Trusts (REITs) has risen sharply since the turn of the century, but as housing tends to be a relatively small—albeit increasing—part of most REITs' portfolios, I will not focus on them here. Rather, I am more interested in the financing of mortgage loans. As I will argue in this paper, the financing of mortgage loans has structurally changed. Although some of these changes are not fully global, housing systems have changed internationally and the convergence of some of these trends is truly remarkable, in particular but not exclusively in western countries.

A disclaimer may be in order at this point of writing. I do not claim that housing systems (e.g. Boelhouwer & Van der Heijden, 1992; Kemeny & Lowe, 1998) have converged across the board and I have demonstrated elsewhere that there is continued divergence, also related to residential mortgage markets (Aalbers, 2009b). I also do not claim that country typologies that have been applied to, or developed for, housing are irrelevant (e.g. Barlow & Duncan, 1994; Esping-Andersen, 1990; Kemeny, 1995; Schwartz & Seabrooke, 2009). What I do claim is that there are some similar trends in different countries that deserve to be studied as international trends. The outcomes of these trends are not easy to interpret. Two countries moving in the same direction does not imply that they are necessarily converging. Let us consider countries A and B. In 1970, A scores 10 and B scores 50 on a certain dimension that runs from 0 to 100. In 2010, A and B score, respectively, 30 and 80. This implies that the trend in both countries A and B is increasing, but also that the difference between A and B has not diminished but increased. This is of course a very hypothetical example, but the point is this: similar trends and continued divergence can be part of the same structural, international change. Through such 'common trajectories' (Hay, 2004) countries can move in the same direction while maintaining their essential institutional differences.

What causes these similarities in trends? This brings us back to the partially global nature of housing. Not only some if its actors are globalized, some of the thinking about housing is also globalized. The ideology of homeownership (Aalbers & Christophers, 2014; Kemeny, 1981; Ronald, 2008) has spread to so many countries that we could speak of an international, or perhaps even global, trend. More generally speaking, we see that the thinking about states and markets has changed throughout the world. That does not imply that, say Sweden and China, have converging political economies, but we do see the same tendencies towards commodification in both countries (e.g. Christophers, 2013; Hsing, 2010).

On a more ideological level, one could think of the global spread of neoliberalism in the last three to four decades. The globalization of ideology is related directly and indirectly to the globalization of certain aspects of housing markets. It is related directly as some of the agents of housing market globalization also further the ideology of homeownership and marketization and are fundamentally enabled by this ideology and the policies based on it. It is related indirectly as the often-abstract ideas associated with dominant ideologies selectively feed into real housing policies. Gilbert (2002), for example, discusses how neoliberal ideology travelled from the US to Chile to influence national housing policy and was subsequently adapted at its implementation. This adapted version, still neoliberal in nature, in turn was picked up by the US international developmental agenda and prescribed to the more indebted and 'less sophisticated' countries (Gilbert, 2002). But we are jumping ahead: before introducing the flexible and late neoliberal periods in housing, we first need to discuss the modern period in housing as well as the Great Moderation.

The Modern or Fordist Period

An important characteristic of the modern or Fordist period in housing markets and policies was the production of houses for the masses, i.e., the construction of large numbers of houses for a large cross-section of the population, in particular, the working and middle classes. It is different from the pre-modern period in the sense that the quality of the housing that was constructed in the modern period had become an important feature, whereas this was not regarded as necessary for most social classes in the pre-modern period, at least not by those in power. This resulted in a second important feature of the modern period: the active role of the state in facilitating housing production and finance (see also Florida & Feldman, 1988).

The first experiments with modern housing took place in the late nineteenth and early twentieth centuries. A combination of public, private (e.g. large corporate employers) and non-profit (e.g. philanthropy) organizations started to take up the goal of providing good and affordable housing for the masses. In western countries, these experiments were consolidated into institutionalized structures in the years between the two world wars. Good, affordable housing became a goal of many states and they facilitated the construction of such houses by non-profits (and sometimes also by for-profits) through new legal structures and subsidies. In addition, a variety of local and national governments also started building houses themselves. The focus in this early modern period is on good housing for the skilled working classes, much less for the large numbers of working poor.

The modern period really took off at the end of World War II. Many countries were faced with large numbers of demolished houses, low housing production in the preceding years and a booming population. Expanding the possibilities to build decent and affordable housing for large parts of the population further redrew the institutional map. In some countries, the state privileged the expansion of a social rented sector, in others the expansion of homeownership and in a few, tax breaks, subsidies and tenant protection focused on expanding the private rented sector. In almost all cases, the state took up a more active role in organising and facilitating the respective privileged sectors. Savings and loans institutions, building societies, *bausparkassen*, *cajas*—or more generally speaking, thrifts, savings banks and credit unions—played a major role in providing mortgage loans to the middle and sometimes also to the working classes. States typically treated these organizations favourably in terms of conditions and taxes. At the same time, state provision of rental housing or state-subsidized rental housing was expanded. Most countries saw state facilitation in both mortgage lending and social housing, but typically in each country, one system was dominant.

Early archetypes of modern housing are company towns, philanthropic 'model estates' and garden towns. High-modernist archetypes include the North American suburb; the West-European housing estates, new towns, *villes nouvelles*, *groeikernen* and the like; and the Central and Eastern Europe (CEE) and to some extent Asian housing estates (see Table 4.1). The morphology and densities of these archetypes are quite different, but what they all have in common is that they were built for a large cross-section of the population and with the use of new building techniques and increased levels of standardization. This standardization was also a direct result of the institutions involved: at a national level, both states and mortgage lenders pushed towards more homogenous housing units and environments.

House building for the masses was supported by a redistributive state that focused on full employment, economic growth and a decent wage for all workers and increasingly (but very unevenly, internationally speaking) minimal income and housing conditions for the poor. In this sense, the difference between what were then called 'The First World' and 'The Second World' was not as large as the Cold War rhetoric suggested. The differences between these two worlds on the one hand and what was then known as 'The Third World' on the other, remained vast and developing countries by-and-large did not enter the modern housing period at the same time.

The Great Moderation

Things started to change in the 1970s and in hindsight I believe a range of developments in the 1970s were preparing the world for a new era of flexible neoliberalism or post-Fordism. Some key events in this decade include but are not limited to: the end of the Bretton Woods system of monetary management and the termination of the gold standard in 1971; the sudden hike in interest rates invoked by U.S. Federal Reserve chairman Paul Volcker in 1979, which had repercussions throughout the world, including the Third World Debt Crisis; the 1973 and 1979 oil/energy crises and the associated 1970s recessions; and finally, the onset of neoliberalism with the election of Margaret Thatcher as Prime Minister of the UK in 1979.

In the early and mid-1980s, most western countries recovered from the many blows that the 1970s had dealt, and slowly entered a new era of moderate but

Table 4.1 Periodization of Housing Developments

	Modern/Fordist Period	Flexible Neoliberal/ Post-Fordist Period	Late Neoliberal/ Post-Crisis Period
Key developments	Building for the masses (either through rental or owner-occupied housing)	Homeownership increasingly financialized; 'tenants are losers' discourse	Emerging regime; difficult access to homeownership
Construction	High	Secondary to financial expansion	Low
Rental housing	Very important (but less so in the U.S.) and often heavily subsidized	Privatization and deregulation, scaling back subsidies	So far: continued privatization and deregulation, but potential for change
Relation to welfare policies	Housing is part of, and crucial to, welfare policies	Households increasingly become responsible for their own housing	Spread of asset-based welfare discourse, yet more household excluded from this possibility
Role of state and financial factors	Redistributive state actors and specialized financial institutions facilitate housing	Mortgaged homeownership promoted to keep global financial markets going; deregulation of finance	Austerity measures as well as measures to keep national housing prices and global financial markets up
Archetypes	American suburb, West-European new towns/*villes nouvelles/ groeikernen*, housing estates	American exurb, West-European 'suburbs', Root Shock in CEE, third-wave gentrification, gated communities	Suburbanization and gentrification slowed down but not stopped; call for more sustainable housing environments

steady growth with smaller GDP and interest rate fluctuations than in previous decades. Economists refer to this macroeconomic cycle as the 'Great Moderation'. It is considered to have started in the US in 1984 and somewhat earlier or later in other western countries (e.g. Summers, 2005).

There are different explanations of what caused the Great Moderation. Some economists argue that it was a result of better monetary policies, others that it was a result of a structural economic change, again others that it was a result of financial innovation and finally some argue that it was simply good luck (e.g. Galí & Gambetti, 2009; Giannone, Lenza, & Reichlin, 2008; Keen, 2013). Empirically, at least for the US, the evidence for the monetary explanation is pretty strong as it is easy to see how decisions of the Federal Reserve are related to volatility in interest rates and other key variables. Yet, it could be argued that the Federal

Reserve is also responding to structural changes in the economy and to demands from the financial sector, which would also provide some credence to the alternative explanations. The 'good luck' hypothesis is quite popular among a large subset of economists, but fails to convince as it does not explain why so many western countries underwent very similar experiences within a couple of years. It also ignores the evidence in favour of the monetary explanation. The fact that econometric modelling of the other explanations cannot explain the Great Moderation entirely, is a very weak argument on the side of the good luck economists, although their argument that reduced oil price shocks were more important also has some validity—i.e., they were also important, although more to some countries than to others.

A great deal of financial innovation is built on leverage. It could be argued that for some years, the combination of a counter-cyclical monetary policy and financial innovation/leverage kept growth numbers up and business cycle fluctuations down. But leverage also has the potential to magnify developments, multiplying both growth and decline, and this is exactly what happened in the run-up to the financial crisis when monetary policy became pro-cyclical in the upswing as well as in the crisis itself when losses were magnified as a result of excessive leverage. The Great Moderation had come to an end.

Even though financial innovation may not have caused the Great Moderation, it has still been important in the mortgage sector where new suppliers of credit entered the market and non-traditional lenders increased their market share. After 1985, savings banks, specialized mortgage banks, credit unions and buildings societies generally lost market share or were acquired by or changed into general or commercial banks. In selective countries, this was followed by the entry of non-bank lenders into the mortgage market, often enabled by securitization. In a larger, but still selective number of countries, the commercial banks also started securitising their mortgage loans—i.e., they resell their mortgage portfolio in the secondary mortgage market and clean up their balance sheets, implying that they become more important as mortgage originators than as mortgage holders. The move to securitization is far from a global phenomenon, but the sale of, and trade in, MBS rapidly became a global market, with investors coming from almost any country in the world, including many institutional investors such as pension funds.

The Flexible Neoliberal or Post-Fordist Period

The changes in the 1970s and the start of the Great Moderation in the 1980s meant the end of the modern or Fordist period in housing structures and the beginning of the flexible neoliberal or post-Fordist period in western countries. CEE entered the post-Fordist period soon after the revolutions of 1989. In most countries, housing construction never reached the heights of the modern period again. Furthermore, the housing market in the post-Fordist period is more stratified than in the Fordist period. This is in part a direct effect of the increasing inequality of income distribution in most countries, and it is in part a result of new housing policies that no longer aim at standardization and that put decent, affordable housing for everyone much lower on the political agenda than was the case in the modern period.

Under neoliberalism, housing becomes increasingly marketized and commodified. Not only is there a shift away from social housing and subsidized rental housing towards mortgaged homeownership, differences within each sector also bear witness to the effects of neoliberalization. Increasingly, but not everywhere, tenants are seen as losers in the popular and political discourses. Where social housing is allowed to subsist, it is either subject to stigmatization and marginalization or its management is commodified and rents are raised. Homeownership, on the other hand, is discursively supported almost everywhere and fiscally supported in many countries. The ideology of homeownership is constructed through supporting ideologies of wealth accumulation and markets (Kemeny, 1981; Ronald & Elsinga, 2012; cf. Smith, 2008). At the same time, neoliberalism 'undermined the integrative and stabilising dimensions of home ownership' (Forrest & Hirayama, 2015: 9). In some cases, states become more interested in supporting mortgage markets than supporting homeowners directly. The promotion of homeownership slowly changes from a policy goal into pure rhetoric: homeownership is no longer a goal in itself, but becomes a derived goal, a means to an end. Mortgaged homeownership increasingly is there to keep mortgage and financial markets going, rather than being facilitated by those markets.

Where credit once enabled growth and wealth, it now comes to replace wealth creation in the real economy. In the US, credit to the real estate and financial sectors increased from 81% of GDP in 1984 to 260% in 2008. Over time, credit changes from being a stabilizer of the economy that supports the real economy into a de-stabilizer that blows asset and financial bubbles, not only in the US but also in places like Iceland and Spain, and to a more limited extent elsewhere as well. The economy becomes increasingly financialized and homeownership forms a keystone in the financialization of both national economies and individual households (Aalbers, 2008). Homeownership is valued less for its use value and more for its exchange value. Not only do lenders and investors prioritise exchange value, but even homeowners increasingly come to think of their home in terms of investment rather than consumption (Langley, 2007; Watson, 2009). This is not a total shift—housing remains important for its use value—but it is nonetheless an important one and illustrates (not validates) the hyperbolic idea that 'we are all capitalists now'.

Archetypes of this flexible neoliberal or post-Fordist period are the North American exurb, the West-European 'suburbs', 'Root Shock' (Klein, 2007) in CEE, 'Capitalism with Chinese Characteristics' (Huang, 2007) and third-wave gentrification (i.e., government-supported, debt-financed class restructuring of cities) (see Table 4.1). In addition to advanced suburbanization and sprawl as well as renewed and government-sponsored investment in cities, we see the rise of gated communities throughout most of the globe. Although it is not necessarily the rich who live in gated communities, proportionally speaking they tend to accommodate richer groups and are more numerous in places where the differences between the poor and the rich are either enormous (including many places in the Global South) or on the rise (including many English-speaking western countries).

Many places in the Global South now have a housing system that has one foot in the pre-modern period and one foot in the post-Fordist period, some of them entirely skipping the modern or Fordist period in housing. This is further evidence to suggest that developing countries do not simply follow the path of developed countries with a lag of a number of decades. As Rolnik (2013) has argued, the neoliberalization and financialization of housing is not limited to the US or to western countries more generally speaking, but has rapidly spread throughout the developed and developing world. Mortgage lending and securitization may remain very limited in most of the Global South, but there is a significant increase in the more developed among them, and decent, affordable housing is hardly provided for the masses as it was in many western countries during the modern/Fordist period. As a result, the housing markets in most of the Global South are extremely stratified.

From Bubble to Crisis

The combination of new types of mortgage lenders, low and less volatile interest rates, and the acceptance of high leverage (for both financial institutions and households) resulted in a massive growth of mortgage lending. The increase in mortgage lending far outpaced real income growth and generally speaking it also outpaced the rising house prices that it enabled. While the expansion of mortgage lending is often presented as necessitated by rising house prices, the causation largely goes in the opposite direction: a greater availability of mortgage credit, both in terms of the households who could acquire such loans and in terms of average loan size (compared to house value and in particular to income level), meant that households could now acquire more expensive properties, but since this was the case for most and ever more households, this simply hiked up the bid rent curve. The idea that house prices would keep rising was not entirely constructed out of thin air—in a sense, this time was different ... at least for the time being (cf. Reinhart & Rogoff, 2009). Never before had interest rates been so steadily low and never before was housing credit so widely available and distributed. Money had never been this cheap for so many people. There really appeared to be a Great Moderation as far as interest rates and access to mortgage credit was concerned.

It is hard to underestimate the combined effects of low interest rates and larger available mortgage loans. As the Central Bank of the Netherlands has calculated, in five years' time (1994–1999), credit limits widened by 86 per cent for the average Dutch household (DNB, 2000). The same development happened throughout the western world, albeit sometimes later or less dramatic and with the exception of Germany. As a result, not only did house prices increase, homeowners also began to carry more debt, both in terms of loan-to-income and loan-to-value. As long as interest rates stayed low, employment high and house prices steady or rising, this caused no structural problems. Individual home-owners, even the most over-indebted ones, could sell their house, pay off their mortgage and cash a nice profit. This lured people into taking on even more debt, making no or tiny down-payments—i.e., to become more leveraged—and to bid up house prices even further. We all know what happened when the music stopped playing and overleveraged households went underwater.

The impact of the housing crisis could first be felt in the US where the housing crisis preceded the financial crisis and a full-blown recession. Although the national housing crisis in the US was only one of the triggers of the global financial crisis, it was a crucial one as it tied individual homeowners in the US not only to Main Street banks but also to Wall Street banks, and through the latter it tied their fate to investors in mortgage-backed securities (MBS) across the globe. The market for MBS froze almost overnight, not only in the US but also in other countries where mortgages were repacked and sold on to investors. Relatively speaking, securitization was more limited in those countries than in the US, but it nevertheless induced a significant shock: as it became more difficult to resell mortgages, it also became more difficult to acquire one as an (aspiring) homeowner.

The global financial crisis also brought to the foreground many weaknesses in the global economy as well as in many national debt-infused economies. House prices started to go down, in particular, in places where they had been going up rapidly in the 1990s and 2000s, and the number of households that were underwater increased in those countries where down-payments had been practically phased out. The near global recession also increased unemployment, which meant that more homeowners who had lost their jobs and were underwater could no longer sell their houses without losing out. And since the number of employed households went down and, even for those that had a job, mortgage credit was heavily constrained, it also became harder to buy a house.

The Emerging Post-Crisis or Late-Neoliberal Period

In many western countries, younger cohorts are now less likely to be or become homeowners than the cohorts before them when they were the same age (cf. Forrest & Yip, 2011). For decades, the trend was towards increasing homeownership amongst younger cohorts. Widely available mortgage credit had enabled their homeownership pursuits, but since the 1980s in some places, and since the 1990s in others, young people also had less choice: social housing was reduced in size and increasingly hard to get access to, even in countries where social housing previously tended to be more widely available, of higher quality and less stigmatized. The private rented sector had steadily decreased in most countries and often their only alternative was to buy a house. Since younger generations after the Great Moderation had seen less income growth than the younger generations before them, the only way they could afford to become homeowners was to take on massive amounts of debt. For many people, the entry into home-ownership was less of a choice than a necessity.

Now that mortgage debt has dried up and employment is both in smaller supply and more casualized, many young households (and increasing numbers of less young households as well) now simply cannot become homeowners. The social housing sector remains barred to most young households, so the alternatives are private rented housing—which is again on the rise in some countries, in particular English speaking ones (e.g. Forrest & Hirayama, 2015)—but it is often under-maintained, overpriced or both. This results in delaying leaving the nest or even returning to one's parents, to doubling up, house sharing and prolonged room renting. Renting a room has for decades been considered a typical condition for both students and young people everywhere (including professionals in their 30s) in global and other high-priced cities, but it is increasingly becoming normalized as employment, in particular of the permanent kind, is harder to obtain (e.g. Laparra & Pérez, 2011).

Construction is at an all-time low in many western countries but not necessarily elsewhere. In many non-western countries, large numbers of houses are being constructed, mortgage lending is being expanded, but vacancies are also on the rise. Such characteristics suggest that these countries may not have entered the post-crisis period yet, but there may be a looming crisis. It is, for example, hard to see how Chinese housing prices could not go down in the near future as vacancies rise rapidly because most units are built for more well-off citizens whose numbers do not increase as fast as the number of houses being constructed for them. In addition, many local governments are heavily indebted (e.g. Yang & Yanyun, 2012), suggesting they soon will be forced to stop propping up local property markets.

In western countries, there is little evidence of the oft-heralded end of neoliberalism. To the contrary, austerity urbanism (Peck, 2012) in combination with the abovementioned casualized labour force (Puno & Thomas, 2010) and the practice of socialising financial risks and privatising housing risk, implies that neoliberalism is alive and kicking (Aalbers, 2013). Right now, it is hard to see a structural change in how western societies deal with housing. But then again, structural changes are often hard to see without hindsight. It is easy to be pessimistic and see housing markets and policies becoming even more exploitative. At the same time, there is the potential for more equitable and sustainable housing markets and policies (Hodkinson, 2012), but the political will is often lacking and needs to be mobilized before structural change in housing commodification will start to be a reality (see Table 4.1).

Conclusion: The End of The Great Excess

The 1970s and early 1980s as well as the post-2007 crises were critical junctures in the development of housing. The Great Moderation was a game changer, but we can only see in hindsight to what extent. Even though some variables were showing moderation, it would be a mistake to characterise the 1980s through the early 2000s as a period of moderation. If anything, these were the decades of the Great Excess in which income and wealth inequality in many countries increased rapidly (e.g. Piketty, 2014). In western countries, the lack of (or limited) real income growth was matched with a rapid rise in household debt, and in particular, mortgage debt for the middle—and in the US also for the lower—classes. What respectively Crouch (2011) and Watson (2010) have dubbed 'privatised Keynesianism' and 'house price Keynesianism' is essentially a way both to fuel the economy by propping up consumption and to 'compensate' labour for decades of negligible or even negative real income growth.

The Great Moderation is a nice and politically neutral sounding label for what was in fact the introduction of a new, finance-led regime of accumulation (Boyer, 2000) in which capitalism has become increasingly dependent on the growth of finance to enlarge money capital (Foster, 2007; Sweezy, 1995). Financialization not only refers to the growth of financial actors such as banks, lenders, private equity and hedge funds, but is reflected in the operations of both non-financial firms and households. Financialization of housing is not limited to homeownership, but, increasingly, also affects rental housing (Aalbers, 2008; Fields, 2015; Forrest & Hirayama, 2015). Despite the fact that the Great Moderation (low interest rates) and the Great Excess (excessive debt and over-leveraging) expanded homeownership to groups hitherto excluded, the gains and losses of homeownership have become skewed, with early homebuyers (both older generations and higher income households) generally better off and more recent ones (younger generations, moderate income households and also ethnic minorities) worse off (see also Forrest & Yip, 2011; Hamnett, 1999).

It is, by definition, challenging to introduce a periodization to housing development, in particular to international developments. Not only do different countries enter a new stage at different times in history, they often enter parallel stages rather than the same stage. Akin to other housing periodizations (e.g. Harloe, 1995), it is easy to point to the weaknesses of such periodizations or even to question the possibility of periodization entirely (Mayhew, 2005). Allow me to remind the reader that the periodization presented here is a heuristic device to help make sense of a messy world. It is not the result of some theoretical exercise in housing models, but the result of an inductive reading of recent and contemporary, international housing histories. That reading is flawed for the simple reason that one cannot know the complex histories of all western countries, let alone all countries in the world.

These disclaimers notwithstanding, the housing periodization opens up several new avenues for research. First, we could hypothesise that the post-2007 housing crisis has been the first global housing crisis, but not in the sense that all countries around the globe were faced with declining house prices, but in the sense that never before have so many countries faced a housing crisis at the same time. Part of the explanation for this is that housing markets are now more (but far from fully) interconnected than in the past. This is because some housing markets actors have internationalized, the funding market for housing has also internationalized (partly but not exclusively through mortgage securitization) and the global economy is now more interconnected than ever before. The implication of the latter is that financial crises and economic recessions, which at the national level are heavily tied to housing markets, are increasingly international in nature.

The second promising avenue would be to more deeply scrutinise the periodization and the shifts for different countries, or alternatively, improve the periodization through country case studies, the goal of which would not be to confirm the periodization as a model for different countries, but to problematize, amend and enrich the analysis presented here. Critically, a periodization can help us understand the ways in which housing connects to the political economy (Aalbers & Christophers, 2014) of different places as well as the crucial role of housing in both sustaining and challenging existing state/market/civil-society/household configurations. A third and equally attractive direction of research would be to investigate further emerging post-crisis housing regimes.

Although the dominant policy response has been to restore 'business as usual' in housing and mortgage lending (Smith, 2010), the current crisis has the potential to be a game-changer as well—'the good old days' are unlikely to return. So far, we have seen a decline in homeownership rates in selective countries and a decline in home-buying younger households in most western countries. It remains to be seen whether this is a conjunctural development that will soon be reversed. The shift towards a casualized workforce suggests homeownership rates are unlikely to start rising again, but the lack of affordable and accessible alternatives also casts doubt on an accelerated decline in homeownership rates. As long as states are undermined discursively as well as materially (austerity, tax flight, etc.), and as long as the financialized regime of accumulation is not rolled back, households that can get mortgage credit are destined to be indebted while those who cannot will remain on social housing waiting lists, in sub-standard housing or doubled up. A decommodified housing alternative is needed more than ever before, but it would already be a great improvement if existing decommodified housing were allowed to subsist and not commodified any further.

Acknowledgements

This work was supported by the European Research Council under grant number 313376. Earlier versions of this paper were presented at the following conferences: 'Home Ownership: During and After the Great Financial Crisis' (Delft, November 2012), 'At home in the Housing Market' (RC43, Amsterdam, July 2013), 'Housing Finance' (EMF-ENHR, Brussels, September 2013). I would like to thank the participants to these events as well as Callum Ward, and the IJHP editors and referees for providing critical feedback.

References

Aalbers, M.B. (2008). The financialization of home and the mortgage market crisis. *Competition & Change*, 12(2), 148–166.
Aalbers, M.B. (2009a). Geographies of the financial crisis. *Area*, 41(1), 34–42.

Aalbers, M.B. (2009b). The globalization and Europeanization of mortgage markets. *International Journal of Urban and Regional Research*, 33(2), 389–410.

Aalbers, M.B. (Ed.). (2012). *Subprime cities: The political economy of mortgage markets.* Oxford: Wiley-Blackwell.

Aalbers, M.B. (2013). Neoliberalism is dead … Long live neoliberalism! *International Journal of Urban and Regional Research*, 37(3), 1083–1090.

Aalbers, M.B., & Christophers, B. (2014). Centring housing in political economy. *Housing, Theory and Society*, 31(4), 373–394.

Barlow, J., & Duncan, S. (1994). *Success and failure in housing provision: European systems compared.* Oxford: Pergamon.

Boelhouwer, P., & Van der Heijden, H. (1992). *Housing systems in Europe: Part I, a comparative study of housing policy.* Delft: Delft University Press.

Boyer, R. (2000). Is a finance-led growth regime a viable alternative to Fordism? A preliminary analysis. *Economy and Society*, 29(1), 111–145.

Christophers, B. (2013). A monstrous hybrid: the political economy of housing in early twenty-first century Sweden. *New Political Economy*, 18(6), 885–911.

Crouch, C. (2011). *The strange non-death of neoliberalism.* Cambridge: Polity.

DNB. (2000). *Het bancaire hypotheekbedrijf onder de loep. Rapport over de ontwikkelingen op de hypotheekmarkt in de periode 1994–1999 gebaseerd op onderzoek naar de hypothecaire kredietverlening bij Nederlandse financiële instellingen.* Amsterdam: De Nederlandse Bank.

Esping-Andersen, G. (1990). *The three worlds of welfare capitalism.* Cambridge: Polity Press.

Fields, D. (2015). Contesting the financialization of urban space: Community-based organizations and the struggle to preserve affordable rental housing in New York City. *Journal of Urban Affairs*, 37(2), 144–165.

Florida, R.L., & Feldman, M.M.A. (1988). Housing in US Fordism: The class accord and postwar spatial organization. *International Journal of Urban and Regional Research*, 12(2), 187–210.

Forrest, R., & Hirayama, Y. (2015). The financialisation of the social project: Embedded liberalism, neoliberalism and home ownership. *Urban Studies*, 52(2), 233–244.

Forrest, R., & Yip, N.-M. (Eds.). (2011). *Housing markets and the global financial crisis.* Cheltenham: Edward Elgar.

Foster, J.B. (2007). The financialization of capitalism. *Monthly Review*, 58(11), 1–12.

Galí, J., & Gambetti, L. (2009). On the sources of the great moderation. *American Economic Journal: Macroeconomics*, 1(1), 26–57.

Giannone, D., Lenza, M., & Reichlin, L. (2008). Explaining the great moderation: It is not the shocks. *Journal of the European Economic Association*, 6(2–3), 621–633.

Gilbert, A. (2002). Power, ideology and the Washington consensus: The development and spread of Chilean housing policy. *Housing Studies*, 17(2), 305–324.

Gotham, K.F. (2009). Creating liquidity out of spatial fixity: The secondary circuit of capital and the subprime mortgage crisis. *International Journal of Urban and Regional Research*, 33(2), 355–371.

Hamnett, C. (1999). *Winners and losers. Home ownership in modern Britain.* London: UCL.

Harloe, M. (1995). *The people's home? Social rented housing in Europe and America.* Oxford: Blackwell.

Hay, C. (2004). Common trajectories, variable paces, divergent outcomes? Models of European capitalism under conditions of complex economic interdependence. *Review of International Political Economy*, 11(2), 231–261.

Hodkinson, S. (2012). The return of the housing question. *Ephemera*, 12(4), 423–444.

Hsing, Y.-T. (2010). *The great urban transformation: Politics of land and property in China*. Oxford: Oxford University Press.

Huang, Y. (2007). *Capitalism with Chinese characteristics: Entrepreneurship and the state*. New York, NY: Cambridge University Press.

Keen, S. (2013). A monetary Minsky model of the Great Moderation and the Great Recession. *Journal of Economic Behavior & Organization*, 86(1), 221–235.

Kemeny, J. (1981). *The myth of home ownership*. London: Routledge & Kegan Paul.

Kemeny, J. (1995). *From public housing to the social market: Rental policy strategies in comparative perspective*. London: Routledge.

Kemeny, J., & Lowe, S. (1998). Schools of comparative housing research: From convergence to divergence. *Housing Studies*, 13(2), 161–176.

Klein, N. (2007). *The shock doctrine: The rise of disaster capitalism*. New York, NY: Picador.

Langley, P. (2007). Uncertain subjects of Anglo-American financialization. *Cultural Critique*, 65, 67–91.

Laparra, M., & Pérez, B. (2011). The impact of the crisis on social cohesion or Spanish households surfing a "Liquid" model of integration. *Revista de Asistenţă Socială*, 9(3), 21–51.

Mayhew, D.R. (2005). Suggested guidelines for periodization. *Polity*, 37(4), 531–535.

Peck, J. (2012). Austerity urbanism: American cities under extreme economy. *City*, 16(6), 626–655.

Piketty, T. (2014). *Capital in the twenty-first century*. Cambridge, MA: Harvard University Press.

Puno, N.J., & Thomas, N.P. (Eds.). (2010). *Interrogating the new economy: Restructuring work in the 21st century*. Toronto: University of Toronto Press.

Reinhart, C.M., & Rogoff, K.S. (2009). *This time is different: Eight centuries of financial folly*. Princeton, NJ: Princeton University Press.

Rolnik, R. (2013). Late neoliberalism: The financialization of homeownership and housing rights. *International Journal of Urban and Regional Research*, 37(3), 1058–1066.

Ronald, R. (2008). *The ideology of home ownership: Homeowner societies and the role of housing*. Basingstoke: Palgrave Macmillan.

Ronald, R., & Elsinga, M. (Eds.). (2012). *Beyond home ownership: Housing, welfare and society*. London: Routledge.

Sassen, S. (2009). When local housing becomes an electronic instrument: The global circulation of mortgages—a research note. *International Journal of Urban and Regional Research*, 33(2), 411–426.

Schwartz, H.M., & Seabrooke, L. (Eds.). (2009). *The politics of housing booms and busts*. Basingstoke: Palgrave Macmillan.

Smith, S.J. (2008). Owner-occupation: At home with a hybrid of money and materials. *Environment and Planning A*, 40, 515–519.

Smith, S.J. (2010). Housing futures: A role for derivatives. In S.J. Smith & B.A. Searle (Eds.), *Companion to the economics of housing* (pp. 585–607). New York, NY: Wiley.

Summers, P.M. (2005). What caused the Great Moderation? Some cross-country evidence. *Federal Reserve Bank of Kansas City Economic Review*, Third Quarter, 5–32.

Sweezy, P.M. (1995). Economic reminiscences. *Monthly Review*, 47(1), 1–11.

Watson, M. (2009). Planning for a future of asset-based welfare? New labour, financialized economic agency and the housing market. *Planning Practice and Research*, 24(1), 41–56.

Watson, M. (2010). House price Keynesianism and the contradictions of the modern investor subject. *Housing Studies*, 25(3), 413–426.

Wu, F. (2015) Commodification and housing market cycles in Chinese cities. *International Journal of Housing Policy*, 15(1), 6–26.

Wyly, E., Moos, M., Hammel, D., & Kabahizi, E. (2009). Cartographies of race and class: Mapping the class-monopoly rents of American subprime mortgage capital. *International Journal of Urban and Regional Research*, 33(2), 332–354.

Yang, H.E., & Yanyun, M.A.N. (2012). Risk control of local debt financing—an analysis from the land public finance perspective. *Finance & Trade Economics*, 2012–05 (unpaged).

5 Financialization and Housing

Between Globalization and Varieties of Capitalism

With Rodrigo Fernandez

Introduction

In the literature there are various explanations for the rise of financialized capitalism. Many financialization scholars situate the beginning of financialization in the 1970s with the industrial crisis in the West, the breakdown of the Bretton Woods system and the rise of neoliberalism. Others have pointed to financial deregulation and the associated changes in the City of London and on Wall Street in the 1980s, including technological developments and the rising influence of institutional investors such as pension funds. More generally speaking, financialization is *part of* and *key to* structural transformations of advanced capitalist economies. We here define financialization as 'the increasing dominance of financial actors, markets, practices, measurements and narratives, at various scales, resulting in a structural transformation of economies, firms (including financial institutions), states and households' (Aalbers, 2016).

The financialization literature is commonly divided into three different strands: financialization as a regime of accumulation, financialization as the rise of shareholder value, and the financialization of daily life. In these different strands housing either plays a minor role or is simply seen as one of the bearers of financialization. Yet, there is a small, but growing literature on the financialization of housing which has demonstrated how housing is a central aspect of financialization. Authors have focused on financialization through overpriced and overextended loans (Langley, 2008; Newman, 2009; Waldron, 2014; Walks, 2013), mortgage securitization (Aalbers, 2008; Gotham, 2009; Wainwright, 2009), credit scoring of (potential) homeowners (Aalbers, 2008; Hall, 2012), land use planning (Coq-Huelva, 2013; Kaika and Ruggiero, 2014; Savini and Aalbers, in press), housing rights (Rolnik, 2013), private serviced residences (Trouillard, 2013), and subsidized housing (Heeg, 2013; Fields and Uffer, 2014). Despite these varied analyses of the financialization of housing and the importance of housing to financialization, the relations between housing and financialization remain under-researched and under-theorized.

The main research question is to examine the interaction of global financialization and national systems of housing and housing finance and explain why its impacts have been uneven and differential. By doing this, the article moves beyond housing as vehicle for financialization and instead focusing on systemic linkages between housing as store-of-value, overaccumulation and the debt-led accumulation regime. The argument is developed in two stages. First, it is argued that the absorption of capital by the housing sector and real estate more generally was one of the defining characteristics of the current age of financialization, exceptionally inflating the balance sheet of households and banks in the process. Instead of being merely an object of financialization—a carrier of its practices, logic and ideological foundations—housing was the main collateral for the debt-driven process of financialization. The build-up of private debt on the back of residential real estate, however, is neither infinite nor without frictions: house prices and debt service costs cannot fully and indefinitely decouple from income levels. The role of real estate in temporally 'solving' or managing the 'capital absorption problem' of capitalism in a state of overaccumulation is rarely mentioned in the broader modifications that shaped our age of financialized capitalism.

Second, the article demonstrates how the housing-centeered process of financialization is uneven in nature resulting from the interaction of a global pool of capital and national systems of housing and housing finance. There is a need to focus on systemic transformations rather than on the fundamental diversity of national models. Whereas some national models, leaning towards an Anglo-American, liberalized mode of housing finance, started to experience the influx of capital into housing in the 1990s and early 2000s, other models followed later (IMF, 2008). Although significant differences remain, a gradual system-wide shift across national models is observable towards the partial integration of *national* systems of housing finance in *global* financial markets, expanding the footprint of a housing-centered financialization. The overall picture displays 'common trajectories' (Hay, 2004) of national models moving in the same direction, but from different starting points, different starting times and at a different pace (Aalbers, 2015; Chapter 4): *all* national models experienced a shift from regulated mortgage and capital markets, limited cross-border capital flows and a low private-debt-to-GDP-ratio towards higher private debt levels and an increasingly 'liberalized' financial environment.

This article, then, contributes not only to the literature that stresses the central role of housing in political economy in general and the Varieties of Capitalism (VoC) literature in particular, but also to the small but burgeoning literature on the financialization of housing. By constructing trajectories of financialized residential capitalism, it indirectly also contributes to the literature on comparative housing systems (i.a. Allen *et al.*, 2004; Doling and Ford, 2003; Kemeny and Lowe, 1998). The VoC approach firmly acknowledges how seemingly unrelated institutional domains become historically intertwined as they co-evolve and develop complementarities that bind them together into a national 'model'. However, the VoC approach originates in the welfare state and industrial relations literatures, where institutional change remains slow and politically sticky. Finance and housing finance have proven to be far more dynamic than these literatures allow. In the last two decades, housing finance in many countries transformed radically, and even though some contributions to the VoC debate have raised this issue (Deeg and Jackson, 2006; 2007; Hay, 2004; Streeck and Thelen, 2005), methodological nationalism is still predominant. The fixation on the national scale has been an obstruction to appreciate supranational, systemic processes, such as the build-up of a wall of money and how this may influence national systems of housing finance. Strong path dependencies of national models are at odds with external pressure causing institutional change.

This article first looks at the role of financial globalization in the rise of housing finance. Section 2 discusses how the build-up of a large global pool of capital, a wall of money, gave rise to domestic credit booms. Sections 3 and 4 discuss the uneven nature of the absorption of excess liquidity in the housing market across national models. The final section discusses what this tells us about the histories and geographies of financialized capitalism and its relations to debt, housing, mortgage markets and the spatial fix.

Housing and the Capital Absorption Problem

Housing finance represents both an asset and a liability—each of these are discussed in turn.

Housing as an Asset

The asset side is discussed in the literature on housing asset-based welfare (Doling and Ronald, 2010; Kemeny, 2005; Toussaint and Lessing, 2009; Watson, 2009) and as collateral in the flexible neoliberal (Aalbers, 2015; Breathnach, 2010) or post-Fordist finance-led accumulation regime (Boyer, 2000; Stockhammer, 2004; 2007) or 'privatized Keynesianism' (Crouch, 2009). The liability side is associated with risk shifts and signs of financialization in daily life and the introduction of systemic risk and as a root cause of the financial crisis (Ansell, 2014). Housing-based wealth, that is housing valued at current market prices minus mortgage debt, has risen to historically unprecedented heights, implying that real estate has become more important as store-of-value for households in the age of financialization. Thomas Piketty has described the rise of housing-based wealth in the last four decades as a 'metamorphosis of capital'. While economies in Europe were characterized by a large stock of agriculture-based capital in the 18th and 19th centuries, the stock of capital relative to income declined from WWI up until the 1970s, only to return in the shape of real estate based wealth (Piketty, 2014). In the Eurozone, for example, housing wealth grew from €3.7 trillion in 1980 to €13.2 trillion in 1999 and €24.2 trillion in 2006 (BIS, 2009; ECB, 2006).

On the asset side, housing plays a critical role as collateral for debt. The rising share of housing finance in overall financial assets demonstrates the pivotal role of the built environment in the expansive phase of finance of the last three decades—a process recognized by Harvey (1985) early on. A historical study including data from 1870 to 2010, partly based on historical data from Bank for International Settlements (BIS) data for seventeen selected advanced economies, found that private-debt-to-GDP ratios remained in the range of 50–60 per cent until 1980, but increased to 118 per cent in 2010 (Jorda *et al.*, 2014). This swelling debt was primarily based on mortgage debt. The ratio of mortgage-debt-to-outstanding-private-loans increased from around 30 per cent in the period 1900–1960 to 60 per cent in 2010. While non-mortgage bank loans remained stable around respectively 41 and 46 per cent of GDP between 1914 and 2010, mortgage loans increased from 20 to 64 per cent of GDP in the same period (Jorda *et al.*, 2014). These statistics clearly show that the increase in private debt was formed primarily on the back of real estate. This should have implications for the way in which political economic changes are perceived in the age of financialization.

Mortgage debt, as any other type of debt, serves as an investment outlet. However, unlike other forms of debt, mortgages rely on land, bricks and mortar as collateral—a familiar store-of-value—well-established calculative practices, and a highly standardized institutional framework to collect future income streams. Compared to alternatives, such as unsecured loans, the size of real estate markets, even if they are largely *nationally*-bound, enabled investors to create a liquid marketplace that serves to diversify portfolios *globally*. Next to public debt from core economies, particularly US T-bills and bonds from blue chip companies, mortgages and real estate are strategic 'fixed income' products for institutional investors such as pension funds. These three categories of investments are considered high-quality collateral (HQC) that act as a safe haven in a complex world of risk (BIS, 2013b). The growing scarcity of HQC means that the 'real' economy is unable to meet the demands of the financial sector for safe, tradable financial assets.

Housing as a Liability

From a different perspective, the supply-side, we see that a 'wall of money', a global pool of liquid assets, seeks investment opportunities. There are four different sources that have been feeding this wall of money. First, the increasing pool of assets by institutional investors, characterized as 'pension fund capitalism' (Blackburn, 2002; Clark, 2000; 2003; Drucker, 1976) or 'money manager capitalism' (Minsky, 1996). This rise represented an increase from 36 per cent of global financial assets in 1995 to 44 per cent in 2005 (BIS, 2007) and 114 per cent of global GDP in 2009 (IMF, 2011a). The main argument in this debate is that the build-up of funded pension schemes in particular countries—notably the US, the UK, the Netherlands, Switzerland, Singapore and Chile—and other institutionalized savings vehicles, like insurance companies and sovereign wealth funds, resulted in a growing pool of savings relative to their respective GDPs. These vast pools of capital lacked the required liquid domestic markets and therefore started to diversify globally in search of yield in the 1990s. This source is directly linked to demographic change.

A second source of the wall of money is the recycling of the growing trade surplus of emerging economies of $5 trillion, coined as the 'savings glut'

(Bernanke, 2011; BIS, 2012). While the supply of HQC in the US increased with $3.1 trillion between 1998 and 2002, and with $5.1 trillion between 2003 and 2007, the share that was acquired by non-residents increased from 22 per cent in the first period to 55 per cent in the second (Bernanke *et al.*, 2011: 8). Third, loose monetary policies such as quantitative easing sharply increased demand for HQC, in particular government bonds that are held as collateral for quantitative easing policies. The BIS (2013b) expects that as a result of central bank activities there will be a structural rise in high-quality demand in the range of 4 trillion dollars worldwide.

The final source feeding the wall of money is the rise in accumulated profits (so-called 'corporate savings') of transnational corporations in tax havens that amount to roughly 30 per cent of global GDP (Henry, 2012). This growing pool of corporate savings was related to the improved profit share and the decline in fixed capital investments (OECD, 2007). This rise in the capital share is the flipside of the decline in the global wage share and reflects neoliberal policies taking shape across the globe. In the period from 1980 to 2008, 17 out of 24 OECD countries experienced a decline in the wage share (ILO, 2011). This decline translates into an annual loss in household income of 6 trillion dollars in 2011, or almost half of US GDP at the global scale. This fourth source is a direct sign of overaccumulation, pointing to the problematic nature of the absorptive capacity of capitalism in the face of rising corporate profits. Combined, these dynamics created a wall of money that gradually pushed for the financialization of housing finance.

Global Finance and National Systems of Housing Finance

Having discussed how housing served to absorb the global pool of excess liquidity and became a focal point in broader political economic processes, the uneven nature of this development is explored. The strong boom and bust scenario observed in Ireland and Spain was much weaker in France and Italy, and completely absent in Switzerland and Germany. Between 1985 and 2006 the accumulated house price increases in these countries were respectively 339, 307, 127, 110, 5 and 11 per cent. This suggests that the impact of the global pool of liquidity on housing markets varies significantly across institutional settings. The nature of this uneven process and the mediating forces between national housing systems and external financial developments remains under-theorized. This section will discuss existing approaches to the interaction between global finance and national systems of housing finance to understand the role of housing in the variations of financialized capitalism.

First, we have a body of literature centered on comparative housing markets, mostly policy-driven and dominated by econometric methods that emphasize the critical role of the variety of systems of housing finance (André, 2010; Andrews *et al.*, 2011; BIS, 2004a; 2004b; IMF, 2008; OECD, 2011a). These empirically rich studies focus on the institutional differences to explain the different outcomes in 'liberalized' economies compared to 'rigid' economies that obstruct mortgage debt financing. Figure 5.1 shows the mortgage market index compiled by the IMF and portrayed in its *World Economic Outlook* (2008). This index is a tool to measure institutional differences in housing finance systems. It includes how housing wealth can be used for consumption, by looking at the possibilities for mortgage equity withdrawal schemes and the ease of refinancing. Secondly, it measures the credit restrictions for households by incorporating the typical loan-to-value and the average term. A third element is the use of non-bank financing channels such as covered bonds and securitization. These three domains are condensed into an index ranging from 0 to 1. These variables represent how accessible mortgage credit is in each country (IMF, 2008).

In Figure 5.1 we can see that the correlation between the mortgage market index and mortgage-debt-to-GDP levels is very strong. Countries with rigid mortgage market regulation have lower mortgage-debt-to-GDP levels. On the top-right corner we find the US, the UK, Denmark, Australia and the Netherlands, that is the high-debt liberalized housing economies. Moving towards the bottom-left corner mortgage-debt-to-GDP decreases and we find countries that are more restrictive in their systems of housing finance. An important drawback of this type of analysis is that it does not inform us how these institutional characteristics are produced and how they relate to a broader set of institutional characteristics of these economies. Indeed, it clearly demonstrates how different models of housing finance relate to levels of mortgage debt, but it is limited in explaining causality or change. Furthermore, the broader transformative processes of our time—globalization, cross-border capital flows and financialization—are difficult to relate to such isolated indices.

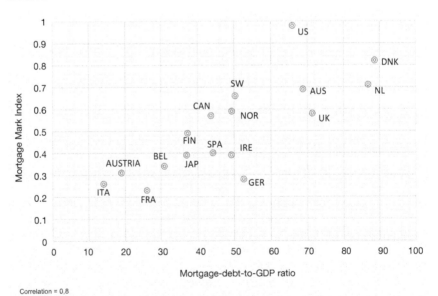

Correlation = 0,8

Source: Based on IMF (2008).

Figure 5.1 Mortgage Market Liberalization and Mortgage Debt

A second approach is found in comparative housing studies in which different national housing systems are compared to each other. One subset of this literature is quite similar to the econometric and statistical analyses described above. In this case, comparative housing researchers have simply included more statistics, for instance on different forms of tenure. Another subset makes use of in-depth historical and institutional analysis, often comparing anywhere between two and six countries (i.a. Allen *et al.*, 2004, Harloe, 1985; 1995; Lawson, 2006; Lujanen, 2004; Ronald, 2008). Such comparisons are richer as they strive to arrive at an explanation or understanding of differences as well as historical developments in individual countries and groups of countries. These studies provide rich historical-institutional explanations of convergence and divergence in housing systems, and although most of these pay attention to national housing finance systems, they rarely focus on the interaction with global finance.

Schwartz and Seabrooke (2009) developed, what we consider, a third approach. They conducted pioneering work in highlighting the critical role of housing in the contemporary international political economy. Their analysis focused on creating an understanding of, what they labeled, the 'Varieties of Residential Capitalism' (VoRC), thereby inserting the institutional domain of housing into the debate on varieties of capitalism (VoC). In their analytical framework housing finance is operationalized by the size of mortgage-debt-to-GDP ratios and the size of the market for securitization, while housing itself is approached by looking into housing tenure (homeownership versus rental housing). Once these two axes, that is the degree of financial liberalization and the homeownership level, are crossed, four ideal-types of residential capitalism emerge (Table 5.1).

We regard the VoRC exercise as a valuable step, but would like to invite the reader to take a step back and first acknowledge system-wide changes, before

Table 5.1 Typology of Residential Capitalism

(Figures in each box are unweighted average % for group for the indicator level)		*Owner-Occupation Rate (Average of 1992 and 2002)*			
		Low		*High*	
Mortgages as a % of GDP (average of 1992 and 2002)	High	**Corporatist Market**		**Liberal Market**	
		Mortgage-GDP:	58.3	Mortgage-GDP:	48.5
		Owner-occupation:	47.0	Owner-occupation:	70.1
		Social rental:	20.7	Social rental:	9.4
	Low	**Statist-Developmentalist**		**Familial**	
		Mortgage-GDP:	28.2	Mortgage-GDP:	21.6
		Owner-occupation:	58.3	Owner-occupation:	75.5
		Social rental:	16.8	Social rental:	5.5

Source: Adapted from Schwartz & Seabrooke (2009: 10).

focusing on the diversity of national models. In an early collection that tried to develop the conceptual apparatus of the VoC debate, centered on the question of diversity versus convergence, Susan Strange was a dissonant voice:

> It has always seemed to me that comparative social scientists are misnamed; they do not compare nearly as much as they contrast; this seems true whether economists, sociologists, or political scientists. That is to say, their attention is mainly directed at the differences between states or economies or societies rather than their similarities. They seldom bother to inquire into what seems to me the rather more important question—Why is it that all these states adopted broadly similar system-sustaining policies and institutions at about the same point in their social, economic and political development?
>
> (Strange, 1997: 183)

Therefore it is more useful to discuss the type of convergence in the housing systems in terms of 'common trajectories' (Hay, 2004) in which countries move in the same direction (albeit from a different starting point) and maintain their essential institutional differences.

There is a need to focus on the dynamic nature of the interaction between global finance, national housing markets and institutional models. While the Schwartz and Seabrooke typology is effective in speaking to an audience of political economists, and firmly implants housing in comparative political economy debates, it lacks the flexibility to incorporate Kindleberger and Aliber's ([1978] 2005) periods of 'manias, panics and crashes', a recurrent theme in the history of capitalism. It is necessary to consider and construct a typology that is open to periods of rapid transformation led by housing booms, manic periods, that always involve abundant credit and often end with panics and crashes. This typology should not be stuck in the world of welfare state regimes, but should move with the speed of transformations in the sphere of housing finance, in particular the rise of private debt.

Trajectories of Housing-Induced Financialization

This section presents an exercise in grouping countries according to their housing-induced type of financialization. First, statistics on private debt are used to demonstrate a degree on convergence. Second, differences between countries are highlighted. The purpose is not to present clear-cut categories, rather countries are grouped together to illustrate how they represent different trajectories in the fast changing landscape of global finance. While clear institutional filters that limit the financialization of the housing sector exist in some countries, the absorptive capacity of individual countries is typically multidimensional. There is no single variable that can explain the multitude of variations. Therefore, the categorization of countries presented here is drawn on wider data to enable the use of more variables. The combination of these variables allows for different outcomes in terms of typologies. The aim is to propose a set of trajectories, that also share a common trajectory, to help the debate to move beyond fixed two-dimensional typologies, such as those of the VoRC approach. Although the VoRC's two dimensions capture essential characteristics of different national models that enable creating clear-cut categories, they leave out elements that may be variegated in different ways.

Obstacles and Filters of Global Structural Pressures

The existing variety of financialized capitalism is closely related to the remaining obstacles and institutional filters that insulate particular national housing markets from the global forces of finance. These obstacles are multidimensional and complex. First, there are filters in the domain of housing finance, such as the tax deductibility of interest payment, loan-to-value ratios, and mortgage equity withdrawal schemes. Second, there are filters in the welfare state arrangements that shape the dominant type of tenure and levels of commodification expressed in homeownership levels and the relative share of the provision of social rented housing. Third, there are filters in the openness and sophistication of the financial sector expressed in the size of cross-border capital flows, in particular in providing domestic private credit and the size of the market for securitization. This section sets out to develop a number of trajectories based on these filters.

Crucially, the variations of financialized capitalism are here considered as a system in motion, moving towards more national housing markets absorbing ever-larger shares of the rising global pool of capital. Some countries were early in opening the floodgates to global capital and experienced a strong rise in cross-border capital flows into their systems of housing finance. The absorptive capacity of these 'early movers' has proved to be problematic since 2007. The financial crisis left a large debt overhang in combination with substantially lower house prices. This discontinued the hitherto smooth process of growing private debt. The Netherlands and Denmark are examples of these saturated housing-induced models of financialized capitalism with extremely high levels of private debt, outpacing those of the all other countries. The US and the UK have been able to stretch the lifetime of the housing-centered economic model by extremely loose monetary policies and fiscal support. It is to be expected that this group of early movers will not emulate the type of credit fueled boom it experienced in the last two decades. This will increase pressure on models on the other side of the spectrum, in Mediterranean countries like Italy, new EU member states in Central and Eastern Europe (CEE) like Poland, and developed countries like Germany and Switzerland, that for different reasons have low mortgage debt and modest price-to-income ratios.

Key Variables

This section focuses primarily on OECD countries for which long-term data are generally more available, but since the global financial crisis emerging economies—notably China, Turkey and Brazil—are increasingly amassing mortgage debt, and have recorded rising price-to-income and price-to-rent levels. In May 2014 the IMF issued a warning of the re-appearance of housing bubbles in a new set of countries, largely related to the global context of excess liquidity, the search for 'safe havens' and cheap money. The global house price index declined from 2007 onwards, but has been on the rise since 2011 and reached the 2006 level in 2013 (IMF global housing watch Data).

The key variable, the levels of private debt-to-GDP, portrays a pattern of common trajectories (BIS, 2012; 2013a). Table 5.2 shows the development of total private credit, including non-bank intermediaries. The dominant view is that that irrespective of 'bank-based' (Germany, Spain, France, Japan) or 'capital market-based' (US, UK) financial systems, or the national model of capitalism, overall private debt increased, either through the banking system or by market-based intermediation (2012; 2013a). Countries that 'missed' the first housing boom show significantly lower levels of private debt, i.e. Belgium, France, Germany and Italy.

The strong growth of credit-to-GDP ratios meant that in many countries domestic deposits could not cover the growth in private debt (BIS, 2011). This difference between credit and deposits, the 'funding gap', is a reflection of credit growth beyond the domestic deposit base and correlates to a growing inflow of foreign capital and the use of non-deposit based finance like securitization. In countries that experienced a strong growth of credit-to-GDP ratios, such as the Netherlands, Ireland and Denmark, this was most pronounced. Countries that only had a modest rise in credit-to-GDP ratios (France, Germany, Italy) also show a modest rise in foreign bank claims. These developments are visible in Table 5.3 that displays the consolidated foreign claims of BIS reporting banks, which include the claims of banks' foreign affiliates but exclude intragroup positions. The BIS constructed these statistics to provide comparable measures of cross-border debt relations and national banking systems' exposures to country risk (BIS, 2005).

Table 5.2 Private Credit by Deposit Banks and Other Financial Institutions as % of GDP

	1961	1980	2000	2010		1961	1980	2000	2010
Australia	17.8	25.1	80.8	130.1	**Japan**	51.5	125.1	222.3	177.2
Belgium	9.1	27.2	77.2	94.2	**Netherlands**	21.5	61.2	125.4	205.5
Brazil	*	25.7	30.7	57.1	**Russia**	*	*	10.9	41.5
France	44.3	96.2	81.3	111.5	**South Africa**	*	48.8	127.0	146.4
Germany	*	*	116.3	107.1	**Spain**	*	69.7	90.1	211.3
Greece	12.7	39.2	42.2	108.4	**Turkey**	*	13.1	14.6	38.2
Ireland	31.5	43.7	95.7	228.2	**UK**	*	*	119.6	201.7
Italy	*	52.4	70.3	115.7	**US**	74.9	93.8	168.8	193.8

Source: Global Financial Development Database, World Bank.

Table 5.3 Consolidated Foreign Claims of BIS Reporting Banks as % of GDP

	1999	2001	2003	2005	2007	2009	2011
Australia	39.1	42.7	55.2	47.2	75.5	67.1	45.4
Belgium	84.7	84.6	113.3	117.1	153.6	144.0	95.8
Brazil	19.9	25.7	19.5	18.1	22.5	24.2	21.8
France	31.7	40.3	41.8	53.6	76.6	66.5	57.9
Germany	33.2	42.1	50.4	55.9	68.9	64.0	53.5
Greece	45.1	52.6	57.4	71.7	93.3	73.3	39.8
Ireland	125.3	150.9	177.5	238.6	387.1	392.9	263.2
Italy	37.6	42.5	43.4	47.3	79.0	67.3	41.4
Japan	15.1	13.3	15.3	17.2	21.8	19.9	19.0
Netherlands	75.8	94.4	108.7	132.8	179.2	135.7	116.2
Spain	28.6	31.9	44.4	56.5	80.4	78.8	46.5
Turkey	16.0	18.6	12.5	16.1	26.0	25.8	26.8
UK	83.1	98.7	109.7	125.3	161.5	171.9	140.1
US	21.8	26.4	31.7	38.7	46.5	39.4	40.5

Source: Global Financial Development Database, World Bank.

Different Trajectories

The question is whether this dynamic transformation, the common trajectory towards higher levels of debt and a more prominent role for cross-border capital flows, will translate in a housing-centered process of financialization in those models where this development was so far absent. For this purpose countries are sorted into trajectories of national institutional structures that relate in similar ways to the influence of the global pool of liquidity and hence share character-istics of housing-induced financialization. These models are discussed without offering an explanation of the persisting diversity or providing an analysis of how the institutional filters have changed in each country. Basically two different trajectories (1 and 4) are identified that resisted moving towards a debt-fueled economic model for different reasons and two trajectories (2 and 3) that experienced a housing-induced type of financialization with different outcomes. Trajectory 1, discussed below, resisted by having a large stock of mortgage-free residential real estate. Trajectory 4 resisted by having low homeownership levels. Trajectories 2 and 3 both allowed private debt to increase but to different degrees.

The key variables are the homeownership rates and mortgage-debt-to-GDP, also used in the VoRC approach. In addition, the size of fixed capital formation and the employment of the construction sector is used to differentiate between national models where the housing-induced form of financialization led to an increase in the stock of real estate and those where the size of the stock was relatively unaffected. This shows a mixed pattern across trajectories. A third variable is the IMF mortgage market index that operates as proxy for the absorptive capacity of these national models. Trajectories 1 and 4 have significant lower scores on this index, confirming that both a high and a low degree of homeownership can be accompanied by low mortgage-debt-to-GDP. But also

Spain and Ireland, both in trajectory 3, show that a medium score on the this index, measuring the institutional support for housing finance, is no guarantee, for escaping the reach of the wall of money. Our classification, based on a broader set of variables largely follows the same lines as the VoRC approach, with some exceptions. In Schwartz and Seabrooke's (2009) analysis, Germany is included in the same group as the Netherlands and Denmark. However, Germany, with its relatively low mortgage-debt-to-GDP levels, fits better in another group. Furthermore, the familial model of the VoRC typology is extended to include a larger set of countries that combine high homeownership rates with low mortgage-debt-to-GDP.

The first and largest trajectory includes CEE countries, some Mediterranean EU countries (Greece, Portugal and Italy) and some emerging economies (Brazil, Mexico and Turkey). These countries combine high to very high rates of homeownership (69–96 per cent) with comparatively low to very low cross-border capital flows and a modest financial sector in terms of diversification and size (World Bank, 2009; 2012). The dominance of a privately-owned housing stock, mostly free of mortgage debt, means that the housing market has not been financialized yet. However, it is critical to note that Spain was once following this trajectory and also had low private debt levels and cross-border capital flows, but transformed radically in the brief period from the late 1990s to the collapse of the bubble. This shows that a large stock of privately-owned, mortgage-free dwellings is not a guarantee to keep the global forces of financialization from entering the national system of housing finance. The case of Spain is crucial to understand institutional change in this trajectory. A final element is the absence of institutional support for mortgages, portrayed by the low score on the mortgage market index and the absence of equity withdrawal schemes.

The second trajectory, including Iceland, Ireland, Spain, Canada, Australia, the UK and the US, has high levels of homeownership in combination with high to very high mortgage-to-GDP levels (Tables 5.2 and 5.4). These countries have large cross-border capital flows (Table 5.3) and, with the exception of Spain, a deep and sophisticated financial sector (World Bank, 2012). The outlook of the countries following this trajectory is mixed. The US and the UK have continued, pushed by monetary policy, on the previous path. This seems unlikely in Iceland, Ireland and Spain where the housing boom produced a large overcapacity of residential real estate. Spain and Ireland have in common that their housing booms were not only accompanied by a sharp rise in private debt, financed by cross-border flows, but also by a construction boom. In Spain and Ireland the gross fixed capital formation as a percentage of GDP rose from, respectively, 20 and 15 per cent in 1993, to 31 and 26 per cent at the top of the boom in 2007. In contrast, other countries that also experienced a house price boom, like the UK, the US and the Netherlands, had an unchanged gross fixed capital formation as percentage of GDP in 1993 and 2007 of respectively 18, 19 and 20 per cent (World Bank data).

The third and smallest trajectory, including the Netherlands and Denmark has moderate homeownership levels combined with very high mortgage-to-GDP

Table 5.4 Selected Characteristics of Housing Finance Systems

	Mortgage Equity Withdrawal[1]	Mortgage Market Index[2]	Tax Gap[3]	Home Ownership Rate[4]	Rate of Mortgage-Free Homeowners[5]	Change in Price-To-Income[6]	Construction as Share of Total Workforce[7]
Australia	Yes	0.69	..	65	..	32	9.0
Austria	No	0.31	0.18	57	56	..	..
Belgium	No	0.34	0.81	72	42	29	6.9
Canada	Yes	0.57	..	69	..	13	7.2
Denmark	Yes	0.82	1.20	67	21	36	6.8
France	No	0.23	0.54	62	53	28	6.9
Germany	No	0.28	..	53	48	-30	6.6
Greece	No	..	1.05	77	77	..	8.7
Hungary	..	..	..	90	73	..	8.4
Ireland	Limited	0.39	0.31	73	53	47	13.4
Italy	No	0.26	0.15	72	79	15	8.4
Japan	No	0.39	..	..	..	-36	8.6
Netherlands	Yes	0.71	1.62	67	12	42	5.9
Portugal	..	..	0.23	75	57	..	..
Spain	Limited	0.4	0.60	83	57	..	13.3
Switzerland	..	..	0.65	44	10	-16	..
UK	Yes	0.58	..	70	37	44	8.2
US	Yes	0.98	0.96	65	..	16	8.1

Source: compiled by authors from various statistics

Notes:
1. OECD
2. IMF, The mortgage market index ranges from 0 and 1 (IMF 2008).
3. OECD, Gap between market interest rate and after tax debt-financing cost (the larger the figure. the greater the tax relief) in 2011.
4. Eurostat (2010); UN (2006).
5. Eurostat (2010); UN (2006).
6. OECD, price-to-income, level of 2010 minus level 1985.
7. ILO, The share of the construction sector (including infrastructure and commercial real estate) of total workforce in 2007.

levels, reflecting an extremely low share of privately-owned houses that are free of mortgages, respectively 12 and 22 per cent. These mortgage markets are the opposite of those in Mediterranean and CEE countries, where mortgage-free homeownership is the norm, e.g. 79 per cent in Italy, 77 per cent in Greece and 73 per cent in Hungary. It is important to note that the Netherlands and Denmark had the largest increase in homeownership rates in the boom period of all OECD countries, reflecting the institutional changes of higher LTV ratios combined with a very high tax gap (OECD, 2011). Table 5.4 shows that Denmark and the

Netherlands enjoy the largest tax gap (fiscal stimuli for mortgage debt) and that both countries have an institutional framework in place that is geared towards a housing-based form of financialization. These countries have extremely high cross-border capital flows and very high funding gaps making these countries vulnerable to economic downswings, as domestic deposits are not able to cover debt levels (Fernandez, 2014). An important characteristic of the countries following this trajectory is the small economic footprint of the real estate sector in terms of employment. These countries seem to have reached the limits in terms of housing-based financialization.

The fourth trajectory includes countries with very low to medium homeownership rates, low mortgage-debt-to-GDP levels and extremely low price-to-income levels (Germany, Switzerland, Austria and France). Germany shows a rare change in its credit-to-deposit share, only shared with Argentina (for different reasons). Whereas the international trend was an increase in the credit-to-deposit ratio, as leverage surged across developed economies, in Germany this ratio decreased from 178 per cent in 1998 to 80 per cent in 2011 (World Bank financial development and structure dataset, November 2013). Table 5.4 shows that Germany and Switzerland are outliers that experienced a decline in the price-to-income-ratio of respectively 30 and 16 per cent in 2010 compared to 1985. These countries have deep and sophisticated financial markets and medium to (very) large cross-border capital flows. In 1974, Germany was one of the first countries to liberalize its international capital flows. This shows that openness to cross-border capital flows as such is not a guarantee for a housing-centered form of financialization typical of trajectories 2 and 3. Trajectory 4, however, has strong institutional barriers against the inflow of foreign capital into the national housing sector. The conditions for mortgages are strict, reflected in the low mortgage market index score. Also the share of the construction sector in overall employment is below average. While countries following this trajectory largely evaded the recent housing boom, they all saw an increase in house prices between 2005 and 2011. These are all signs that the process of a housing-induced type of financialization may be starting to take hold in these countries (IMF, 2014). Furthermore, evidence from Germany suggests that foreign capital is entering Germany's subsidized rental market (Aalbers and Holm 2008; Fields and Uffer 2014; Heeg 2013; see Chapter 7).

Conclusion

Housing is central to the real-world political economy, but remains peripheral to academic political economy (Aalbers and Christophers, 2014; Chapter 2). This article not only demonstrated how housing links into the real-world political economy, but also how in can be placed in political economy. The Varieties of Capitalism literature is an important school in contemporary political economy, but is still coming to grips with both housing and finance. In order to extend and deepen the analysis and understanding of these varieties in real-world political economies, VoC needs to open up further. In particular, to the literatures of financialization and housing, and more specifically to the crucial role of the financialization of housing, not only as a bearer of financialization processes, but as one central to understanding contemporary real-world political economies.

A growing imbalance between the growth rate of the stock of capital and GDP has resulted in a wall of money looking for profitable investment. This wall of money is one of the key drivers of financialization and explains partially why so many assets have been opened up to financialization, including residential and non-residential real estate but also infrastructure, raw materials, food and so on. As a result, mortgage debt has exploded in most developed countries since the 1980s. To echo David Harvey, the overaccumulation of capital leads capitalists to seek new outlets, including the built environment. The resulting 'spatial fix', while trying to resolve the internal contradictions of capitalism, 'transfers its contradictions to a wider sphere and gives them greater latitude' (Harvey, 1985: 60). Under financialized capitalism, Harvey's overaccumulation has transformed into a more structural wall of money. Unlike Harvey, we do not really see capital 'switch' into real estate from production. The wall of money has different sources and dynamics, as has been explained in section 2. Moreover, this wall of money fuels a variety of traditional and 'innovative' financial instruments and could perhaps better be characterized as a 'financial fix': an emergent financial landscape in a permanent state of stable instability that enables a continuous circulation of capital outside the sphere of production.

The long-term effects of relying on a housing-finance elixir to boost growth have surfaced since the global financial crisis. Housing became a political drug, highly addictive as it *temporarily* allowed political elites to overcome capitalist contradictions: boosting corporate profits by lowering the wage share while increasing private consumption and achieving fiscal surpluses. The problem is how you get off the drug that growing housing wealth produced. In the wake of the 2008 crisis the response in countries such as the US, the UK and the Netherlands has been geared towards reviving housing markets instead of moving into alternative policies. The question is how sustainable these policies are as the housing-finance elixir ultimately depends on growing private debt levels.

Although housing has the ability to absorb the global pool of excess liquidity, the impact of the wall of money on housing markets varies significantly across institutional settings. The variation is multidimensional and dynamic. An underdeveloped system of housing finance and large debt-free stock of privately-owned houses are no guarantees for remaining insulated against the pressures of cross-border capital flows. Moreover, as the case of Spain shows, countries can open up relatively rapidly to global capital flows and change their housing systems accordingly. At the other end, there is a group of countries with highly developed and interconnected financial systems that have tried to insulate their housing systems from global forces of financialization but are now beginning to see the penetration of their rental housing markets by global capital, as the case of Germany illustrates.

The approach to housing systems taken here based on variations of financialized capitalism, is better equipped to account for periods of rapid transformation led by housing booms, manic periods, that always involve abundant credit and often end with panics and crashes. Political economists need to take on board the critical role of housing and study more closely what determines the rapid changes in some countries but the lack thereof in others. Our approach, focused on housing-centered processes of financialization, needs to be complemented with in-depth historical-institutional analyses that not only focus on the development of the welfare state but also on national politics *vis-à-vis* international finance.

Although this article primarily focused on developed countries, it is noted how a process of housing-induced financialization may be starting to take hold in emerging and (rapidly) developing countries. A great deal of research needs to be done for each of these countries to see how their real-world political economies are (not) integrating financialization and residential capitalism (see Jones, 2012; Rolnik, 2013). The pathways followed and to be discovered will, no doubt, be different from those in developed countries and they will be very different from one country to the next, as they also have been and continue to be in developed countries. The key question is how does housing (not) become financialized in these countries and what does this tell us about the development of these political economies. Although financialization is a global process it remains highly uneven—varieties of residential and financialized capitalism subsist, but that does not imply one cannot witness similar changes and therefore joint mechanisms at work.

Finally, more research is needed on how housing and the built environment function as a store of value. Presently, we know too little about the politics, geography and consequences of the ability of cities, like London, to absorb massive global savings into the urban environment (Fernandez *et al.*, 2016). This also implies research is needed that connects global political economy to urban political economy. Three decades of neoliberal urban transformation are part of how the process of the urbanization of capital took shape, and how, as response to local frictions, cities may have become the new global reserve currency.

Acknowledgments

The authors would like to thank the referees, the editor of this journal and the members of the research group for constructive feedback. The work of both authors is part of "The Real Estate/Financial Complex" research project, which is supported by the European Research Council [grant number 313376].

References

Aalbers, M.B. 2008. The financialization of home and the mortgage market crisis. *Competition & Change* 12(2): 148–166.

Aalbers, M.B. 2015. The Great Moderation, the Great Excess and the global housing crisis. *Journal of Housing Policy* 15(1): 43–60.

Aalbers, M.B. 2016. Corporate financialization. In: D. Richardson, N. Castree, M.F. Goodchild, A.L. Kobayashi and R. Marston (Eds), *The International Encyclopedia of Geography: People, the Earth, Environment, and Technology*. Oxford: Wiley.

Aalbers, M.B. & Christophers, B. 2014. Centring housing in political economy. *Housing, Theory and Society* 31: 373–394.

Aalbers, M.B. & Holm, A. 2008. Privatising social housing in Europe: The cases of Amsterdam and Berlin. In: K. Adelhof, B, Glock, J. Lossau and M. Schulz (Eds) *Urban trends in Berlin and Amsterdam*, pp. 12–23. Berlin: Berliner Geographische Arbeiten, Humboldt Universität zu Berlin.

Allen, J., Barlow, J., Leal, J., Maloutas, T. & Padovani, L. 2004. *Housing & Welfare in Southern Europe*. Oxford: Blackwell.

André, C. 2010. A bird's eye view of OECD housing markets. *OECD Economics Department Working Articles,* No. 746.

Andrews, D., Caldera Sánchez, A. & Johansson, A. 2011. Housing markets and structural policies in OECD countries, *OECD Economics Department Working Articles,* No. 836.

Ansell, B. 2014. The political economy of ownership: housing markets and the welfare state, *American Political Science Review* 108: 383–402.

Bernanke, B., Bertaut, C., DeMarco, L.P. & Kamin, S. 2011. International capital flows and the returns to safe assets in the United States. *Banque de France financial Stability Review* 15.

BIS. 2002. Housing markets and economic growth: lessons from the US refinancing boom. *BIS Quarterly Review.* September 2002

BIS. 2004a. Twin peaks in equity and housing prices? *BIS Quarterly Review*, March 2004.

BIS. 2004b. What drives housing price dynamics: cross-country evidence. *BIS Quarterly Review*, March 2004

BIS. 2005. The BIS consolidated banking statistics: structure, uses and recent enhancements. *BIS Quarterly Review*, September 2005.

BIS. 2007. Institutional investors, global savings and asset allocation. *CGFS Articles* 27.

BIS. 2009. EU housing statistics. *IFC Bulletin* 31: 111–120.

BIS. 2011. *Global credit and domestic credit booms. BIS Quarterly Review*, September 2011.

BIS. 2012. The great leveraging. *BIS Working Articles* 398.

BIS. 2013. How much does the private sector really borrow? A new database for total credit to the private non-financial sector. *BIS Quarterly Review*, March 2013

BIS. 2013b. Mind the gap? Sources and implications of supply demand imbalances in collateral asset markets. *BIS Quarterly Review*, September 2013

Blackburn, R. 2002. *Banking on Death; Or, Investing in Life: The History and Future of Pensions.* Verso.

Boyer, R. 2000. Is a finance-led growth regime a viable alternative to Fordism? A preliminary analysis, *Economy and Society* 29(1): 111–145

Breathnach, P. 2010. From spatial Keynesianism to post-Fordist neoliberalism: emerging contradictions in the spatiality of the Irish state. *Antipode* 42(5): 1180–1199.

Clark, G.L. 2000. *Pension Fund Capitalism*. Oxford: Oxford University Press.

Clark, G.L. 2003. *European Pensions and Global Finance*. Oxford: Oxford University Press.

Coq-Huelva, D. 2013. Urbanisation and financialisation in the context of a rescaling state: the case of Spain. *Antipode* 45(5): 1213–1231.

Crouch, C. 2009. Privatised Keynesianism: an unacknowledged policy regime. *The British Journal of Politics and International Relations* 11: 382–399.

Deeg, R. & Jackson, G. 2007. Towards a more dynamic theory of capitalist variety. *Socio-economic Review* 5: 149–179.

Doling, J. & Ford, J., eds. 2003. *Globalisation and Home Ownership: Experiences in Eight Member States of the European Union*. Delft: DUP Science.

Doling, J. & Ronald, R. 2010. Home ownership and asset-based welfare. *Journal of Housing and the Built Environment* 25(2): 165–173.

Drucker, P.F. 1976. *The Unseen Revolution: How Pension Fund Socialism Came to America*. New York: Harper & Row.

ECB 2006. *Monthly Bulletin December*. ECB.

ECB 2009. *Euro area private consumption is there a role for housing wealth effects?* Working article series no. 1057.

Fernandez, R. 2014. *Denken over de verzorgingsstaat van morgen; Hoe globalisering en de financiële crisis Nederland vormgeven*. Den Haag: Boom Lemma.

Fernandez, R., Hofman, A. & Aalbers, M.B. 2016. London and New York as a safe deposit box for the transnational wealth elite. Article under review (available from the authors).

Fields, D. & Uffer, S. 2014. The financialization of rental housing: a comparative analysis of New York City and Berlin *Urban Studies*. DOI: 10.1177/0042098014543704.

Gotham, K.F. 2009. Creating liquidity out of spatial fixity: the secondary circuit of capital and the subprime mortgage crisis. *International Journal of Urban and Regional Research* 33(2): 355–371.

Harloe, M. 1985. *Private Rented Housing in the United States and Europe*. New York: St. Martin's.

Harloe, M. 1995. *The People's Home: Social Rented Housing in Europe and America*. Oxford: Blackwell.

Harvey, D. 1985. *The Urbanization of Capital. Studies in the History and Theory of Capitalist Urbanization*. Oxford: Blackwell.

Hay, C. 2004. Common trajectories, variable paces, divergent outcomes? Models of European capitalism under conditions of complex economic interdependence. *Review of International Political Economy* 11: 231–261.

Heeg, S. 2013. Wohnungen als Finanzanlage. Auswirkungen von Responsibilisierung und Finanzialisierung im Bereich des Wohnens. In: *Sub\urban, Zeitschrift für kritische Stadtforschung* 1: 75–99.

Henry, J.S. 2012. *The Price of Offshore Revisited*. The Tax Justice Network.

ILO. 2001. *The Construction Industry in the Twenty-First Century: Its Image, Employment Prospects and Skill Requirements*. Geneva: ILO.

ILO. 2010. *The Global Wage Report 2010/2011: Wage Policies in Times of Crisis*. Geneva, ILO.

IMF. 2006. *World Economic Outlook* April 2006. IMF

IMF 2008. The changing housing cycle and the implications for monetary policy. *World Economic Outlook April 2008*. IMF

IMF. 2009. *World Economic Outlook April 2009*. IMF

IMF 2011. *World Economic Outlook April 2011*. IMF

IMF 2013. *Capital Flows are Fickle: Anytime, Anywhere*. IMF Working Article, WP/13/183

Jones, B.G. 2012. 'Bankable slums': the global politics of slum upgrading. *Third World Quarterly* 33(5): 769–789.

Jordà, O., Schularick, M. & Taylor, A.M. 2014. The great mortgaging: housing finance, crises, and business cycles. NBER Working Article No. 20501.

Kaika, M. & Ruggiero, L. 2014. Land financialization as a 'lived' process: the transformation of Milan's Bicocca by Pirelli. *European Urban and Regional Studies*. DOI: 10.1177/0969776413484166.

Kemeny, J. 2005. 'The really big trade-off' between home ownership and welfare: Castles' evaluation of the 1980 thesis, and a reformulation 25 years on. *Housing, Theory and Society* 22: 59–75.

Kemeny, J. & Lowe, S. (1998) Schools of comparative housing research: from convergence to divergence. *Housing Studies* 13(2): 161–176.

Kindleberger, C. & Aliber, R. [1978] 2005. *Manias, Panics and Crashes: A history of Financial Crashes*. Hoboken, NJ: Wiley.

Langley, P. 2008. *The Everyday Life of Global Finance: Saving and Borrowing in America*. Oxford: Oxford University Press.

Lawson, J. 2006. *Critical Realism and Housing Studies*. London: Routledge.

Lujanen, M., ed. 2004. *Housing and Housing Policy in the Nordic Countries*. Copenhagen: Nordic Council of Ministers.

Minsky, H.P. 1996. Uncertainty and the institutional structure of capitalist economies. Journal Of Economic Issues 30: 357–368.

Newman, K. 2009. Post-industrial widgets: capital flows and the production of the urban. *International Journal of Urban and Regional Research* 33(2): 314–331.

OECD 2007. Corporate net lending: a review of recent trends, OECD Economics Department Working Articles, No. 583, OECD.

OECD. 2008. Households' wealth composition across OECD countries and financial risks borne by households. Financial Market Trends, OECD.

OECD. 2008b. Trends in institutional investors statistics. Financial market trends, OECD.

OECD. 2011. The evolution of homeownership rates in selected OECD countries: demographic and public policy influences. *OECD Journal: Economic Studies* 2011/1.

Piketty, T. 2014. *Capital in the Twenty-First Century*, Harvard College.

Rolnik, R. 2013. Late neoliberalism: the financialization of homeownership and housing rights. *International Journal of Urban and Regional Research* 37(3): 1058–1066.

Ronald, R. 2008. *The Ideology of Home Ownership Homeowner Societies and the Role of Housing*. Palgrave.

Savini, F. & Aalbers, M.B. (in press): The de-contextualization of land use planning through financialisation: urban redevelopment in Milan. *European Urban and Regional Studies*. DOI:10.1177/0969776415585887.

Schwartz, H.M. & Seabrooke, L., eds. 2009. *The Politics of Housing Booms and Busts*. Basingstoke: Palgrave Macmillan.

Stockhammer, E. 2004. Financialization and the slowdown of accumulation, *Cambridge Journal of Economics* 28(5): 719–741.

Stockhammer, E. 2007. Some Stylized Facts on the Finance-dominated Accumulation Regime. Political Economy Research Institute, University of Massachusetts Amherst, working article series number 142.

Strange, S. 1997. The future of global capitalism; or will divergence persist forever?. In: C. Crouch & W. Streeck eds, *Political Economy of Modern Capitalism: Mapping Convergence and Diversity*. London: Sage Publications.

Streeck, W. & Thelen, K. 2005. Introduction: institutional change in advanced political economies. In: W. Streeck & K. Thelen eds, *Beyond Continuity; Institutional Change in Advanced Political Economies*. Oxford: Oxford University Press.

Toussaint, J. and Elsinga, M. 2009. Exploring 'housing asset-based welfare'. Can the UK be held up as an example for Europe? *Housing Studies* 24.

Trouillard, E. 2013. Development of a financialized rental investment product: private serviced residences in the Paris region (Île-de-France). Working paper, Transforming cities: urban processes and structure. URL: researchrepository.ucd.ie

Waldron, R. 2014. Mortgage stress and the impact of the Irish property crash. Doctoral thesis. Dublin: University College Dublin.

Walks, R.A. 2013. Mapping the urban debtscape: the geography of household debt in Canadian cities. *Urban Geography* 34(2): 153–187.

Wainwright, T. 2009. Laying the foundations for a crisis: mapping the historico-geographical construction of RMBS securitization in the UK. *International Journal of Urban and Regional Research* 33(2): 372–388.

Watson, M. 2009. Planning for a future of asset-based welfare? New Labour, financialized economic agency and the housing market. *Planning Practice and Research* 24(1): 41–56.

World Bank. 2009. Financial institutions and markets across countries and over time. Policy Research Working Article, 4943.

World Bank. 2012. Benchmarking financial systems around the world. Policy Research Working Article, 6175.

6 Mortgage Lending and House Price Developments in Germany, Italy, Spain, the Netherlands and the US

Four Housing Trajectories and One Outlier

In this chapter I will discuss four countries (Germany, Italy, the Netherlands and the US), each representing one of the four trajectories discussed in the last chapter, and one outlier, Spain, a country that "jumps groups" (see Chapter 5). I will demonstrate that the financialization of housing is not happening in the same way and to the same degree in all countries. The fact that four of these countries are considered to be "representing" four different groups of countries does not imply that these countries should, in any way, be considered to be average cases within each group. These countries are selected because they help illustrate the different trends and due to the availability of comparative data.

The comparative data are limited in (1) scope, only available for some of the relevant developments (e.g. house price development or mortgage-debt-to-GDP ratio), and (2) time. Most only go back to 1995 and do not include the most recent years. These limitations only allow us to say something about a relatively short period of time—not even including the entire period of "flexible neoliberalism", introduced in Chapter 4. Although older data sets are available for some countries, they may not be available or comparable for all five countries. This brings us to the last limitation, (3) the limited comparability of the data. Some statistics that seem to represent the same thing in different countries are in fact differently constructed. For example, we had to exclude data on loan-to-value ratios because they are measured and collected in a different way in each country and are difficult to compare and interpret.

The country comparison is not meant as a full overview of the housing policies and practices in these countries, but merely as an illustration of how different—and sometimes, how similar—the financialization of housing is between countries. Anyone familiar with one or more of these countries will recognize that I ignore a great deal of housing policies and practices that, if included, would help to understand the development as well as the contemporary housing situation in these countries. My purpose here is not to explain these developments or understand why and how differences between countries (and between different decades within each country) are shaped, but rather what the idea of "common trajectories" (Hay, 2004) in the financialization of housing actually means.

Homeownership and Mortgage Markets

First, when we look at the homeownership rates in these five countries in 2013, we see Mediterranean Spain and Italy on top, with 78 per cent and 73 per cent respectively (Table 6.1). The US, often thought of as a country of homeowners, has a rate of 65 per cent; the Netherlands' is slightly higher, 67 per cent; and the German one is significantly lower, 53 per cent. These significant differences are, as discussed extensively in the literature, a result of decades of variegated policies. Yet, with the possible exception of Germany, homeownership has been discursively and fiscally privileged in each of these countries, suggesting a common trend. Since the Second Word War homeownership rates have generally increased, also in the traditionally homeownership-focused Mediterranean countries. The most spectacular increase took place in the Netherlands, where in 1955 only 15 per cent of housing units were owner-occupied. The 50 per cent mark was only passed in 2002, which implies that the homeownership rate went up recently by 17 percentage-points in only 11 years. As Dutch and German homeownership rates continued to increase, while Spanish, Italian and US rates declined somewhat in recent years, divergent trends emerge between these countries.

The German homeownership rate continues to be comparatively low, even though it has also increased markedly in recent years. In fact, Germany has the second lowest homeownership rate of any European or North American country, after Switzerland (44 per cent). CEE countries Romania, Lithuania, Slovakia and Hungary (all over 90 per cent homeownership) are on the other end of the spectrum. All other CEE counties have very high homeownership (77–90 per cent). Whereas the Mediterranean and more recently the English-speaking countries had some of the highest homeownership rates in the world, they have been surpassed by not only the former communist states of CEE, but also by China (90 per cent), India (87 per cent) and Mexico (80 per cent). The homeownership rates in Mediterranean countries look rather average these days while those in predominantly English-speaking countries such as—listed from high (70 per cent) to low (65 per cent)—Ireland, Canada, Australia, New Zealand, the UK and the US, are now below average; several continental European countries where 20 years ago most households were still renting their homes have now joined their ranks (e.g. Sweden, the Netherlands, Denmark, and France).

In Italy and in particular Spain it is financially difficult for households to acquire their first owner-occupied home, but with very few other alternatives, there is no significant decline in the homeownership rate:

> Buying a home becomes a necessary practice when rented housing is scarce or inappropriate in terms of price or condition. But buying a home means taking a greater risk given a labour market characterised by temporary and precarious working contracts.

> (Leal, 2003: 176)

Table 6.1 Homeownership Rate (%)

Rank	Country	Home Ownership Rate (%)	Year of Information (if not 2013)	Rank	Country	Home Ownership Rate (%)	Year of Information (if not 2013)
1	Romania	96		23	Brazil	74	2008
2	Lithuania	92		24	Portugal	74	
3	Slovakia	91		25	Cyprus	74	
4	Singapore	90	2014	26	Finland	74	
5	China	90	2012	27	Italy	73	
6	Hungary	90		28	Luxembourg	73	
7	Croatia	89		29	Belgium	72	
8	India	87	2011	30	Ireland	70	2011
9	Bulgaria	86		31	Sweden	70	
10	Russia	84	2012	32	Canada	68	
11	Poland	84		33	Turkey	67	2011
12	Norway	84		34	Netherlands	67	
13	Latvia	81		35	Australia	67	2011
14	Estonia	81		36	New Zealand	65	
15	Malta	80		37	United Kingdom	65	
16	Czech Republic	80		38	United States	65	2014
				39	France	64	2012
17	Mexico	80	2009	40	Denmark	63	
18	Spain	78		41	Japan	62	2008
19	Iceland	78		42	Austria	57	
20	Slovenia	77		43	South Korea	54	2010
21	Trinidad & Tobago	76		44	Germany	53	2012
				45	Hong Kong	51	2014
22	Greece	76		46	Switzerland	44	

Source: https://en.wikipedia.org/wiki/List_of_countries_by_home_ownership_rate (accessed November 15, 2015).

In Italy, young people continue to leave their parents' house at a comparatively late age, while Spain has seen many of its young people "boomerang" back to the parental home or migrate to other countries where they typically rent a flat in the private market. This represents a major shift in Spanish society: homeownership is increasingly becoming denormalized for young Spaniards. It remains a question if this is indicative of a continued drop in homeownership rates in Spain (and possibly elsewhere) or rather a delay of their entry into homeownership. As long as rental alternatives are extremely constrained, it is hard to imagine a more significant drop in homeownership.

There is no strong correlation between the homeownership rate and the size of the mortgage market (Aalbers, 2009), the latter measured by the mortgage-debt-to-GDP ratio. At an internationally comparative level it does not appear to be the size of the mortgage market that pushes homeownership to high levels. If we look at each country individually, however, we cannot be so sure. The Netherlands, which saw a sharp rise in homeownership, saw an even sharper increase in the size of its mortgage market: from a ratio of just under 40 per cent in 1995 to 105–110 per cent in the post-crisis years (Figure 6.1). The Netherlands' only other "group member", Denmark, looks remarkably similar: from 68 per cent in 2000, up to 104 per cent in 2007 and then down slightly to 101 per cent in 2011.[1] In other words, although the growth of mortgage lending may have significantly contributed to the rise in homeownership, the massive expansion of the mortgage market cannot only be explained by the rise in homeownership.

The US, Italy and Spain did not see a large increase in homeownership in the last 20 years (and even note a decline in recent years), but they did see an enormous growth in the mortgage market, a pattern familiar throughout Europe and North America. The US mortgage-debt-to-GDP ratio nearly doubled from 47 per cent in 1995 to 93 per cent in 2008, while its homeownership rate in 2014 was back to its 1994 figure, 64 per cent, after it reached an all-time high in 2004 at 69 per cent.[2] The subsequent drop in the US is remarkable and, as far as I am aware of, unique: the mortgage-debt-to-GDP ratio went down to 76 per cent in 2011, a decline of 27 per cent percentage-points in only three years.

This cannot be only a result of new homeowners taking out smaller mortgage loans, which would not affect the stock of outstanding mortgages sufficiently to account for such a steep decline. The high number of foreclosure proceedings and sales in the US is of greater importance. Foreclosure sales not only predominantly hit households with relatively large mortgages (compared to other homeowners in their housing market area) but also eliminated a large number of outstanding loans from the books, resulting in a rapid decrease of the overall mortgage debt. Since the US is unique in cancelling out the outstanding loan when it is foreclosed, the drop in the national mortgage debt is much more intense than in other countries with high rates of foreclosure, like Spain, where the affected households still have to pay off the remaining debt on their mortgage loan.

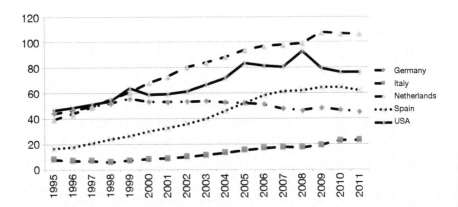

Figure 6.1 Mortgage-Debt-To-GDP Ratio (%)

Perhaps a simple example can help illustrate the national differences in dealing with foreclosures. Imagine an American household that bought a house for $200,000 and has an outstanding $160,000 mortgage loan. If house prices go down by 40 per cent in their housing market area, and they are, for whatever reason, unable to pay off the mortgage loan and therefore foreclosed on, the bank may sell the house for $100,000 and cancel out the loan completely. The household can walk away from *both* the house and the mortgage loan. Getting a new mortgage loan for a house or even renting a house or flat will be difficult for the family in the future, as many landlords in the US conduct credit checks and may decide not to let to persons with a foreclosure history. However, on the upside, the household does not have to pay off the remaining $60,000 of their mortgage loan ($160,000 minus $100,000) and can start off with a clean slate.

Their Spanish (and almost all other) counterparts face radically different conditions. Imagine a Spanish household who bought their house for the same price, took out an equally large mortgage loan, were faced with an equally dramatic fall in house prices and also lost their house due to foreclosure. The Spanish mortgage lender, however, will not cancel out the mortgage loan when they sell the house through a foreclosure sale. The Spanish household will still need to pay the Euro equivalent of the remaining $60,000 (roughly €50,000) and will remain indebted even though they have lost their collateral to the loan. Contrary to the American household, the Spanish household cannot start with a clean slate and will be faced with financial difficulties in the years to come as they need to keep paying for a loan that does not guarantee them any housing services in return while at the same time they need to budget for new housing expenses.[3]

Where the US was remarkable for its steep decline of the mortgage-debt-to-GDP ratio between 2008 and 2011, Spain was remarkable for the increase from 16.6 per cent in 1995 to 64.7 per cent to 2010—an almost fourfold increase—and then down slightly to 62.1 per cent in 2011. In relative terms, the rise in the mortgage-debt-to-GDP ratio in Spain even surpasses the hyper-mortgaged Netherlands, despite the fact that the homeownership rate remained somewhat stable in Spain during those years. The trajectories of the Netherlands, the US, Spain and even Italy look quite similar even though the increase in Italy looks much more modest at first: from 8 per cent in 1995, down to 6 per cent in 1998 and then up to 23 per cent in 2011. But in fact, the Italian mortgage-debt-to-GDP tripled in 1995–2011 and quadrupled in 1998–2011, something that within Europe only happened in Italy, Malta and several CEE countries, but the latter came from even lower levels in the 1990s.

In relative terms, the increase in many CEE countries looks spectacular: the mortgage-debt-to-GDP ratio in Estonia, for example, went up from 4.6 per cent in 2000 to 44.2 per cent in 2009 and then down to 36.7 per cent in 2011, an almost tenfold increase in seven years and still an eightfold increase in 11 years, including the slight decline in recent years. Real modest development of mortgage debt is only visible in Germany, where the mortgage-debt-to-GDP ratio increased from 44 per cent in 1995 to 54 per cent in 2003 and then decreased again to 45 per cent in 2011—up 10 percentage-points in eight years and then down 9 percentage-points in a further eight years. Even change in Germany appears not only modest but also balanced.

The Netherlands, the US, Spain, Italy and most of the "non-focus countries" follow a common trajectory of increasing mortgage debt (with some developments in the opposite direction since the crisis), indicative of the increasing financialization in these countries (and possibly some de-financialization in recent years), while Germany is the outlier with a very different trajectory, one of relative stability. The mortgage-debt-to-GDP level in Germany, the Netherlands and the US was remarkably similar in 1995 but the development since has been rather different. And whereas the difference between the level of the German mortgage debt on the one hand, and the Spanish and Italian on the other, appears to have become smaller between 1995 and 2011, indicative of convergence, this is not a result of similar trends but rather of different trends. Finally, where Spain appears to "walk away" from Italy in Figure 6.1, indicative of divergence, they follow a common trajectory and in relative terms the increase in the mortgage-debt-to-GDP ratio is remarkably similar, with Spain starting at a higher level in 1995 and also reaching a higher level in 2011.

Mortgage Market Funding

Throughout the history of mortgage markets different kinds of institutions have issued mortgage loans.[4] Historically, most of these lenders have been "depository institutions": not only providing loans but also taking in deposits from savers. It may seem obvious that lenders need to accumulate deposits as a reserve from which to provide loans, but this is not necessarily true. It is also possible for a lender to acquire funding in other ways. "Non-depository institutions" only need a small amount of "working capital" to originate loans if they sell these loans in the secondary mortgage market as bonds or mortgage-backed securities. Every time they sell a portfolio of loans they have freed up capital that they can use to originate new loans. Most non-depository lenders are so-called non-bank lenders, which means nothing more than that they are not considered banks by law.[5] These non-bank lenders include insurance companies and pension funds. However, this does not imply that depository lenders do not use the secondary mortgage markets to sell the mortgage loans they originated. Many commercial banks in developed countries not only take deposits from savers but also sell a significant share of the loans as bonds or mortgage-backed securities.

Another important distinction can be made within the group of depository lenders. On the one hand, there are commercial and general banks, and on the other, "savings and loans institutions" (US), "building societies" (UK), "Bausparkassen" (Germany), "cajas" (Spain) and other specialized lending institutions sometimes known as "thrifts". The main difference between the former and the latter is that the latter are financial institutions *specializing* in residential mortgage lending, as their names also indicate. For commercial, general and many other types of banks (the labels depend on the country) mortgage lending is only one of their many typical banking activities. Historically speaking, commercial banks were excluded from issuing mortgage loans in many countries. In 1913, the Federal Reserve Act in the US authorized federally chartered banks to lend money on real estate. Many other developed countries followed suit decades after the Second World War, with aspiring homeowners mostly relying on some sort of thrift institution.

Another important development took place in the late 1980s. "Regulated deregulation" (see Chapter 7) and hyperinflation in the US undermined the savings and loans institutions. Many of them first fell into a liquidity crisis, followed by a solvency crisis, and finally, they either went bankrupt or were bailed out by the federal government. The commercial banks briefly became the most important source of mortgage credit before the non-bank lenders took over this role.

In the UK, building societies traditionally held the monopoly on the supply of mortgage credit. However, from 1986 onwards, commercial banks were allowed to provide mortgage credit. At the same time, building societies were allowed to "demutualize" and become banks. Only ten of them did and those ten are now all owned by commercial banks or were nationalized as a result of the 2007–2009 financial crisis. Similar developments took place in several other countries, where the entry of commercial banks into the mortgage market combined with deregulation sometimes undermined thrift-like institutions. Only half of the savings and loans institutions in the US survived the crisis years, and those that did generally lost market share. In both countries, many of those that survived the crisis of the 1980s and early 1990s became active in the secondary mortgage market, sometimes even as buyers rather than sellers.

The regulated deregulation of mortgage lenders, and of finance more generally, coupled with the rise of non-bank lenders (which in the US were often heavily involved in subprime lending), was at the root of the 2007–2009 global financial crisis. In part this was because so many lenders had sold the mortgage debt they originated in the secondary mortgage market, thereby externalizing risk and responsibility. The crisis halted the rise of non-bank lenders; many went bankrupt while others were snapped up by commercial banks.

Looking back at the last 20 years, the visible trend is the decrease of depository lending and the rise of both mortgage bonds and mortgage-backed securities. In several countries mortgage lenders rely heavily on mortgage bonds, and between 2000 and 2011 the popularity of so-called covered bonds for funding mortgage lending increased markedly in Europe. Whereas in 2000 only 12 per cent of outstanding mortgage lending was financed by covered bonds in the EU27, the figure more than doubled by 2011 reaching 27 per cent.

Within the EU27, Denmark makes the most use of mortgage bonds. In fact, Danish covered bonds made up a stunning 143 per cent of outstanding Danish mortgage loans in 2011 (up from 132 per cent in 2000 and 115 per cent in 2007–2008, but down from 156 per cent in 2002). We will not go into the peculiarities of Danish mortgage lending that underpin this situation (see Frankel *et al.*, 2004; Mortensen and Seabrooke, 2009) but have included these figures here to point at the largest contributor (in relative terms) to Europe's covered bond market and also to point out how different Denmark is from the Netherlands regarding mortgage bonds. Although we grouped the countries together in the last chapter as examples of hyper-mortgaged, and therefore highly financialized housing markets, covered bonds only entered the Dutch market in 2005 (0.4 per cent) and grew rapidly to 8.5 per cent by 2011 (still a very modest figure compared to Denmark's 143 per cent). Italy is, by exception, rather similar to the Netherlands in this respect: from 2 per cent in 2008 going up to 14 per cent in 2011.

There is a huge gap in the reliance on covered bonds to finance mortgage lending between Denmark and *all* other countries. In Europe (not only in the EU27) other countries that rely relatively heavily on covered bonds are Sweden (69 per cent in 2011, up from 27 per cent in 2006), Spain (55 per cent in 2011, up from 4 per cent in 2000), the Czech Republic (42 per cent in 2011, down from 73 per cent in 2005), Norway (38 per cent in 2011, up from 4 per cent in 2007), Slovakia (32 per cent in 2011, down from 53 per cent in 2006), France (29 per cent in 2009, up from 10 per cent in 2003) and Portugal (28 per cent in 2011, up from 0 per cent in 2005 and 2 per cent in 2006). On the other hand, many countries shy away from covered bonds: the share in Poland and Latvia in 2011 does not even reach 1 per cent (down from respectively 4 per cent and 5 per cent in the early 2000s), while the share in the US is a negligible 0.1 per cent. Whereas generally speaking the use of covered bonds has gone up, it has gone down in most CEE countries. Germany, the last of our five focus countries is again a beacon of stability and moderation: the share of covered bonds of outstanding mortgage lending in 2000–2011 fluctuated between 18 per cent (2002) and 23 per cent (2000–2002), reaching 19 per cent in 2011.

The use of covered bonds can be measured by looking at the value of outstanding covered bonds as a share of GDP. Unsurprisingly, Denmark is again the "winner" with 144 per cent in 2011, up from 90 per cent in 2000. Next come Sweden (54 per cent in 2011, up from 17 per cent in 2006), Spain (34 per cent in 2011, up from 1 per cent in 2000) and Norway (26 per cent in 2011, up from 2 per cent in 2007). Suddenly Spain has "become" a Nordic-type country, by virtue of the unprecedented mortgage boom. In the US, Italy, Germany and the Netherlands covered bonds as share of GDP in 2011 are respectively 0.1 per cent, 3 per cent, 9 per cent and 9 per cent.

Indeed, the European and North American covered bonds picture is extremely mixed, both in their reliance on mortgage bonds and in the development of the use of them in the early twenty-first century. Nordic European countries appear to rely on covered bonds either heavily (Denmark) or substantially (Sweden, Norway and Finland, but not Iceland), and the share of mortgage bonds has been increasing in all these countries. CEE countries rely on covered bonds substantially (the Czech Republic, Slovakia, Hungary) or marginally (Poland, Latvia), but in both groups the use of covered bonds is decreasing or non-existent or not recorded in the EMF dataset (Estonia, Lithuania, Romania, Russia, Ukraine). It is hard to see any general patterns in the rest of Europe and North America, although increasing use of covered bonds is the dominant trend, with a marked jump in 2008 (e.g. France, Ireland, Portugal, Spain, UK, but also Norway). The growth is possibly aimed at replacing the reliance on mortgage-backed securities which had become difficult amidst the global financial crisis and the mass defaulting and mass dumping of mortgage-backed securities around the globe.

This brings us to the use of mortgage-backed securities to fund mortgage lending. Figure 6.2 shows the issuance of mortgage-backed securities per capita. Commonly, the issuance of mortgage-backed securities in shown in absolute numbers, but in order to compare relative levels between countries, I use a line graph instead. In absolute terms, the issuance of mortgage-backed securities in the US reached its peak in 2003[6] and at that point was more than 43 times as large as in the second largest issuing country, the UK. Of course, Figure 6.2 understates the massive size of the US market for mortgage-backed securities, but it also allows a comparison between the five focus countries.

Figure 6.2 illustrates the collapse of the market for mortgage-backed securities in 2008 (US) and 2009 (primarily Spain but also other countries) along with the spectacular rise of new mortgage-backed securities in the Netherlands (despite minor setbacks in 2009 and 2011). What this figure does not show is that issuance of new mortgage-backed securities has continued to rise in the Netherlands in recent years (Engelen, 2015). Looking for a common trajectory in the issuance of mortgage-backed securities, we can note growth in the early 2000s (even in Germany, although on such a small scale that it is hardly visible here) and a decline starting either before the financial crisis (starting 2004 in the US and 2006 in Germany) or at the height of the crisis in Europe (2009 in the Netherlands, Spain and Italy). So far, the recent decline has been smaller than the earlier rise in mortgage securitization. The Netherlands first followed the common trajectory but then charted a different course from 2010 onwards, with rapid but volatile growth in issuance of mortgage-backed securities.

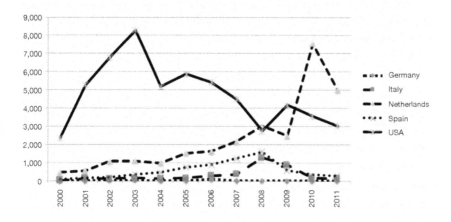

Figure 6.2 RMBS Issuance Per Capita (EUR thousands)

Outside the five focus countries, the common trajectory is widely shared, namely in the countries where mortgage securitization already existed or was introduced in the first years of the twenty-first century, for example Greece, Ireland (albeit more erratic), Norway, Portugal, Sweden and the UK. Yet, only the UK, and to some extent Ireland, have seen relatively high levels of securitization during the boom years. France, and in particular Belgium, appear to be following the Dutch trajectory, although at much lower levels. In these countries, small declines in the issuance of mortgage-backed securities during the crisis have been more than compensated by the growth in recent years. In terms of absolute size in 2011 (the latest year with comparative figures), the Netherlands (16.7 million people) surpassed the UK (62.4 million people) as the second largest issuer of mortgage-backed securities (still lagging far behind the US). In terms of total outstanding mortgage-backed securities in absolute terms, it will be a while before the "top 4" of 2011—namely the US, the Netherlands, the UK and Spain—will change position.

Housing Construction and House Prices

To explain house price development, both housing economists and the popular media typically look at housing construction as well as the number of housing units compared to population size. The general idea is that increasing house prices reflect a lack of housing supply. The reader will, by now, be familiar with my argument: house prices are not primarily driven by the development of the demand and supply of housing units (although they can surely make a difference of secondary order) but rather by the demand and supply of finance to both housing consumers (primarily in the form of mortgage loans) and housing producers (through a range of financial instruments to real estate developers, construction firms and different types of landlords).

Figure 6.3 presents the house price developments since 1995 in the five focus countries. The clear trend is a rise in prices in all five countries, although a very modest one in Germany. There is also a second trend: in the crisis years house prices went down in the three countries where they increased the most and they flattened off in the two countries where the house price development was more moderate, namely Italy and Germany. In the late 1990s the price growth is particularly impressive in the Netherlands and in the early 2000s even more spectacular in Spain. By comparison, the developments in the other three countries look rather modest, but are still substantial: house prices in the US almost doubled over the course of ten years, with Italy close behind.

If we look beyond these five countries and focus only on the first 12 years of the twenty-first century (the comparative data for a deeper review is lacking), the house price developments in other European countries are remarkable. Estonia is again an extreme case: taking 2001 as 100 (Estonia's figures for 2000 are not available), by 2007 the index was up to 450 and down to 249 by 2011, a 45 per cent drop from its peak. Prices more than doubled between 2000 and the subsequent respective peak years in many European countries, namely Latvia,

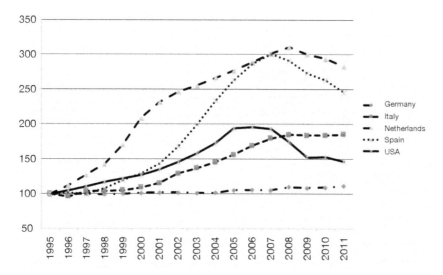

Figure 6.3 Indexed House Prices (1995=100)

Slovakia, Iceland, Belgium, France, Sweden, Norway, the UK and Poland. However, post-crisis prices continued to rise only in Belgium, France, Sweden and Norway. Considering the severe impact of the crisis in Iceland, the modest decline may seem surprising. Similarly, the drop in Greek house prices between 2008 and 2011 is also rather modest. The conclusion is that Estonia's extreme house price development is a real outlier. The other two outliers are Germany and Ireland. In Ireland house prices doubled between 1998 and 2006, but then halved again between 2007 and 2011.

To see how house price developments relate to housing construction figures, we will now look at the figures for housing units and housing construction per country. Figure 6.4 shows the number of housing units per 1,000 inhabitants for the five focus countries. The common trajectory for the four European countries is an increase in the relative number of housing units. The US also shows an increase in this period, but it is almost negligible, from 422 in 1995 to 424 in 2011. The increase in the Netherlands (from 409 to 427) is also rather modest. The increase in Germany (from 438 to 495) is more pronounced, and Italy (from 461 to 550/1,000) and Spain (from 477 to 585) show spectacular growth, especially if one considers that they did not experience rapid population growth in this period.

Comparing Figures 6.3 and 6.4, we can see that there is no relation between the expansion of the number of housing units per 1,000 inhabitants and house prices. Indeed, the only constant trend is that the biggest house price increases are recorded in years when the housing stock increased the most. The empirical evidence invalidates the economic truism that oversupply must lead to declining prices and that rising prices are a result of undersupply.

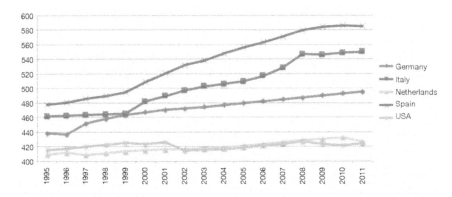

Figure 6.4 Number of Housing Units Per 1000 Inhabitants

To further illustrate the inverse—and for some, counterintuitive—relationship described here, we take a closer looks at annual housing construction numbers. The advantage of Figure 6.5, housing construction (operationalized as housing completions) per 1 million inhabitants, is that it shows much more clearly the rise and fall of housing construction, something that stock figures, such as those presented in Figure 6.4, never can. Spotting a common trajectory in Figure 6.5 is more difficult. The only clear pattern is the fall of housing construction in the crisis years in all five countries, although this is part of a constant decline in Germany 1995–2011.[7]

Whereas in Germany housing construction is slowly but steadily declining, the picture for the other countries is more mixed. In the US the effect of the crisis is clearly visible: new construction per million inhabitants drops suddenly and sharply in 2006 and through the following years, bringing it down to the

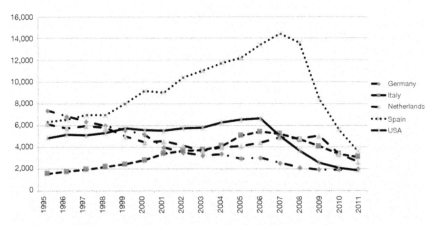

Figure 6.5 Housing Completions Per One Million Inhabitants

German level, although the American population continues to grow. In the early 2000s, the US added the second highest number of units per million inhabitants, but by 2011 it added the fewest, a fall by a factor of 3.5. If the US population keeps growing, construction numbers will eventually have to start increasing again.

The Netherlands shows a somewhat counterintuitive development: housing construction declined for most of the late 1990s and early 2000s, but this actually reflects a minor increase in the number of housing units per 1,000 inhabitants (see Figure 6.4). Yet, house prices explode in the late 1990s and keep growing steadily until 2008, as Figure 6.3 shows. Indeed, house prices in the Netherlands double in less than five years and triple in about 12 years, even though the number of housing units per 1,000 inhabitants increases slightly in that period, which clearly illustrates that prices did not rise due to growing housing demand.

As seen in Figures 6.3 and 6.4, both house prices and the number of housing units per 1,000 inhabitants increase steadily in Italy. In fact, Italy represents a very clear, straightforward picture with only a temporary levelling off of the house prices after 2008. And although Figure 6.5 shows a significant decline in housing construction from 2007 onwards, Italy continues to add more units per 1,000 inhabitants (see Figure 6.4). Together, these figures depict Italy as a steady (i.e. non-volatile) growth area. Ironically, this is not the popular image of the Italian economy and society, but it is the reality of the development of housing construction, finance and prices. That being said, the effects of steady growth are not all positive. The increase in land and house prices hits those households that are traditionally most vulnerable and in particular those that cannot rely on financial (and other forms of) support to climb the housing ladder.

Spain is marked by spectacular yet volatile growth—and to some degree also contraction. Figure 6.4 shows that the expansion of the Spanish housing sector clearly outpaces the other four focus countries, and indeed, almost all other countries. Figure 6.5 shows how extreme the rise and fall in new construction really was. In 2007, at the height of the Spanish building boom, Spain (44.5 million people) added more new units to its housing stock in absolute terms than France, Germany, Italy and the UK (with a combined population of 265 million, i.e. almost six-fold Spain) *together*. In fact, housing "boom" is an understatement in the Spanish case; "frenzy" is more accurate. Figure 6.4 also shows that "bust" is an understatement for the decline of housing construction in Spain; "collapse" is much more appropriate. Yet, even after the collapse, Spain, up to 2011 at least, continued to add relatively more housing units to its stock than each of the other four countries.

Conclusion

This chapter provides empirical illustrations of the analysis presented in the previous two chapters. In that sense, this chapter's conclusions have already been read. The data presented here clearly illustrate that demand and supply of housing units does not adequately explain fluctuations in house prices. In the age of financialized capitalism, house prices are primarily, but never exclusively, driven by the supply of housing finance. Even when with relatively stable populations and income levels, it is not merely possible but highly likely that house prices will go up if the supply of housing finance goes up. If the wall of money, described in the previous chapter, enters a country it will feed the housing finance bubble, which in turn will feed the house price bubble.

The differences between countries can be large, but nonetheless common trajectories are evident—and not only within the four groups of countries defined in the previous chapter, but also across groups of countries. Until the beginning of the global financial crisis in 2007, homeownership rates increased across the board. Likewise, mortgage debt soared and, as a result, so did house prices. Germany is the exception where the homeownership rate increased but mortgage debt and house prices remained somewhat stable.

Spain, in many ways, is the opposite of Germany. The homeownership rate remained almost the same, while housing finance, housing construction and house prices soared. In a way, Spain left the development trajectory of one group of countries and joined another group, the highly financialized and highly volatile housing markets of the US and the UK. Iceland and Estonia, like Spain, also seem to have "jumped groups", following a rapid, highly financialized pattern. The development in the US (and many other English-speaking countries) looks somewhat moderate when compared to Spain, but is rather volatile when compared to Germany. The Italian market is much more stable than the US and Spanish markets, with impressive growth in both mortgage debt and house prices.

The Netherlands and Denmark represent a small group of extremely financialized housing markets with mortgage-debt-to-GDP ratios of over 100 per cent, despite moderate or average homeownership rates. Yet, a great deal of the rise of homeownership is very recent, in particular in the Netherlands, which implies limited multigenerational housing equity. Moreover, since the early 1990s households in the Netherlands and Denmark are used to buying property with little or no down-payment. Both countries saw a significant drop in house prices but continue to rely heavily on non-depository mortgage funding. In fact, in relative terms Denmark has the biggest market for mortgage bonds, and the Netherlands has the largest for mortgage-backed securities. As a result, while house prices may have fallen in both countries, their mortgage debt continues to soar.

Many other countries with rapidly rising house prices and even faster growing mortgage debt, experienced what economists like to call a "correction", namely a fall in both house prices and mortgage debt following a steady substantial rise in preceding years. Other less volatile countries, including Italy but also Belgium, France and several Nordic as well as developing countries, did not see their house prices collapse in the crisis and continued to experience rising house prices and in particular rising mortgage debt in the post-crisis years as they became (or already were) popular with the agents behind the wall of money. At the time of writing—fall 2015—however, it appears that in many of these countries are beginning to see the end of ever-rising house prices and ever-soaring mortgage debt. It is becoming clear that the financialization of housing does not produce continuously rising house prices but rather volatile house prices and an addiction to mortgage credit.

Notes

1   The only other country besides the Netherlands and Denmark that at some point in time surpassed the symbolic 100 per cent mortgage-debt-to-GDP ratio is Iceland. Its ratio doubled from 57 per cent in 2000 to 119 per cent in 2007 and then dropped somewhat to 110 per cent in 2011. Iceland also recorded the largest increase in percentage-points in a single year: from 74 per cent in 2006 to 119 per cent in 2007, an unprecedented almost doubling of the market (45 percentage-points) in a single year.

2   The US homeownership rate between 1960 and 1997 hovered between 62.0 and 66.0 per cent.

3   In reality, actual prices in foreclosure sales are typically significantly lower than for "normal" sales, which implies that the $100,000 price in the example is rather optimistic. The range $70,000–$90,000 is more realistic, which means that the losses are usually even greater.

4   The first five paragraphs of this section are adapted from Aalbers (2012).

5   Confusingly, non-bank lenders are also known as mortgage banks, although in several countries they are, legally speaking, not banks.

6   Indeed, the peak was four years before the outbreak of the global financial crisis.

7   Despite the consistent fall in housing construction in Germany, from the highest level among the five focus countries in 1995 to the second-lowest level in 2011, Germany still witnessed a substantial increase in the number of housing units per 1,000 inhabitants (see Figure 6.4). This is the result of a modest but continued expansion of the housing stock during a period of near-zero population growth.

References

Aalbers, M.B. (2009) The Globalization and Europeanization of Mortgage Markets. *International Journal of Urban and Regional Research* 33(2): 389–410.

Aalbers, M.B. (2012) Mortgage Lenders and Loans. In: S.J. Smith, M. Elsinga, L.F. O'Mahony, O.S. Eng, S. Wachter and R. Ronald (Eds), *International Encyclopedia of Housing and Home: Vol. 4*, pp. 389–393. Oxford: Elsevier.

Engelen, E. (2015) Don't Mind the "Funding Gap": What Dutch Post Crisis Storytelling Tells Us about Elite Politics in Financialized Capitalism. *Environment & Planning A* 47(8): 1606–1623.

Frankel, A., Gyntelberg, J., Kjeldsen, K. and Persson, M. (2004) The Danish Mortgage Market. *BIS Quarterly Review* (March): 95–109.

Hay, C. (2004) Common Trajectories, Variable Paces, Divergent Outcomes? Models of European Capitalism under Conditions of Complex Economic Interdependence. *Review of International Political Economy* 11: 231–261.

Leal Maldonnado, J. (2003) Spain. In: J. Doling and J. Ford (Eds), *Globalisation and Home Ownership: Experiences in Eight Member States of the European Union*, pp. 160–184. Delft: DUP Science.

Mortensen, J.L. and Seabrooke, L. (2009) Egalitarian Politics in Property Booms and Busts: Housing as Social Right or Means to Wealth in Australia and Denmark. In: H.M. Schwartz and L. Seabrooke (Eds), *The Politics of Housing Booms and Busts*, pp. 122–145. Basingstoke: Palgrave Macmillan.

7 The Financialization of Subsidized Rental Housing

As returns begin to falter in a specific asset class and bad news, for example, on collateralized debt obligations, begins to travel fast, institutional investors seek diversification and move into a new class of asset. As that asset class begins to inflate and surpass the now declining returns in the old asset class, the pace of withdrawal quickens as more and more investors attempt to enter the new asset class, thus stoking the new bubble. In this way, the new bubble is partially at least caused by the deflation [of the] old bubble, which becomes the spur for its own further cannibalization. Thus we move from one bubble to another, one asset class to another, as part of the politics of permanent bubbles of which housing is just one, albeit very important, part of the story.

(Blyth, 2008: 403–404)

In many ways then, the story is familiar: poor people and minorities are bearing the brunt of a housing market crisis. Which is why it's important to point out what's *different* here: there has been a fundamental change in the key actors involved, and this transforms the social relations of rent. Today, private equity funds and equity stakeholder, global banking and financial services companies, and issuers of mortgage-backed securities are responsible for exploitation, rather than the inner city slum landlords of the 1970s.

(Fields, 2013: 125)

Introduction

The financialization of housing is usually studied in relation to mortgage debt and mortgage securitization, and this book has so far also followed this approach. Chapter 3 in particular looks at how mortgage debt exploded in the Netherlands and the US, and examines the different drivers underlying this process. Mortgage securitization, in particular, was singled out as driver of the financialization of housing. Since securitization increases the supply of housing credit, thereby enabling not only bigger mortgage loans but also the inclusion of more households in the mortgage market, it directly leads to higher house prices. This house price inflation further increased the demand for mortgage loans (How else can one afford a house?) and in turn more securitization. This need was met by a demand for high-quality collateral (HQC), discussed in Chapter 5. Through techniques such as credit scoring and risk-based pricing, discussed in Chapter 3, mortgage lenders were able to answer the investors' call for HQC.

In the final months of 2007, when I wrote Chapter 3, the collapse of the US housing and mortgage market was clearly visible. Very few people in Europe anticipated a similar fate for Europe. As we have seen in Chapter 6, house prices in a number of European countries went down, especially in the Netherlands and Spain, but other countries did not experience this trend, for example Germany and Italy. Germany is the outlier as it did not follow many of the common trajectories that resulted in the financialized, overindebted housing markets of the US, the Netherlands and Spain. Yet, it would be too easy to conclude that the German housing market did not become more financialized in the past decades.

As I will argue in this chapter, the German housing market has also become increasingly financialized but through different means. And for once, Germany is not the exception. In the past 15 years, Germany witnessed a massive (but far from total) financialization of its rental housing stock. In Germany and parts of the US, large, financialized investors, such as private equity firms and publicly listed real estate companies, buy up entire city blocks or even entire social housing companies. The UK and the Netherlands are experiencing a secondary financialization of the rented social housing stock, not by financialized landlords (although this is beginning to change) but primarily through the participation of social housing associations in financial markets, either social housing bond markets or financial derivatives.

In each of these cases, financialization is made possible by a combination of economic circumstances, conscious government decisions, unforeseen consequences ("negative externalities" in economist speak) of government decisions, and financial-technical possibilities. And at least in one case, some big egos stepped into the picture as well. In this sense, this chapter not only contributes to the literature on the financialization of housing but also to the literature on the financialization of the state and semi-public institutions, which investigates financialization processes in a range of sectors, including education, health care, infrastructure and housing.

The dominant critique of these developments is that they are the consequence of privatization and deregulation. Although I am sympathetic to this critique, it is an oversimplification of the situation. While privatization is the prevailing condition, this in itself does not explain what happened in these semi-public sectors. The combination of privatization and financialization—"financialized privatization" if you will—provides a better explanation of what did and continues to happen in these sectors. The specific way privatization was carried out did create triggers for financialization; however, there is another more important factor at play. Financialization typically needs a favourable regulatory framework to get off the ground. I argue that "deregulation" is not the proper regulatory environment in which we observe financialization. Rather, regulation had to be reinvented to foster, and sometimes to officially allow in legal terms, the financialization of the semi-public sector.

This demands a reconceptualization of deregulation, which is amply covered in the next section. I propose the term "regulated deregulation" to express the paradox of more legal regulation doing less *régulation*. The subsequent sections will first discuss the German and US cases (as well as a short excursion to Spain) and then go on to the British and Dutch cases. The concluding section will attempt to answer the question: What does this tell us about the financialization of housing as well as the financialization of the state and semi-public institutions?

Regulated Deregulation

Deregulation is not a clearly defined term, mostly serving to encompass "the opposite of regulation".[1] In economics and popular media, regulation is seen as anything that limits the workings of market mechanism. To most mainstream economists, regulation has a negative connotation; it is only deemed beneficial if it addresses market failures. Political economists generally use a more open definition of regulation, such as "setting rules and establishing an enforcement mechanism designed to control the operation of the system's constituent institutions, instruments and markets" (Spotton, 1999: 971). Here, regulation is not set in opposition to the market mechanism, even viewing it as necessary for market stability and growth. In Spotton's terms, deregulation would then refer to removing rules and reducing the role of enforcement mechanisms.

Bob Jessop, was one of the key authors in political economy and human geography who did define deregulation. In 2002, he defined deregulation as the "reduced role of law and state" (Jessop, 2002: 461), that is in line with my reading of Spotton's definition. In another paper, Jessop (2003) defined deregulation as "giving economic agents greater freedom from state control and legal restrictions", similar to liberalization. Furthermore, it may be argued that deregulation should be read in the tradition of the French Régulation School and that deregulation is not the opposite of regulation but of *régulation*, which could better be translated into English as regularization or normalization (Jessop and Sum, 2006). In this particular interpretation, deregulation should be rephrased as "deregularization" or "denormalization". Although I do not exclude the possibility that some have conceptualized deregulation as opposed to *régulation*, the dominant use of deregulation seems closer to Jessop's definitions or to my reading of Spotton's definition.

Because of the problems associated with the term deregulation, I propose an alternative concept: "regulated deregulation". The "deregulation" part of it refers to deregulation-as-liberalization, namely giving some economic agents greater freedom from state control and legal restrictions (cf. Jessop, 2003), while the "regulated" part refers to "setting rules and establishing an enforcement mechanism designed to control the operation of the system's constituent institutions, instruments and markets" (Spotton, 1999: 971). In other words, under regulated deregulation some economic agents are given greater freedom from state control, but the market framework itself is regulated. In fact, regulation gives some economic agents this freedom (often at the expense of other agents). Regulated deregulation may seem like a contradiction in terms, but this is intentional—an oxymoron that breaks down the false dichotomy between *régulation* and deregulation. It problematizes the faulty understanding of deregulation-as-liberalization and of regulation-as-constraining-markets.

The notion of regulated deregulation also implies that regulation in the age of neoliberalism does not have to diminish. Typically these forms of regulation facilitate markets at least as much as they constrain them. Authors using the term deregulation often focus on the repeal of legislation such as Glass-Steagall Act in the US, but pay less attention to all the new and expanded regulation that has replaced it, that is they have a selective and limited understanding of actually existing regulation. In fact, regulation in most markets is actually increasing and often at a rapid pace, tempting Levi-Faur (2005) to speak of a "regulatory explosion". New regulation tends to be more specific, more detailed and therefore complex. There is also a tendency for formal laws and acts to be complemented by massive volumes of different types of regulation (by-laws, statutes, ordinances, controls, codes, rules, principles and standards), which are all increasingly institutionalized in law.

Economic historians, sociologists, geographers, anthropologists and political economists have all argued, in some way or another, that the state principally shapes—not constrains—markets. Vogel (1996) summarized the debate quite nicely: "Freer markets, more rules". Capitalism is furthered through regulation. The corporatization, and more recently the financialization, of the global economy is a product of regulation, of which the growth of states can be seen as a by-product (Braithwaite, 2005; Levi-Faur, 2005). To illustrate the meanings and implications of regulated deregulation, I will now briefly discuss one example of regulated deregulation that led to securitization: the regulation of American and British housing finance.

Kevin Fox Gotham (2006, 2009) discussed how mortgage securitization in the US was created by government intervention and was subsequently expanded through an active redrawing of the boundaries between different parts of the housing and financial sectors. Some of these changes can be characterized as deregulation-as-liberalization, but since significant regulation-as-rulemaking was required at each step of the rolling out of securitization, it is another case of regulated deregulation. Mortgage securitization in the US dates back to the late 1960s and early 1970s when new legislation allowed the two so-called "government-sponsored enterprises" (GSEs), Fannie Mae and Freddie Mac, to securitize the mortgages and loans they were legally obliged to buy from local banks and thrifts, and to sell the bonds issued on the back of these assets to private investors. This became known as "public label securitization" (Gotham, 2006, 2009).

During the 1970s, these GSEs were involved in a large-scale experiment of constructing a smoothly running securitization machine, which ground to a halt in the late 1970s because of disadvantageous macroeconomic conditions. The political response was to introduce additional deregulation to roll out securitization nationwide. In the mid-1980s a package of legislative measures was initiated to increase the accessibility of the primary mortgage market for an ever larger slice of US households (Gotham, 2009; Aalbers, 2012). What has happened since is a gradual transformation of local legislative frameworks, techniques, expertise and relationships into a "private label securitization machine", namely-securitization by investment banks rather than by the GSEs. This resulted in a step-by-step extension of the securitization technique to other assets, markets and jurisdictions.

Subsequently, Thomas Wainwright (2009) demonstrated that the transfer of US securitization techniques to the UK required multidimensional organizational, institutional and legal adaptations, which were actively negotiated by market insiders and regulators. Wainwright described how Salomon Brothers established a specialized structuring firm in London in 1986, called the Mortgage Corporation, which issued mortgage-backed securities and sold them to UK based investors. Wainwright stressed that the technique of securitization did not travel well across borders: rolling it out on a mass scale in the UK required fiscal, legal and accounting adaptations, which in turn required extensive negotiations between market insiders and regulators. Wainwright's paper counters head on the mainstream economists' view of financial markets, by pointing out that securitization did not develop in an institutional void but required institutional, organization and cultural preconditions for which state intervention was crucial.

The concept of regulated deregulation enables us to see how liberalization of selective economic agents was only made possible by the introduction of a new regulatory system that replaced or amended the existing one. Regulated deregulation allows for the combination of competition and economic incentives, on the one hand, and the coordination and regulatory authority-led making and shaping of different economic sectors and industries. Regulated deregulation negates the "contradiction" between liberalization and state control. Under regulated deregulation some economic agents are given greater freedom from state control, but the market framework itself is regulated.

Private Equity and Publicly Listed Real Estate Firms in New York and Berlin

In Germany, the US and elsewhere, a new set of landlords has entered the housing market: financialized landlords. These private equity firms and publicly listed real estate firms are financial companies that only recently have become interested in subsidized rental housing. While homeownership rates in almost all countries are now well over 50 per cent (see Chapter 6), many big cities, including New York and Berlin remain "tenants' cities". Whereas public housing amounts to only 6 per cent of New York's housing stock and has remained stable for decades, the public housing share in Berlin went down from 30 per cent in 1990 to 15 per cent in 2008. And, whereas financialization in New York targeted the large rent-stabilized housing stock rather than public housing, in Berlin the public housing stock was not only privatized but also financialized.

In the first decade of the twenty-first century private equity firms acquired around 10 per cent of New York City's rent-stabilized housing stock, approximately 100,000 units (Fields, 2013) heavily concentrated in a few predominantly low-income neighbourhoods in the Mid and South Bronx and Upper Manhattan (Harlem, Washington Heights) as well as smaller concentrations in Downtown Manhattan and several Brooklyn and Queens neighbourhoods.[2] Acquisitions included portfolios of around 50 multistorey buildings. The New York Rent Stabilization Board sets the maximum rent and the annual rent increase for these buildings. A few of these buildings are owned by non-profit landlords, such as community development corporations, a type of locally embedded housing association that became important providers of affordable housing in cities like New York following the crisis of the 1970s and 1980s. For-profit landlords, however, own most of the rent-stabilized stock.

With capped rents, a few notable trends are visible in rent-stabilized buildings. First, some landlords do not invest much in maintenance, not necessarily because rents are too low but primarily because tenants often have few alternatives. Second, some landlords will selectively upgrade units; sometimes small investments are profitable as they can provide legal grounds for a rent increase. New York is awash with stories of landlords who do minimal improvements and label these as "major capital investments". Third, landlords try to push the rent over the $2,000–2,500 threshold which allows them to "deregulate" the unit and charge the market rate if the unit becomes vacant or the household presently living in the unit can afford a higher rent. Fourth, some landlords aim at high turnover so that they are allowed to raise rents. This practice can lead to the paradox of a studio apartment being more expensive than a three-bedroom one in the same building. Fifth, some landlords will illegally raise rents and or evict tenants. Wyly and colleagues (2010: 2609) described such tactics as "an automatic deregulation machine".

Rent-stabilized buildings can be bought and sold. Due to the restricted rents, sales prices have historically been lower than for other buildings, although some landlords are prepared to pay more and make up the difference by subsequently squeezing out higher rents through the techniques described above. Fields (2015) provided several examples of how private equity firms operate in New York. The Los Angeles-based private equity firm Milbank, for example, acquired 18 buildings in the Bronx in 2007 for $35 million. The acquisition was enabled by a loan from Deutsche Bank that was subsequently securitized. LaSalle Bank operated as the trust for the securitization and sold the loan to Wells Fargo in 2008. When Milbank defaulted on its loan one year later, the service agreement was transferred to a subsidiary of the construction firm Lennar Corporation, named LNR Partners. In the meantime the buildings deteriorated and tenants and community organizations took the landlord to court. LNR, however, was unwilling or unable to make the repairs ordered by the court, which subsequently pushed LNR to sell the buildings to a landlord that is willing and able to make the required repairs (Teresa, 2015). In 2011, the Finkelstein Timberger East Real Estate acquired the buildings for just under $28 million and promised the court to make the necessary repairs while limiting the rent increases. In 2012 Milbank declared bankruptcy.

Private equity firms operate in a financial web of multiple actors, loans and securitizations, which makes it difficult to conceptualize who really is the landlord and to whom tenants should address their grievances. Private equity firms have a short-term focus (three to five years), are highly leveraged (i.e., loaded with borrowed money and little equity) and typically invest little in maintenance (Fields, 2015). Some of their real estate acquisitions are so over-leveraged that the average rent per unit is lower than the cost of servicing the debt per unit, namely the rent does not even cover the interest on the loans that were taken out to acquire these properties in the first place. Under these circumstances, the high rate of poor maintenance should come as no surprise, as reported by Fields (2013) and Teresa (2015). New York is rather exceptional within the US context, for the simple reason that most other cities do not have any rent-stabilized housing stock.

In Germany privatization and financialization happened throughout the country, but more intensely in Berlin because of the large public housing stock and the dire budgetary crisis of the City of Berlin. Of the 212,000 public housing units privatized since 1990, 125,000 were sold in the first five years of the new millennium (Aalbers and Holm, 2008). Not only did the 19 different public housing companies sell off thousands of units, two companies were completely privatized (GSW and Gehag, with a combined stock of more than 100,000 units).

With the 2004 purchase of GSW and its 65,000 units, Cerberus, an American private equity firm valued at $24 billion, became the largest landlord of Berlin overnight. Valued at €405 million, the deal allowed Cerberus to purchase the stock at a mere €6,230 per housing unit, although I should add that Cerberus also took on GSW's debt. The company acquired another 30,000 units in at least nine different transactions (Aalbers and Holm, 2008). Cerberus was backed by Goldman Sachs' real estate subsidiary Whitehall Funds, According to Goldman Sachs' website, Whitehall Funds has raised approximately $29 billion in capital since 1991, and it "invests globally across a broad range of markets, acquiring real estate companies, real estate projects, loan portfolios, debt recapitalization and direct property". Cerberus and Whitehall Funds had planned to hold GSW and the other 30,000 units for a few years, raising rents, upgrading and selling a number of units in gentrified neighbourhoods (Uffer, 2014), while reducing maintenance costs elsewhere. Due to the crisis it was harder than expected to sell off all units, but in 2011 Cerberus managed to bring GSW to the stock exchange. The IPO of GSW was valued at €468 million, undoubtedly less than Cerberus and Whitehall Funds had counted on, but assuming these firms have loaded GSW further with debt than it already was when Cerberus bought it in 2004, both companies probably still realized a handsome profit.

Both Cerberus and Whitehall sold their stakes in GSW in a number of transactions and reinvested their money in real estate in, for example, Spain where Cerberus acquired Bankia Habitat, a real estate management subsidiary of

Bankia, a conglomerate of seven former *cajas* (Spanish building societies), which was partially nationalized in 2012. Cerberus paid €90 million for Bankia Habitat in 2013 and combined this portfolio with properties acquired from Gesnova and Reser Subastas in a new company, Promontoria Plataforma, headquartered in Madrid but registered in Netherlands for tax-related reasons. In the next year, €17 million of real estate assets acquired from "bad bank" SAREB are also transferred to Promontoria, which is subsequently rebranded as Haya Real Estate. Haya is controlled, but apparently not fully owned, by Cerberus and was valued at €32.7 billion—yes billion, not million—in 2014 and 2015. It was estimated that in 2014, Haya managed approximately 10 per cent of all Spanish real estate for sale.[3] Goldman Sachs followed suit in 2014, acquiring a former Bankia portfolio of residential, commercial and logistics assets for €355 million. Again, Cerberus and Goldman Sachs snapped up property from government institutions facing budgetary problems.

In the meantime in Germany, and not just in Berlin, a new generation of landlords has stepped in: publicly traded housing firms (i.e., companies listed on the stock exchange). Their strategy is to "hold" properties rather than to offload them in opportunistic reselling within a few years, like private equity firms. Within a few years, companies like Deutsche Wohnen, Gagfah and Vonovia acquired over 800,000 units, including the portfolios of private equity funds GSW and Deutsche Annington (Kofner, 2012). Deutsche Annington was the German branch of UK's largest landlord, Annington Homes, which has been converting former British Defence housing since 1996. Annington Homes is a subsidiary of Terra Firma Capital Partners, a British private equity firm. It formed Deutsche Annington out of the combined portfolios of 11 out of 18 German *Eisenbahn-Wohnungs-baugesellschaften* (Railway Housing Companies) (65,000 units, acquired in 2001), the Heimbau publicly listed company (10,000 units, acquired in 2003), the RWE electric utilities company (4,500 units in 2004) and the Viterra publicly listed company (152,000 units in 2007). With over 230,000 units, it became the largest landlord of Germany.

As a result of the crisis, accessing external finance, crucial for the business models of private equity real estate firms, became so difficult that Deutsche Annington was in need of €4.7 billion to keep its business afloat. In July 2013, Terra Firma took the German branch of its subsidiary public, and by May 2014 it had sold off most of its shares. As a publicly listed company, it continued to acquire additional portfolios and entire companies. In March 2015, it acquired another large listed housing company, Gagfah, for €3.9 billion. The new company, named Vonovia, owned 370,000 housing units. Gagfah had started as the housing company of a pension fund, but was sold to Fortress Investment Group, a hedge fund based in New York, which continued to expand the portfolio though acquisitions of public housing companies, including all 47,600 units of the city of Dresden. In October 2015, Vonovia announced the takeover of Deutsche Wohnen, the company that had acquired GSW a few years earlier.

In both New York and Berlin the financial expectations of the private equity firms often did not materialize. Making money on subsidized rental housing turned out to be harder than expected. Some of these firms simply collapsed; others had to readjust their strategies: both rents and sales brought in less money than expected and buy- hold- and sell-plans had to be adjusted accordingly (see also Fields and Uffer, 2014). Tenants, especially in New York, often waited in limbo, sometimes living in dangerously unsafe conditions, without a landlord to approach (Fields, 2013). In Berlin, gentrification pressures resulted in the displacement of both the poor and immigrants (Uffer, 2014). Indeed, the financialization of these rental buildings by private equity firms was often a deception for both the financialized landlords and the financialized subjects. Poor maintenance remains an issue under Deutsche Wohnen and Vonovia (e.g. Kretz-Mangold, 2010); at least now tenants know where to complain, as these listed firms appear to be in it for the long run and, at least in Germany, they seem to have fully replaced private equity firms.

Social Housing Bonds and Derivatives in the UK and the Netherlands

The privatization of social housing (including council housing) in the UK and the Netherlands primarily took place through a transfer to homeownership. Since 1980 council housing tenants in the UK have had a "Right to Buy" their unit from their landlord, typically at a substantial discount. The Netherlands does not have a similar scheme; there housing associations were pushed by national and sometimes also local governments to sell units, either at market prices or at a small 10 per cent discount, both to their sitting tenants as well as to new owner-occupiers (e.g. Murie *et al.*, 2005). Both the British Right to Buy and the Dutch "Offer to Buy", however, do not directly result in the financialization of subsidized rental housing. Instead, housing is transferred to another tenure, which usually will require households to take out a mortgage loan, contributing to rising mortgage debt and the financialization of home ownership.

The housing associations that continued to manage the remaining social housing stock are, however, financializing because they increasingly rely on either bonds (UK) or derivatives (the Netherlands). In the UK, the shrinking of the market for mortgage-backed securities has resulted in a search for new HQC, with investors becoming interested in social housing bonds. This is not a new product (on offer since the late 1980s), but its popularity has grown substantially in recent years. The market was created by the state to replace government funding by private sector finance. During its first two decades the social housing bond market remained small as housing associations could easily get low-interest, long-term bank loans (Wainwright and Manville, 2016).

The global financial crisis hit British banks hard, and they retreated from granting large loans to housing associations. In addition, government funding cuts further increased the need for housing associations to find alternative sources of finance (Wainwright and Manville, 2016). Their funding needs were matched by the wall of money searching for new HQC. In recent years the market quickly expanded and internationalized, with investors not only from the UK, but also the US, Canada, Asia and elsewhere. Insurance companies, in particular, are fond of social housing bonds as these are rated as very low-risk, which is more important to these investors than the relatively low yields that these bonds generate. But as the market has expanded, demand expanded even further, as one financial services manager explained:

> When you reach £250 million of issuance on a bond, especially a rated listed bond, it goes on the index, and then its benchmark bond. And once it's on the index, then a number of other insurance companies have to buy it essentially, because they track these indices […] and you see Canadian pension funds coming in as well; they like the product; they understand property and the social consequences. […] This is actually a very attractive product as a Double A, Single A level, as most of these investors can't buy below investment rate.
>
> (Interviewee R21 in Wainwright and Manville, 2016)

Wainwright and Manville continue to argue that the reliance on the bond market impacted the housing policies of housing associations, especially larger ones and those based in London, where operational and development costs are higher. At every turn, the question being asked is: How does this affect our bonds? Even diversification strategies outside social housing are frowned upon "as this introduces more risk by moving away from stable revenues provided by social welfare spending, which is perceived to be low risk" (Wainwright and Manville, 2016).

Housing associations in the Netherlands found themselves in a similar squeeze to their UK counterparts.[4] Although a decade later than in the UK, Dutch housing associations were cut loose by the national and local governments. The *Waarborgfonds Sociale Woningbouw* (WSW), a Triple A-rated Social Housing Guarantee Fund, was created to guarantee loans for the development of new social housing, thereby enabling housing associations to borrow at favourable conditions. In the early 2000s, the WSW decided to also guarantee derivative contracts between housing associations and banks, and even started promoting them.

For banks, derivatives are interesting to sell because the fees are high and all risks are often transferred to counterparties or are covered by collateral. Thanks to the WSW, the banks are offered full security. Derivatives can be a useful instrument to decrease interest rate risks. In the words of a board member of a Dutch housing association, "Of course we have derivatives. Every large housing association has them, or at least, should have them" (Personal communication, 2011). Housing associations are, however, prohibited from speculating with derivatives, something that the sector's regulator appears unaware of, even after the 2001 debacle of housing association Woonzorg, which lost €33 million on complex financial products (Berentsen, 2014).

Vestia, a housing association active throughout the Netherlands but primarily in the Rotterdam-The Hague metropolitan area, originated in the public housing company GWB from The Hague, privatized into a non-profit housing association in 1992. In the following 20 years, CEO Erik Staal expanded GWB from a local public housing company with just over 20,000 units into the largest housing association of the Netherlands, managing 90,000 units. By the late 1990s, Vestia had also become a large property developer, investing €150–170 million annually. After Staal appointed Marcel de Vries as treasurer in 2002, Vestia effectively became a derivatives-trading house. In his first years as treasurer, De Vries bought derivatives contracts from ABN Amro and Fortis to mitigate the interest risks related to Vestia's many real estate development projects. In 2005 Deutsche Bank and other foreign banks started selling more complex products to Vestia. Meanwhile, De Vries, believing that the current interest rate was so low that it could only go up, started to trade in other, more complex and more speculative derivatives.[5] Many of these contracts did temporarily lower Vestia's interest rates, but carried the risk of considerably higher costs if interest rates would increase (Smit, 2014).

The first cracks appeared in late 2008 when, as a result of a sudden decrease in the interest rate, the negative value of Vestia's derivatives portfolio jumped to €762 million. However, as Vestia had a buffer of €1 billion in liquid capital, it was able to answer the bank's margin calls to provide more collateral. Dutch banks, which had only sold it non-speculative derivative contracts, discovered that Vestia had also bought very risky derivatives from foreign banks, and stopped selling derivatives to Vestia in 2009. In the summer of 2011 interest rates fell rapidly, thereby increasing the negative market value of the derivatives portfolio leading to margin calls that quickly amounted to €1 billion in September 2011. The national government hired financial consultancy firm Cardano to make sense of Vestia's more than 400 derivative contracts with 13 banks. Cardano concluded that Vestia's portfolio was extremely sensitive to interest rate changes; it carried 70 per cent speculative derivatives and lacked proper risk management.

Meanwhile, De Vries expanded the portfolio further to €23.6 billion. He believed that rates were certain to rise in the future, which would compensate for the negative market value of the derivatives portfolio at the time. In November 2011 Vestia was put under guardianship. The two new CEOs decided to restructure €1.7 billion of complex derivatives into normal loans with a fixed interest rate, taking a loss of €700 million. To force the banks into negotiation, the WSW executed its first right to collateral. This came as a big surprise to the banks, and the CEO of ABN Amro, a state-owned bank since the crisis of 2008, threatened to stop financing *all* housing associations. After a couple of months of tough negotiations, all banks except Credit Suisse agreed to a solution in which the remaining derivatives, valued at €1.9 billion, were transformed into regular loans, roughly a third of it to be paid by all other Dutch housing associations through a remediation support fund.

To repay its debts, Vestia initially sold off many development projects to municipalities or other housing associations (Verbraeken, 2015). In 2014, Vestia presented its restructuring strategy for 2014–2021: lowering operating expenses (including staff costs) by 15 per cent, selling 32,000 of its 90,000 housing units, and maximizing rents on social and commercial units after vacancies. By February 2015 Vestia had already sold 5,500 units to Patrizia, a publicly listed German real estate investor, for €577 million, and 6,000 student rooms to another housing association, Woonstad. Since Vestia is the largest landlord in the Rotterdam-The Hague metropolitan region, this will have a considerable impact on the regional housing market. In addition, the social housing sector's regulator has labelled Vestia as insolvent, making it extremely difficult for the association to secure credit for new projects.

The case of Vestia highlights the inherent problems with self-regulation, the excessive freedom of housing association CEOs, and the far-reaching impacts of mismanagement and financial losses. The regulator first reported that Vestia was part of a small group of approximately 20 housing associations that had entered into derivatives contracts, but it soon had to publish a much higher figure of 162 out of 380 housing associations, representing a nominal value of €17.9 billion (not including Vestia) by the end of 2011. The regulator also came to the conclusion that many housing associations did not have adequate knowledge to enter into many of the derivatives contracts on their books and that the derivatives portfolios of eight other associations were problematic (CFV, 2012).

Not only in the Netherlands but also in the UK, some housing associations have nearly collapsed. In 2013, for example, the Cosmopolitan Housing Association had to be rescued by the Sanctuary Housing Group after Cosmopolitan was overextended in the bond market and plagued by accounting errors (Altair, 2014). But not only outright failures like Vestia and Cosmopolitan have affected the social housing sector. Housing associations' reliance on bonds and derivatives is part of a larger shift, moving further away from the state, step-by-step, to the point when they no longer function as an extension of the state. As the ties between housing associations and the state were loosened in a process of regulated deregulation, it became easier for housing associations to explore tempting unconventional financial instruments, thereby potentially jeopardizing their public mission.

Conclusion

In the introduction of this chapter I wrote that financialization is made possible through a combination of economic circumstances, conscience government decisions, unforeseen consequences of government decisions, and financial-technical possibilities. Governments in the US, Germany, the UK and the Netherlands all took steps towards "deregulating" their subsidized rental housing stocks through new regulation. New York City required only modest intervention; Rent-stabilized housing was already largely owned by for-profit landlords, many trying to minimize or end rent stabilization for decades. NYC landlords, those from other cities that participated in the programme, and the real estate industry as a whole are intensively lobbying New York State to end rent stabilization and allow landlords to demand market rents.

Over the years, rent stabilization has been curtailed (DeFilippis and Wyly, 2008) but some of its fundamentals have remained, largely due to the continued efforts of an alternative lobby movement that continues to laud the benefits of a rent-stabilized housing stock. Indeed, recent Rent Acts (2011 and 2015) include some improvements for tenants that make it harder to "deregulate" a unit, and limit rent increases. Since no new units are being added to this stock, and more and more landlords find ways to skirt existing regulations, rent stabilization now applies to fewer units than one or two decades ago. Combined with the pressure on the NYC housing market the very reason for the existence of rent stabilization in the first place!) this makes it harder to keep housing outside the fully "free" market. In NYC very little re-engineering by the state was necessary to enable private equity firms to buy up large numbers of rent-stabilized buildings.

The situation is quite different in the other three cases. In all three, privatization was a conscious policy choice. Budgetary arguments played a part, especially in the Berlin case with its crushing €50 billion state debt (Vesper, 2003). The local budget crisis resulted in a political decision to mobilize and activate municipal assets. In 2000 the Berlin State Parliament approved the sale of no less than 50,000 housing units. This was one of the last political decisions of the "black-red big coalition" of the Christian Democratic Party (CDU) and the Social Democratic Party (SPD). However, the left-wing "red-red" coalition, formed by the SPD and the Party of Democratic Socialism (PDS), which took office in 2001, kept on the same course, implementing the resolution and selling the public housing company GSW in 2004. Yet, the housing privatization had only a very small effect on the budget. The 212,000 housing units brought in only €4 billion in Berlin's coffers (at an average price of less than €20,000 per unit). A close look at the legislative directives for privatization of public housing enterprises reveals the key role of sub-national governments. In Berlin, more than 85 per cent of all housing privatizations have their roots at the local and only 14 per cent at the national policy level (Aalbers and Holm, 2008).

In the UK, the privatization of the council housing sector goes back to the Thatcher years, during which the budgets for council housing were deliberately cut and social landlords forced into accepting a Right to Buy from their tenants. The wholesale privatization of British social housing was the intended goal; the rise of housing associations was not. The British housing associations are a typical response to the political marginalization of council housing and the normalization of private housing. The idea of housing associations enabled the British government, on the one hand, to continue their privatization efforts and, on the other, to safeguard the continued existence of some social rental housing— a typical Third Way "solution".

In the Netherlands, privatization was, at least in part, presented as a financial-technological fix to a budgetary problem. Through a so-called deleveraging operation, the future operating subsidies that the housing associations were entitled to based on earlier agreements (€15.9 billion) were cancelled out against government loans (€18.6 billion) in 1995, cleaning up the balance sheet of the Dutch state, thereby making it a little easier to fulfil the entry criteria of the European Monetary Union (EMU). The bigger story was a massive privatization of public and semi-public institutions throughout the 1980s and 1990s. Social housing was not the first and would not be the last sector earmarked for "independence", a euphemism for privatization. Other sectors where privatization provided no financial-technological advantages under EMU entry rules, suffered the same fate. For each of these sectors, the government has since produced a continuous stream of regulatory documents, both to enable the market and mitigate negative consequences. Advancing insights as well as trouble and outright fraud have also contributed to the regulatory explosion.

In these three cases government directives enabled not only privatization but also financialization. Unlike in the UK, the resulting financialization through derivatives was largely unforeseen in the Netherlands. In Germany the state actors responsible for the sale of social housing units and entire housing companies knew that they were selling to private equity and listed firms. Since these firms were able to pay the highest price, this was considered the best outcome for the local treasury. Markets were not privatized with the idea of financializing them. The privatization had ideological as well as budgetary roots, while the financialization happened almost by chance. The regulated deregulation of social housing not only enabled financialization, but in some ways also pushed social landlords towards bonds and derivatives, whether for budgetary or speculative reasons.

Popular historians and journalists often prefer a "great men" version of history (or, in the case of the UK, perhaps an "Iron Lady" version). Social scientists and most academic historians typically prefer to look at the deeper roots, motivations, institutions and mechanisms underlying change. This book follows the latter approach, but it also argues that powerful persons often play pivotal roles. The derivatives heist at Vestia took place in a setting in which CEO Staal and treasurer De Vries could act almost autonomously. Vestia's supervisory board was made up mostly of friends of Staal, while national supervisors and regulation were ignored, and accounting firms neglected the many shortcomings in the annual reports. Other housing associations were in the same position, but none of their CEOs was as brash as Staal, who is quoted as saying "My supervisory board has only one task: it appoints and dismisses me. Otherwise, I decide myself" (Verbraeken, 2014) and "Finance is our core business. [...] We know the financial markets, minute by minute" (in: Cobouw, 2011). Even though Staal and De Vries clearly did not understand financial products and the devastating impact they would have on their organization, they still steadfastly pursued this course.

Many social scientists use the word deregulation to refer to liberalization and the freeing up of markets. I suggest we need to break out of the framing of the deregulationist perspective and its ambiguities by systematically referring to the increasing regulation of markets to facilitate one set of agents over other sets of agents by the label "regulated deregulation" (Aalbers, 2016). This will minimize the chance that the label deregulation is misunderstood as freeing up markets from government regulation. I hope the relabeling will also facilitate a more widespread understanding of actually existing regulation as increasingly dense, specialized and juridical and therefore less accessible. Regulation is increasingly facilitating the rise of one set of market agents over others, typically but not necessarily aiding big, powerful corporations at the expense of less powerful small enterprises and the population at large.

In recent decades, with the financialized privatization of semi-public institutions, these "private organizations with public goals" became entangled in a web of debt and derivatives. Whereas many semi-public institutions moved into the world of finance due to financial constraints, Dutch housing associations moved in to capitalize on the possibilities offered by their asset-rich portfolios. Yet, the introduction of external financial templates and managerial practices into the public institutions demands a transformation of the organization and a redesign of the institutional setting. Financialization is a dynamic and interactive process that continuously reshapes the market. The state actively promoted this competitive attitude and the associated movement away from the public sector and into financial markets (Aalbers *et al.*, forthcoming). The financialization of formerly semi-public organizations did not reduce the state's involvement but rather expanded its "role of 'risk absorber' for the private market sector rather than for the citizenry" (Christopherson *et al.*, 2013: 352).

Notes

1   This section is an abridged version of Aalbers (2016).
2   See the map at www.benteresa.org/#!research/c17b1.
3   See: www.auraree.com/real-estate-news/haya-real-estate-takes-lead-reo-asset-management-spain/.
4   The next eight paragraphs are adapted from Aalbers *et al.* (forthcoming).
5   Including speculative interest swaps, writing swaptions, and cancellable swaps.

References

Aalbers, M.B. (Ed.) (2012) *Subprime Cities: The Political Economy of Mortgage Markets.* Oxford: Wiley-Blackwell.

Aalbers, M.B. (2016) Regulated Deregulation. In: S. Springer, K. Birch and J. MacLeavy (Eds) *Handbook of Neoliberalism.* London: Routledge.

Aalbers, M.B. and Holm, A. (2008) Privatising Social Housing in Europe: The Cases of Amsterdam and Berlin. In: K. Adelhof, B, Glock, J. Lossau and M. Schulz (Eds) *Urban Trends in Berlin and Amsterdam*, pp. 12–23. Berlin: Berliner Geographische Arbeiten, Humboldt Universität zu Berlin.

Aalbers, M.B., Van Loon J. and Fernandez, R. (forthcoming) The Financialization of a Social Housing Provider. *International Journal of Urban and Regional Research* 40.

Altair (2014) *Cosmopolitan Housing Group Lessons Learned.* London: Altair.

Berentsen, L. (2014) Even vergeten dat derivaten al heel lang taboe waren; Woningcorporaties trokken zich niets aan van circulaires. *Financieel Dagblad*, July 10.

Blyth, M. (2008) The Politics of Compounding Bubbles: The Global Housing Bubble in Comparative perspective. *Comparative European Politics* 6: 387–406.

Boelhouwer, P. and Priemus, H. (2014) Demise of the Dutch Social Housing Tradition: Impact of Budget Cuts and Political Changes. *Journal of Housing and the Built Environment* 29: 221–235.

Braithwaite, J. (2005) Neoliberalism or Regulatory Capitalism. *RegNet Occasional Paper No. 5.* URL http://ssrn.com/abstract=875789.

CFV (2012) *Renterisico's beheerst of financiële risico's vergroot? Derivaten bij woning-corporaties.* Baarn: Centraal Fonds Volkshuisvesting.

Christopherson, S., Martin, R. and Pollard, J. (2013) Financialisation: Roots and Repercussions. *Cambridge Journal of Regions, Economy and Society* 6: 351–357.

Cobouw (2011) Financiën is onze corebusiness. URL www.cobouw.nl/nieuws/economie/2011/05/18/financien-is-onze-corebusiness.

DeFilippis, J. and Wyly, E. (2008) Running to Stand still: Through the Looking Glass with Federally Subsidized Housing in New York City. *Urban Affairs Review* 43(6): 777–816.

Fields, D.J. (2013) *From Property Abandonment to Predatory Equity: Writings on Financialization and Urban Space in New York City.* PhD Dissertation. New York: The City University of New York.

Fields, D. (2015) Contesting the Financialization of Urban Space: Community Organizations and the Struggle to Preserve Affordable Rental Housing in New York City. *Journal of Urban Affairs* 37(2): 144–165.

Fields, D. and Uffer, S. (2014) The Financialization of Rental Housing: A Comparative Analysis of New York City and Berlin. *Urban Studies.* doi:10.1177/0042098014543704

Gotham, K.F. (2006) The Secondary Circuit of Capital Reconsidered: Globalization and the U.S. Real Estate Sector. *American Journal of Sociology* 112(1): 231–275.

Gotham, K.F. (2009) Creating Liquidity out of Spatial Fixity: The Secondary Circuit of Capital and the Subprime Mortgage Crisis. *International Journal of Urban and Regional Research* 33(2): 355–371.

Jessop, B. (2002) Liberalism, Neoliberalism and Urban Governance: A State-Theoretical Perspective. *Antipode* 34: 452–472.

Jessop, B. (2003) From Thatcherism to New Labour: Neo-Liberalism, Workfarism, and Labour Market Regulation. In: H. Overbeek (Ed.) *The Political Economy of European Employment: European Integration and the Transnationalization of the (Un)employment Question*, pp. 137–53. London: Routledge.

Jessop, B., and Sum, N.-L. (2006) *Beyond the Regulation Approach: Putting Capitalist Economies in Their Place.* Cheltenham: Edward Elgar.

Levi-Faur, D. (2005) The Global Diffusion of Regulatory Capitalism. *The Annals of the American Academy of Political and Social Sciences* 598(1): 12–32.

Kofner, S. (2012) *Aktuelle Geschäftsmodelle von Finanzinvestoren auf den Wohnungsmärkten in NRW. Gutachten im Auftrag der Enquetekommission Wohnungswirtschaftlicher Wandel und Neue Finanzinvestoren auf den Wohnungsmärkten in NRW.* Düsseldorf: Nordrhein Westfalen.

Kretz-Mangold, M. (2010) *Der NRW-Wohnungsmarkt nach der Privatisierungswelle. Zur Miete bei "Heuschrecken" Von Marion Kretz-Mangold.* Hamburg: Norddeutsche Rundfunk.

Murie, A., Tosics, I., Aalbers, M.B., and Sendi, R. and (2005) Privatisation and After. In: R. van Kempen, K. Dekker, S. Hall and I. Tosics (Eds) *Restructuring Large Housing Estates in Europe*, pp. 85–103. Bristol: Policy Press.

Smit, J. (2014) *Het Derivatendrama.* Amsterdam: Balans.

Spotton, B. (1999) Regulation and Deregulation: Financial. In: P.A. O'Hara (ed.) *Encyclopedia of Political Economy*, pp. 971–974. London: Routledge.

Teresa, B. (2015) Managing Fictitious Capital: The Legal Geography of Investment and Political Struggle in Rental Housing in New York City. *Environment and Planning A.* doi: 10.1177/0308518X15598322.

Uffer, S. (2014) Wohnungsprivatisierung in Berlin. Eine Analyse verschiedener

Investitionsstrategien und deren Konsequenzen für die Stadt und ihre Bewohner. In Holm, A. (ed.) *Reclaim Berlin: Soziale Kämpfe in der neoliberalen Stadt*, pp. 64–82. Berlin: Assoziation A.

Verbraeken, H. (2014) Oprecht gepassioneerd, maar ook ongeremd megalomaan. *Financieel Dagblad*, September 6.

Verbraeken, H. (2015) *De vrije val van Vestia.* Amsterdam: Business Contact.

Vesper, D. (2003) Berliner Haushalt: Trotz Sparkurs hohe Sanierungshilfen des Bundes erforderlich. *DIW Wochenbericht* 70(23): 363–374.

Vogel, S.K. (1996) *Freer Markets, More Rules: Regulatory Reform in Advanced Industrial Countries.* Ithaca, NY: Cornell University Press.

Wainwright, T. (2009) Laying the Foundations for a Crisis: Mapping the Historico-geographical Construction of RMBS Securitization in the UK. *International Journal of Urban and Regional Research* 33(2): 372–88.

Wainwright, T. and Manville, G. (2016) Financialization and the Third Sector: Innovation in Social Housing Bond Markets. Working paper (available from the authors).

Wyly, E., Newman, K., Schafran, A. and Lee, E. (2010) Displacing New York. *Environment and Planning A* 42(11): 2602–2623.

8 Conclusion

The Twenty-First-Century Housing Question

> There are, no doubt, few markets that are not only so controlled as the housing market is by the state, but indeed so *truly constructed by the state*, particularly through the financial assistance given to private individuals [...] favouring particular social categories and, consequently, particular fractions of builders to differing degrees.
>
> (Bourdieu, [1990] 2005: 89–90, emphasis in original)

Summary on the Argument

A global wall of money is looking for High-Quality Collateral (HQC) investments, and housing is one of the few asset classes considered HQC. This explains why housing is increasingly becoming financialized, but it does not explain the timing, politics and geography. The need for HQC, supported by a neoliberal ideology, discursive tenure practices that favour homeownership, and government policies pushing the financial sector as a key engine of economic growth, have internationally—but far from globally—inflated mortgage finance bubbles.

This is visible in countries like the US and the UK where mortgaged homeownership was financialized relatively early on. Especially in the US, the fate of homeowners was tied to the tidal waves of finance through securitization, with demand for mortgage-backed securities so high that it fed the subprime and predatory mortgage market. Loans that were designed to strip wealth from already poor communities were reinvented to bankroll middle-class Americans. The result was the mass foreclosure of the country, not only hitting the run-down districts of Rustbelt cities like Detroit, Michigan and Cleveland, Ohio but also entire "suburban cities"[1] like Stockton, California and Lehigh Acres, Florida, where house prices dropped two-thirds between 2006 and 2008.

The situation does not look as dramatic in the Netherlands and Denmark where house prices have dropped but, compared to the US, very few people lost their homes. Yet, the Dutch and the Danes have the highest mortgage debt in the world, far higher than in countries hit hard by the housing crisis like the US and Spain. Denmark relies heavily on relatively safe mortgage bonds to finance homeownership, while the Netherlands embraces the riskier mortgage-backed securities.

Both countries, comparatively speaking, have a strong welfare state that traditionally includes people in a formal, non-casualized labour market, limits the risk of unemployment, ensures a decent income when unemployed (especially in the first years), and thereby limits the risk of default and foreclosure as well as their consequences. But as welfare is being restructured and homeownership rapidly expanded to lower income groups, the risks of mortgaged ownership increase while the welfare protection net shrinks.

Spain, a country with a relatively stable and high homeownership rate, moved so rapidly from a country with few and typically small mortgages into one fuelled by mortgage finance, that it was hard to imagine a soft landing. Coupled with a building fever—adding more new houses to the stock than France, Germany, Italy and the UK combined—it was a recipe for disaster. House prices, mortgage debt and housing construction increased much slower in Italy, but they did all increase, and not at a particular slow pace. Yet, Italy's development looks modest compared to the other case countries discussed in Chapter 6.

Germany, by contrast, did not open the floodgates to the wall of money blowing mortgage bubbles. But the wall of money did enter Germany as the country allowed its subsidized rental stock to be financialized at an unmatched scale. First thousands, then tens of thousands, and now hundreds of thousands of social housing and other non-commodified rental houses are being snapped up, chiefly by American and British private equity firms; and then, a few years later, taken on by real estate companies listed on the stock exchange. Similar things are happening in the US and Spain (on a substantial scale), but also in the UK, the Netherlands and elsewhere (so far, at a more limited scale). Furthermore, the UK and the Netherlands are also undergoing a secondary financialization, in which non-profit housing associations partake in bond and derivatives markets, resulting in near bankruptcy at worst and a financialized housing management mindset at best.

The state is far from absent in the process of creating variegated patterns of housing financialization: it is directly implicated in each step that the wall of money takes towards securing HQC in local and national housing market sectors. The state actively—but not always consciously—creates the conditions for the financialization of housing and other assets, sectors and markets, often through a process I have called "regulated deregulation" (Aalbers, 2016). The term indicates that the state is not withdrawing but rather being restructured (increasingly also through finance) in a way that favours the interest of some, often financialized corporations, and at the expense of others. Regulation is not being repealed to make the market mechanism function more smoothly; it is introduced to create new markets that end up looking nothing like the level playing field utopias espoused by neoliberal economists, think tanks, lobbyists and politicians. Of course the state could do other things, and luckily some arms of the state continue to, or start to, do other things—a theme we will revisit in the second half of this chapter.

Colin Crouch describes the situation that governments have created as "privatized Keynesianism", which occurred initially by chance, but gradually became a crucial matter for public policy. Instead of governments taking on debt to stimulate the economy, individuals and families did so, including some rather poor ones. [...] Once privatized Keynesianism had become a model of general economic importance, it became a kind of bizarre collective good, however nested in private actions it was. [...] that very irresponsibility became a collective good.

(Crouch, 2011: 114)

In this book I analysed how privatized Keynesianism was introduced in the years following the Great Moderation, a period that economists think of as one of stable growth and convergence, but which, in fact, was the beginning of the Great Excess, in which income and wealth inequality in many countries increased rapidly (Piketty, 2014). The lack of real income growth was matched with a rapid rise in household debt, and in particular, mortgage debt for the middle and to some extent lower classes.

Privatized Keynesianism, the Great Moderation, neoliberalization and financialization have transformed the nature of homeownership and rental housing, and in turn also the social relations of housing. We arrive here at a fundamental point of contention between Marxist and Weberian housing scholars. As covered in Chapter 2, Marxists maintained that one's position in the housing market is a result of one's position in the labour market, namely social class determines housing position; while Weberians argued that one's position in the housing market determines social class. Kemeny (1992), for example, argued that housing forms the basis for a new explanation of social inequality.

Recent research has generally confirmed the basic tenets of the Weberian view: housing policies and practices have changed attitudes towards homeownership and rental housing, and have transformed social relations (Doling and Ford, 2003; Fields, 2013; Forrest and Yip, 2011; Smith, 2008):

Ironically, home ownership may have become less stable and more risky due to the same changes in welfare and employment which have destabilized the income basis of mortgage repayment. A significant outcome is the re-situating of housing in life-plans and economic strategies.

(Ronald, 2008: 99)

The presumed benefits of homeownership relate to an idea and a time when homes were owned outright or through a combination of significant down payments and smaller mortgage loans with moderate loan-to-value (LTV) and loan-to-income (LTI) ratios. As Bourdieu already remarked in 1990, mortgaged homeownership functions as a trap: "it tends gradually to become the exclusive focus of all investment: those involved in the—material and psychological—work required to come to terms with its reality, which is often so far removed from anticipations" (Bourdieu, [1990] 2005: 189).

The financial crisis and its aftermath have challenged the security of both homeownership (King, 2010) and subsidized rental housing. "Neoliberalism thus undermined the integrative and stabilising dimensions of home ownership" (Forrest and Hirayama, 2015: 241) and social housing. What is known in the policy and academic literature as "asset-based welfare" is a very thinly disguised neoliberal and financialized discourse that is mobilized to break down welfare and replace it by housing wealth. Instead, it should be labelled "asset-based wealth", a fictional construct to be further explored in this chapter. Betting on housing wealth is also a very risky option as the benefits of homeownership are extremely skewed in terms of location, class, gender, generation and ethnicity (Oliver and Shapiro, 2006; Smith *et al.*, 2008). Moreover, putting all one's eggs in one basket—housing investment tends to crowd out other investments, as Bourdieu observed—is the opposite of spreading risk by spreading investments over different assets, markets and locations.

When asked the popular survey question "Do you live to work or work to live", most Americans pick the first and most Europeans the second option (Hofstede, 1984). In fact, both Americans and Europeans increasingly work to pay off their mortgage debt. To Lazzarato, debt has become the fundamental social relation in contemporary, neoliberal societies. The debtor-creditor relationship "intensifies mechanisms of exploitation and domination" (Lazzarato, 2011: 7), and here finance acts as the key enabler of "predatory formations", resulting in displacement, exclusion and expulsions (Sassen, 2014). Indeed, housing markets in general, and financialized housing markets in particular, facilitate secondary exploitation, "which runs parallel to the primary exploitation taking place in the production process itself" (Marx, [1894] 1990: 350; see also Soederberg, 2014). Marx specifically refers to forms of lending and usury that do not contribute to production but exploit modes of production, suggesting that Marx was more open to the Weberian critique than those who purport to speak on his behalf.

Labour, Housing and Construction

If the problem is the financialization of housing, the solution appears easy: the de-financialization of housing. But the problem is actually much bigger: the financialization of housing does not take place in isolation but is tied to a range of other problems related to housing, finance and states that also need to be addressed. Already in the nineteenth century, Friedrich Engels (1887) discussed *the Housing Question*, but, as noted in Chapter 2, his perspective on housing was deeply ambivalent. He recognized its social and political importance but resisted making it a core concern of radical political-economic theory. To Engels, as to many Marxists since, the Housing Question remains something of secondary importance. In the final instance, there was no housing question for Engels: solving the Labour Question automatically resolved the Housing Question. The exploitation in the housing market is *always* secondary to exploitation in the labour market. But is this really the case? Can the Housing Question be completely reduced to being a function of the Labour Question?

Labour movements have had some marked success in improving working conditions, but much remains to be done to truly "solve" the Labour Question. On the contrary, decades of implemented neoliberalism have marginalized many labour rights, exemplified by the increasing numbers of people not covered by collective labour agreements and the "state of exception" (Agamben, 2005) consciously created for them. In places where many labour movements were successful in protecting some or most (depending on the national and economic-sector context) of the acquired labour rights, the number of workers covered by such agreements has been dwindling.

What many labour movements have failed to understand—or failed to address—is that any monetary gains in the labour market are quickly snapped up in the housing market. Earning more does not simply imply that one can afford bigger or better housing, but may also imply that labourers, as a collective although not acting as such, drive house prices up. In a situation where you increase your income but everyone else's stays the same, you can afford a bigger or better house, but in a situation where a large number of households has higher wages, it all too often leads to these households bidding up housing prices, both owner-occupied or rented. In the end, few are better off and those whose wage starting position was similar will eventually lose out as their stagnant income can no longer afford the higher rents and house prices.

In mainstream economic theory, supply will go up as demands goes up. If only economic reality were as simple! If the demand for housing quality goes up, that does not imply that the supply of housing increased. Regarding housing, wage increases usually translate into the quest for a better housing position: a better-equipped residence, a larger house or a better location. But why would housing producers offer higher-quality housing if the existing lower-quality housing (again, in terms of amenities, size or location) sells or rents out just fine? Housing producers, as a collective but again not necessarily acting as one, have no pre-defined interest in providing higher-quality housing. Of course, these producers will compete with each other, but typically in an understanding that if the market thrives, all participating actors can thrive (Fligstein, 2001). It is much cheaper to make small investments and profit on them, than to make large investments and profit.

Most construction firms and real estate developers constantly look for new projects or new building sites to expand their market, but only to the extent that the additional supply of housing will not depress house prices. This is not in the interest of housing producers. These companies will often advocate new construction because it creates jobs, but also because construction can keep house-price inflation down. It is the second reason that is problematic here. In theory—well, in mainstream economic theory, that is, but this is what the media constantly reproduce as "obvious truths"—more supply should result in lower prices. Or, in the case of higher demand, higher supply should keep prices stable.

Is this what happens? Sometimes it does. There are cities and regions where house prices are relatively stable over several decades, but these are the exception. In many—I'm inclined to say in the majority of—cases house prices tend to go up in the long run *regardless* of what happens. In some places rapidly increasing house prices are blamed on the lack of new construction, which gives housing producers some political fire in their quest to expand. In other places new construction outpaces real, quantitative demand and house prices still go up year after year. What happened there?

The General Mechanism and the Specific Conditions

Now that you have hopefully read most of this book, the answer should be clear: housing was financialized. House prices did not skyrocket because demand increased faster than supply (although this can be a contributing factor) but because the supply of money directed towards housing went up, irrespective of the demand for either housing or money. Economists like to say that supply creates its own demand, and they might be correct in this case. The supply of money, namely the wall of money, creates the demand for... well, money. If the price of money, namely the interest rate, is low enough, it will be used either to construct, develop, buy-up, rent out, sell or buy housing. This is the *general mechanism*. The exact workings will depend on many factors, which can be summarized as the structure of the market as a field.

The financialization of housing is the general mechanism that operates under financialized capitalism. My critics will say that a general mechanism cannot explain *anything* but they are wrong: a general mechanism cannot explain *everything*. The general mechanism tells us very little if anything about the *specific conditions and mechanisms* at work in different housing markets and sub-markets. It doesn't tell us anything about specific actors or the structure of the field. But that is fine; we do not need to employ general mechanisms to explain specific situations. We do, however, need the general mechanism to make sense of the remarkable congruence of actually-existing housing situations around the globe, namely in different countries, different local and regional housing markets and different tenure sub-markets.

The question is not *whether* your housing market will be financialized if the wall of money arrives, but rather *how* and *where* it will be financialized when the wall of money starts pushing into your housing market. That does not imply that all housing markets will be financialized all the time. It implies that under conditions of financialized capitalism, those housing segments and sub-markets will financialize that are *able* to financialize, or that are *enabled,* namely made, to financialize. Financialization is not a natural phenomenon and is strongly influenced by context drivers. There are not only geographies of financialization but also politics of financialization. For example, as I have argued in Chapters 3 and 7, mortgage securitization is neither a given nor natural; rather it is enabled by the actions of both public and private actors. Private actors, such as lenders interested in securitizing their loans from investment banks interested in the fees they can charge for handling securitization operations, may lobby actors within the state to adopt regulation, namely to enable mortgage securitization through the expansion of financial regulation.

We have seen that even in a context where the owner-occupied housing market is hardly financialized, the rental housing markets (plural, potentially both private and social) may be pressured to financialize selectively (rather than totally). In Germany, the long-term stability of house prices is quite remarkable, but different segments of the rental housing market did financialize rapidly. This makes Germany exceptional and generic at the same time. In terms of the general mechanism, the German case appears quite generic (i.e., some but not all housing is being financialized), but in terms of the specific conditions and mechanisms, the German case appears exceptional (although not unique). Whereas an analysis of the German mortgage and owner-occupied markets might conclude that the German housing market is not financialized, those analysing the social and private rental markets would come to very different conclusions. It would be incorrect to conclude that Germany is not financializing because it is not financializing like the US or the UK.

Financialization, like the progress of capitalism itself or like neoliberalization, is a fundamentally uneven development that, by definition, will not happen in the same way everywhere. The fact that things happen in different ways in different countries (or within different countries for that matter) does not "prove" that the general mechanism is not at work here. Rather, it demonstrates how the general mechanism operates *despite* fundamental and on-going differences. The plurality of different forms of capitalism implies the plurality of different forms of financialization of housing markets. Some academics, however, are so obsessed with difference that they fail to see the "common trajectories" (Hay, 2004). If we take the argument of the uneven development of capitalism, and by extension of neoliberalization and financialization seriously, it could not be any other way.

Creating and Realizing Housing Wealth

Let us return to the discussion on the housing producers. I have argued that they will advocate for new construction because it will create jobs and because higher supply will make or keep housing affordable. At the same time, producers have an interest in keeping prices up or to raise prices further. Here, housing producers rely on the argument that a house is typically the biggest commodity a household will own and that housing wealth needs to be secured and, if possible, expanded. Thus, housing producers, as well as many politicians and the media, rely on two contradictory arguments. One the one hand, they advocate or push policies that are supposed to curb house-price inflation or even result in more affordable housing, while on the other hand, advocating or pushing policies that are supposed to increase housing wealth and in effect stimulate house-price inflation (resulting in less affordable housing).

The question is: How do higher house prices create housing wealth and for whom? The last part of the question is easy: higher house prices primarily create housing wealth for those who already own a house. And since rental prices are, at least in part, related to house prices, this also benefits those landlords that are legally able to increase rents. Of course this also implies that those who do not own a house and those who are faced with increasing rents are the losers in the housing game. Even if their income goes up, they may not be able to buy a house. And in many housing markets the common knowledge is that the longer you wait, the more expensive houses will become. Households are then faced with at least three choices: a) continue to rent; b) save for a larger down-payment in the future; c) try to get a foot in the door and buy a house (or a less attractive flat), in order to gain from future house-price inflation and then trade up.

Trading up or saving up both sound like viable solutions, but if house prices keep increasing one may not be able to trade up or use one's savings as a sufficient down-payment to acquire the house one wants. A simple example helps illustrate this situation. A couple wants to buy a house for $400,000, but as the house is currently too expensive for them, they decide to get a foot in the door and take out a high LTV mortgage to buy a small $200,000 flat in a less attractive neighbourhood (perhaps also delaying plans to have children).

Their plan appears to work. House prices go up by 50 per cent in the next five years, and the couple wants to sell their flat for $300,000—indeed, this couple has created $100,000 in housing wealth—and they are now ready to use their housing wealth to buy a more expensive house. The only problem is that the price of the house they want to buy has also increased by 50 per cent and is now on the market for $600,000. Even with the $100,000 that this couple has created by buying and selling a flat, they still cannot afford to take out a $500,000 mortgage (and it is a big question whether any lender would even approve such a large loan).

Did higher house prices really create housing wealth in this case? On paper this couple became rich simply by owning a flat for a couple of years. In other words, they appear to have made a great investment: 50 per cent in five years represents a return on investment that is hard to beat in most other markets. But what use is housing wealth to this couple? To buy the house they want, they would need to use all the housing wealth they have created and then they would still fall short of being able to acquire it. They can keep on living in their flat, enjoying the idea that they have created a $100,000 in housing wealth and may be able to create more by staying in their flat in a part of the city they do not like too much and in a flat that they consider too small for a family. (Besides, the schools in the area are not very good, so it would be better to move to another neighbourhood before the children reach school age.)

In some countries, they may be able to take out a home equity loan and use some of their housing wealth to improve the flat, buy some nice consumer goods and go on a trip around the world. This is all great of course but they still need to pay interest on that loan, so their housing wealth only buys them access to affordable credit. That can be a great thing if you need it, as people who have been able to take out a home equity loan to pay for medical expenses have realized, but it creates very little real wealth.

The wealth becomes liquid only when the couple sells the flat, but since their only reason to sell the flat would be to trade up in the market, the housing wealth they have accumulated would again vanish, that is it ends up in the pockets of someone else. So, perhaps someone else is realizing housing wealth. The people who sell the house must be creating wealth. But in most cases people sell a house to trade up, to move to a bigger, better-equipped or better-located house. There are some exceptions, however. Some people may want to scale down and they may be able to use the housing wealth they have created, to buy a smaller house or flat outright, namely without taking out a loan. In some cases there is no other option as older households may find it difficult to obtain a mortgage.

Another exception occurs when someone dies, and their relatives sell the house and divide the housing wealth among each other. This could be a real boost, as it may enable the couple in our example to finally acquire that $600,000 house they have wanted for so long. Most likely, however, children inherit their parents' wealth when they are themselves already in a phase of their lives when their household size is shrinking. This may benefit the grandchildren: they may receive some cash to make a down-payment on a flat or a house. The paradox is that the children *need* help from their parents because house-price inflation has structurally outpaced wage inflation; and the primary reason why the parents are able to help out is because they have created housing wealth as a result of house-price inflation.

This is definitely "pumping money around". This is the multigenerational pumping around of money realized in housing and being used to acquire housing. This is the scenario where parents have built up housing wealth and are willing and able to share some of it. The situation would be different if parents or grandparents did not have good relationships with their children and grand-children, or if they owned or did not own a house, or if they own or owned a house in a housing market where house prices did not go up or even went down. The last example does not sound too problematic as that would imply that the (grand-)children could also acquire a more affordable flat or house. Yes, they could if they wanted to buy in the same housing market but chances are that house prices stayed stable or decreased because there are not many (good) jobs in the local area and the (grand-)children would feel forced to move to a different area where there are more (good) jobs and housing tends to be more expensive. Family, class and geography all matter and interact in unique ways, resulting in a concentration of most of the housing wealth in the hands of select set of families and the exclusion of many other families from the opportunity not simply to create housing wealth on paper but to realize *real* housing wealth.

The funny thing is of course that the narrative here is that people have *created* housing wealth as if they have worked to realize an increase in housing wealth of, in our example, $100,000. It is not the couple or the market that has created housing wealth, but the conditions, mechanisms and structures of the field have created the myth of the creation of housing wealth. In reality, what is created is the shifting of wealth between families, classes and locations. It is, indeed, part and parcel of both the class-based structure of society and the fundamentally uneven development of capitalism. Or, in other words, the workings of the housing market, and the tendency towards house-price inflation under a regime of financialized capitalism reproduce uneven development and class inequality.

The De-Financialization of Society

Now, the challenge is to fight the general tendencies of financialization without losing sight of the specifics—or, to fight the specifics of local or national financialization without losing sight of the general mechanism. This is not easy and my suggestions here are partial at best.

Social movements exist at all levels. Some are better equipped to fight the local or national specifics of the financialization of housing, while others are targeting some of the factors underlying the general mechanism at different scales. Anti- and Alt-globalization movements protest against supranational decision-making that favours neoliberal globalization and financialization. At least as important is the organization of an anti- or alt-lobby network of think tanks, research centres, government and corporate observatories that challenges the corporate-dominated network active at different scales. Organizations in such networks can uncover lobbying, policy agendas and practices in order to inform not only politicians but also the public at large of currently practised neoliberalism.

Such organizations might be considered to have an easy job. The politics are sometimes too obvious, the lobbying so open and the practices so clearly biased that it would be hard not to give the alt-lobby network ample resources and a large platform to share their analyses and conclusions. Although organizations like *Corporate Europe Observatory* and a range of organizations within the *Tax Justice Network* have demonstrated time and time again how biased the policy-making process is, how large corporations are able to avoid paying almost any taxes, and how lobbyists become powerful commissioners and politicians become powerful lobbyists, the media still marginalizes such organizations. They are allowed to report on the specifics of certain policies and practices, but the point that this adds up to a more general picture of how policies are designed and implemented—often clearly articulated in these organizations' reports—is typically ignored. The Inconvenient Truth, clearly spelt out and confirmed multiple times, is considered too difficult, too complicated, too contested by most media. In the name of the legal and journalistic principle of *audi alteram partem* (listen to the other side), they ask different parties to reflect on the conclusions of such reports, and thereby enable them to put up a smokescreen. Sometimes outright lies are published in the name of hearing both sides, as if giving a voice to those who inflict harm is more important that explaining the bigger implications of the findings of the alt-lobby machine.

Moreover, the lobby machine has—and this should be obvious—more means than the alt-lobby machine. The lobby machine simply has more resources to invest in making sure their message is the dominant one, preferably the hegemonic one. To this end, it will not only mobilize traditional lobbyists, but a whole range of actors and organizations to trumpet and multiply their message, giving it an aura of objectivity. Research centres and think tanks are crucial in this exercise, but so are sponsored professorships, preferably at top universities. Such professors are then mobilized to speak out against the conclusions of the alt-lobby machine. This mobilization will not necessarily have to happen actively. Some of these professors have aligned their interests so much with the industry that pays them (and many of them also continue to work for the industry that funds their part-time professorships) that they have internalized the interests of the industry to such a degree that their media messages sound sincere. In most cases the media will conclude that the jury is still out: some organizations may make valid points but there are too many questions surrounding their findings and implications.

We should also consider the formal role of politicians in this process. First, they all have their own ideologies, and some support the agenda of big corporations. Second, in some countries (notably the US), their election is enabled by think tanks, lobby organizations and big corporations. Third, they are constantly and heavily lobbied when in office, even if some are willing to talk to the alt-lobby movement as well, theirs is a much quieter voice. Fourth, politicians regularly come from the industry they need to regulate or are offered jobs in these industries once they retire from politics. Many end up working as lobbyists as they know the people and the informal practices of politics particularly well. To take office at the federal level in the US (and increasingly also at state and lower levels), one often already needs to have become wealthy in a particular industry (or at least be backed by those who have become, or have always been, wealthy). This may not be the case everywhere else, but increasingly, a job in politics is a first step towards a better-paid job on retirement from politics. I am not arguing that this is why people go into politics, but it is often the reason to leave formal politics for informal political work like lobbying.

Housing is Not Finance[2]

How does all of this relate to housing? Well, in direct terms, it does not. But in indirect terms, it does. If we want to understand the general mechanism of the financialization of housing as well as its politics and consequences, we should focus not only on the local and national politics but also at the multi-scalar politics of financialization. It may seem remote from the Housing Question, but this is the arena where some of the conditions of the Housing Question are created and moulded. It is not only easy for the media to conclude that something is "too complicated" for their readers (and I have heard journalists writing for high-quality newspapers use these exact words), but also for housing researchers to consider the politics of financialization as something that does not concern them. This is a key arena of the politics of housing, and as long as housing activists and housing researchers ignore this arena, they will ignore one of the key developments in recent and contemporary housing debates. It also makes activists and researchers more susceptible to myths like "we need to build more housing". But aligning oneself with the build more agenda will typically do little to alleviate housing costs and housing-induced harm. It will rarely bring prices down, and it will rarely improve the housing conditions or the location of that housing for low- and moderate-income households.

The idea that "There Is No Alternative" (TINA) is so deeply internalized that in contemporary debates it is all too easy to sideline someone who advocates non-market (or non-financialized) housing solutions. Such alternatives are often ridiculed, not only by big corporations, right-wing politicians and the conservative media but often *tout court*. Mainstream left-liberal, labour and social-democratic parties in many countries internalized TINA reasoning during the Third Way decade, and even though the "glory years" of the Third Way are long gone and now often criticized, mainstream left-wing political parties still have trouble coming up with alternatives. In this sense Fukuyama (1989) was correct: there appears to be an 'End of History' when socialist parties have 'lost their ideological feathers', to quote a former Dutch social-democratic prime minster, and now preach 'Friendly Capitalism' as if There *Is* No Alternative.

But was it really socialism or communism that many of these parties preached before? Not necessarily. Many post-war, left-wing parties did not fundamentally position themselves against capitalism. In fact, many preached a social capitalism, a softened capitalism, a socio-democratic capitalism and a society in which capitalism existed alongside other ideologies and systems and not everything had to be commodified *per se*. At the dawn of the 1980s even the most conservative and most neoliberal politicians and thinkers could probably not have foreseen the wholesale privatization, commodification and to some extent financialization that has taken places in some countries (the UK being the paradigmatic case)—partly, and in some cases largely, implemented when (formerly) left-wing parties were in power. I do not think any of them could have predicted such a slam dunk in the ideological contest.

But there is, of course, an alternative. Housing does not have to be privatized, commodified or financialized. Is the idea of building, maintaining and renting out public or other forms of social housing really so appalling? Well, if that were the case, we should definitely get rid of owner-occupied housing. At first sight, this may seem like a strange argument: Why do we need to end owner-occupied housing if we find the idea of public provision of housing unattractive? Because, as Wyly and DeFilippis (2010) have persuasively argued for the US (but their argument resonates across many countries), owner-occupation is so heavily supported by public funding, often more heavily than so-called public housing, that owner-occupied housing should be considered the core public housing sector, echoing the idea of a "hidden welfare state"—fiscal policies that primarily benefit middle and higher classes (Howard, 1999). Indeed, the public character of owner-occupied housing has facilitated the financialization of housing.

Tax breaks and government guarantees have perhaps made homeownership more accessible, but they have not made homeownership more affordable. If mortgage default is publicly insured, it makes it easier to grant more and bigger mortgages. Tax breaks on mortgage interest payments bring down "other monthly expenses", leaving more room for additional mortgage payments, whether in the form of higher interest rates (e.g. subprime and predatory loans) or bigger loans (with a larger sum of interest payments). Here we see a familiar principle at work: when a class of households has more to spend, this generally does not result in a relatively lower wage-share spent on housing or on an improved housing situation. Rather, it drives up prices, either directly or indirectly by expanding the availability of mortgage credit.

This brings public and other forms of social housing back into the picture. If the government is spending more money on de facto subsidized owner-occupied housing than on so-called subsidized rental housing (whether in the form of social, public, council or other forms of subsidized housing), it should also be able to spend the same total amount of money by subsidizing different forms of housing equally. In the literature this idea, known as a "tenure-neutral housing policy", has spurred a lively debate among housing scholars (e.g. Balchin, 1996; Kemeny, 1981; Turner and Whitehead, 2002). Unfortunately, it is less popular among contemporary governments. Yet, it would be relatively easy to implement and does not necessarily require a strong progressive coalition.

A tenure-neutral housing policy would only be a first, significant step towards a better housing policy. Further steps do require a progressive majority but such a majority already exists locally in many places and has potential in many other locations, regions and countries. We could actually invest more in social rental housing and shift fiscal support from mortgage loans to building and maintaining social housing. Since the fiscal support of mortgage interest deductions primarily drives up house prices, it would also be a more productive investment. In places where a larger cross-section of the population lives in social or other forms of subsidized housing, that housing stock also tends to be less stigmatized, in part because a larger stock implies that this kind of housing in located in many, and therefore also more mixed, neighbourhoods.

Furthermore, we could promote alternative forms of housing, including limited equity cooperatives, community land trusts, mutual housing associations and other bottom-up, unorthodox housing tenures. These are often based on the principle of "commoning", namely collective, active and strategic groups, which are also anti-capitalist in the sense that they strive towards an actually-existing (rather than a utopian) alternative world (i.a. Gibson-Graham, 2006; Linebaugh, 2008; for application to housing see Hodkinson, 2012). This approach prioritizes housing as a social good over housing as a commodity or financial asset, which is exactly the opposite of the neoliberal or financial perspective on housing, which by definition subordinates use value to exchange value.

The neoliberal logic, which sees housing primarily as a financial asset, has been unable to solve the Housing Question. The neoliberal, financialized version of the market cannot provide decent housing for all, as economist Christine Whitehead has also concluded:

> The two most obvious areas where the neoliberal legacy can be seen to have failed lie with the excesses of the finance market in the 21st century and the outcome of transferring subsidy from bricks and mortar to households. The first appears to be a failure of theory as well as of practice; the second can be interpreted as a failure of government to provide adequate demand-side subsidies and of markets to respond to demand- rather than supply-side incentives.
>
> (Whitehead, 2002: 123)

Under a neoliberal, financialized capitalism, there is a *permanent* housing crisis of affordability, insecurity, exclusion, segregation and environmental degradation (Marcuse with Keating, 2006). If a model cannot supply a need as basic as a decent roof over our heads, should we not be questioning the *public* prioritization of this model? In other words, the state should not support a system that has proven to be dysfunctional. I am not saying that the state should ban a market for housing—although this is certainly open to debate—but it should not push this model of housing in discursive and financial terms.

Another way to stimulate housing commoning would be to legalize squatting by establishing clear rules when and how squatting is allowed. The squatting movement has a rich history of making housing available for those in need, while also fighting housing speculation and providing non-commercial services, including but not limited to restaurants, child care facilities, cinemas, theatre, job training, and support for victims of violence, minorities and a range of other groups. Let us imagine that it is illegal to keep a building empty for more than one year in a housing market where there is a lack of affordable housing and that squatting is legalized after that period. Under this framework, squatters would enjoy clear rights and fewer buildings would stand empty and underused for years. This proposal is, in fact, not that different from the situation that existed for decades in countries like the Netherlands, where squatting was declared illegal in 2010.

The regulation of mortgage markets could also be changed. If households were first provided with an alternative to mortgaged homeownership, the entry bars to mortgaged homeownership could also be raised. Before, it was common to require a down-payment of, for instance 20 or 30 per cent—and in some countries 50 per cent—which forced people to save before buying and made sure that people would have 'skin in the game', which is a healthy idea for a range of, partly moral, reasons. It also protects people against house-price decline and ensures they do not so easily end up 'underwater', namely in a situation where the size of their mortgage is larger than the current market value of their house. In most countries this would currently be a very unattractive policy because there are not enough affordable rental housing units available to accommodate people who, in the new situation, would not become homeowners or would do so at a later age. Therefore, it is crucial that more affordable housing is provided before a higher down-payment requirement is introduced.

Furthermore, the government could introduce maximum LTV and LTI ratios to limit the money people could borrow, which would most likely bring house prices down. In the long term, housing would become more affordable for everyone, but in the short term it would penalize households that recently bought a house on a mortgage with high LTI and LTV ratios. A form of public insurance could be introduced for households at risk of default. If the tax deduction of mortgage interest payments could be cut completely, part of the funds could be transferred to such a public insurance instrument. Indirectly, structurally lower house prices may also bring the rent for privately rented housing down—an added benefit. As with other commodities, especially basic needs, lower prices will ultimately benefit most households. Consumer confidence may initially decrease but once people start to realize that they will spend less on housing and therefore will have more money to spend on other things, the mid- and long-term macroeconomic effects will be positive.

Finally, to avoid future excesses in mortgage markets, rules that exist in some countries regarding mortgage securitization and interest rates could be introduced in more countries. Again, as in the old days (and like today in many countries), usury laws could curb some forms of subprime and predatory lending. Mortgage securitization would not have to be discontinued even though it was, like subprime and predatory lending, responsible for a significant part of the financial crisis. In the US where modern mortgage securitization was invented, securitization worked rather well for a couple of decades. Clear rules about the types of mortgage loans that can be securitized and the design specifics of the securities could take away most of the risk of securitization. In addition, lenders, just like homeowners, could be required to have 'skin in the game', that is lenders could be required to keep a share of all mortgages on their books. This would limit the risk of lenders selling bad loans because they could no longer turn the entire risk over to investors through mortgage-backed securities.

Housing transforms the class and geographical structures of society much more intensively under the mechanism of the financialization of housing. The impact of housing reaches much more deeply into class and geographical structures under financialized capitalism. Since the financialization of housing drives house-price inflation and produces uneven development, housing is fundamental to the nature and outcomes of the transformation of society. To ignore housing at a time of financialized capitalism is to ignore a key driver of class restructuring and uneven development. Today's political economy cannot be grasped without a firm understanding of housing.

Notes

1   I refer to "suburban cities" as relatively recently built cities that look and feel suburban in every way, but that are not a suburb of any particular city, like Stockton, as well as to suburban and exurban areas that are so large that they have either overshadowed their main city or that appear to be socially and economically detached from that city, like Lehigh Acres.

2   I took this subtitle from the title of King's (2010) first chapter.

References

Aalbers, M.B. (2016) Regulated Deregulation. In: S. Springer, K. Birch and J. MacLeavy (Eds), *Handbook of Neoliberalism*. London: Routledge.

Agamben, G. (2005) *State of Exception*. Chicago, IL: University of Chicago Press.

Balchin, P.N. (1996) *Housing Policy in Europe*. London: Psychology Press.

Bourdieu, P. [1990] (2005) *The Social Structures of the Economy*. Cambridge: Polity.0

Crouch, C. (2011) *The Strange Non-Death of Neoliberalism*. Cambridge: Polity.

Doling, J. and Ford, J. (Eds) (2003) *Globalisation and Home Ownership: Experiences in Eight Member States of the European Union*. Delft: DUP Science.

Engels, F. 1979[1887]. *The Housing Question*. Moscow: Progress.

Fields, D.J. (2013) *From Property Abandonment to Predatory Equity: Writings on Financialization and Urban Space in New York City*. PhD Dissertation. New York: The City University of New York.

Fligstein, N. 2001. *The Architecture of Markets*. Princeton, NJ: Princeton University Press.

Forrest, R. and Hirayama, Y. (2015) The Financialisation of the Social Project: Embedded Liberalism, Neoliberalism and Home Ownership. *Urban Studies* 52(2): 233–244.

Forrest, R. and Yip, N.-M. (Eds) (2011) *Housing Markets and the Global Financial Crisis*. Cheltenham: Edward Elgar.

Fukuyama, F. (1989). The End of History? *The National Interest* 16 (Summer): 3–18.

Gibson-Graham, J.K. (2006) *A Postcapitalist Politics*. Minneapolis, MN: University of Minnesota Press.

Hay, C. (2004) Common Trajectories, Variable Paces, Divergent Outcomes? Models of European Capitalism under Conditions of Complex Economic Interdependence. *Review of International Political Economy* 11(2): 231–261.

Hodkinson, S. (2012) The Return of the Housing Question. *Ephemera: Theory & Politics in Organization* 12(4): 423–444.

Hofstede, G. (1984) *Culture's Consequences: International Differences in Work-Related Values*. Second edition. Beverly Hills CA: Sage.

Howard, C. (1999) *The Hidden Welfare State: Tax Expenditures and Social Policy in the United States*. Princeton, NJ: Princeton University Press.

Kemeny, J. (1981) *The Myth of Home-Ownership: Private Versus Public Choices in Housing Tenure*. London: Routledge & Kegan Paul.

Kemeny, J. (1992) *Housing and Social Theory*. London: Routledge.

King, P. (2010) *Housing Boom and Bust: Owner Occupation, Government Regulation and the Credit Crunch*. London: Routledge.

Lazzarato, M. (2011) *The Making of the Indebted Man: An Essay on the Neoliberal Condition*. Los Angeles, CA: Semiotext(e).

Linebaugh, P. (2008) *The Magna Carta Manifesto: Liberties and Commons for All*. Berkeley, CA: University of California Press.

Marcuse, P. with Keating, W.D. (2006) The Permanent Housing Crisis: The Failures of Conservatism and the Limitations of Liberalism. In: R.G. Bratt, M.E. Stone and C. Hartman (Eds) *A Right to Housing: Foundation for a New Social Agenda*, pp. 139–162. Philadelphia, PA: Temple University Press.

Marx, K. [1894] (1999) *Capital. Volume III. The Process of Capitalist Production as a Whole*. Originally published by International Publishers, New York. URL: www.marxists.org/archive/marx/works/1894-c3/index.htm.

Oliver, M.L. and Shapiro, T.M. (2006) *Black Wealth, White Wealth: A New Perspective on Racial Inequality*. New York: Routledge.

Piketty, T. (2014) *Capital in the Twenty-First Century*. Cambridge, MA: Harvard University Press.

Ronald, R. (2008) *The Ideology of Home Ownership Homeowner Societies and the Role of Housing*. Basingstoke: Palgrave Macmillan.

Sassen, S. (2014) *Expulsions: Brutality and Complexity in the Global Economy*. Cambridge, MA: Harvard University Press.

Smith, S.J. (2008) Owner-occupation: At Home with a Hybrid of Money and Materials. *Environment & Planning A* 40(3): 520–535.

Smith, S.J., Searle, B.A. and Cook, N. (2008) Rethinking the Risks of Home Ownership. *Journal of Social Policy* 38(1): 83–102.

Soederberg, S. (2014) *Debtfare States and the Poverty Industry: Money, Discipline and the Surplus Population*. London: Routledge.

Turner, B. and Whitehead, C.M.E. (2002) Reducing Housing Subsidy: Swedish Housing Policy in an International Context. *Urban Studies* 39(2): 201–217.

Whitehead, C.M.E. (2012) The Neo-liberal Legacy to Housing Research. In: D.F. Clapham, W.A.V. Clark and K. Gibb (Eds), *The Sage Handbook of Housing Studies*, pp. 113–130. London: Sage.

Wyly, E. and J. DeFilippis. 2010. "Mapping Public Housing: The Case of New York City." *City & Community* 9(1): 61–86.

Index

For Product Safety Concerns and Information please contact our EU
representative GPSR@taylorandfrancis.com
Taylor & Francis Verlag GmbH, Kaufingerstraße 24, 80331 München, Germany

www.ingramcontent.com/pod-product-compliance
Ingram Content Group UK Ltd.
Pitfield, Milton Keynes, MK11 3LW, UK
UKHW021610240425
457818UK00018B/475